Border Fictions

Border Fictions

GLOBALIZATION, EMPIRE, AND WRITING AT THE BOUNDARIES OF THE UNITED STATES

Claudia Sadowski-Smith

New World Studies

A. James Arnold, editor

University of Virginia Press

Charlottesville and London

University of Virginia Press
Printed in the United States of America on acid-free paper

First published 2008

9 8 7 6 5 4 3 2 1

Library of Congress Cataloging-in-Publication Data

Sadowski-Smith, Claudia, 1968–
 Border fictions : globalization, empire, and writing at the boundaries of the
United States / Claudia Sadowski-Smith.
   p.   cm. — (New world studies)
 Includes bibliographical references and index.
 ISBN 978-0-8139-2677-3 (cloth : alk. paper) — ISBN 978-0-8139-2678-0 (pbk. :
alk. paper) — ISBN 978-0-8139-2689-6 (e-book)
   1. American literature—Mexican American authors—History and criticism—
Theory, etc. 2. American literature—Indian authors—History and criticism—Theory,
etc. 3. American literature—Canadian influences. 4. Canadian literature—American
influences. 5. Boundaries in literature. 6. Mexican-American Border Region—
In literature. 7. Imperialism in literature. 8. Globalization in literature. I. Title.
 PS153.M4S23 2008
 810.9′358—dc22

                                                                    2007035060

To Bryan and Nina

Contents

Acknowledgments

THIS BOOK has been a long time in the making. The project stuck with me throughout many, many moves across the United States that, while draining, also shaped my view of developments along the border territories that are the subject of this book. As someone who moved across international borders and on whom borders also moved, I already knew about the significance of boundaries and of comparative work on this issue. But living in different areas of the United States, especially, and for longer periods of time, along its borders with Mexico and Canada, further opened my eyes to the importance of geography to notions of belonging, affiliation, and politics.

The book would never have been finished without the help and guidance of many colleagues and the support of friends and family. I would especially like to thank my colleagues at Arizona State University—Elizabeth Horan, Márta Sanchez, and also Isis McElroy—who supported me intellectually and emotionally through two summers of completing and revising this manuscript. Thanks for finding the time to read my work amid incredibly busy schedules, for your thorough feedback, for your guidance, and for your belief in my work. Special thanks to my colleague Karen J. Leong, who helped me strengthen the argument of chapter 2, and to Jennifer Andrews, who carefully read and commented on chapter 3. I am also glad to have the opportunity to thank Manuel Martín-Rodríguez for his comments on chapter 1. Thanks also to Erika Lee for her collegiality and for her inspiring historical scholarship on Chinese immigration. Robert McKee Irwin's friendship and his insights on northern Mexican border literature have been equally invaluable to the articulation of my argument. And thanks to the many Canadianists who generously shared their knowledge of the field, including Richard Cavell, Donald C. Goellnicht, Reginald C. Stuart, Marie Lo, and Chris Lee.

The insights I have drawn over the years it has taken to complete this book from exchanges with Claire Fox, Joni Adamson, Jyotsna Singh, and my tireless mentor Ann Ardis animate many of my arguments. Thanks for your unwavering support and for reading and commenting on significant portions of this work. Priscilla Wald, Judith Roof, and Silvia Spitta also have my thanks for their constant professional guidance. Thanks also to Alvina Quintana, Thomas M. Leitch, Barbara Gates, and Charles Robinson for their continuing advice. And thanks to Rachel Adams, Joel Pfister, and Daniel Belgrad for their insights into U.S. American studies and to Djelal Kadir for his hospitality and generosity during a summer visit to the Penn State campus as well as for promoting work on internationalized American studies under the aegis of the International American Studies Association.

I have been fortunate to find colleagues in several programs and departments at Arizona State University who have offered their friendship and support, including Tisa Wenger, Ayanna Thompson, Montye Fuse, Cora Fox, Peter Goggin, Mary Margaret Fonow, Keith Miller, T. M. McNally, Cynthia Hogue, Mark Lussier, Jay Boyer, Gregory Castle, Beth Tobin, Maureen Goggin, Taylor Corse, DoVeanna Fulton, and Dan Gilfillan. Thanks to my colleagues at Texas Tech University who read first drafts of parts of the book and helped me strengthen my argument, especially Jen Shelton, Julie Couch, Yuan Shu, Madonne Miner, and BJ Manriquez. And thanks to my colleagues at the State University of New York, Fredonia—Christina Jarvis, Bob Marzec, and Bruce Simon—who often shared their views of U.S. and contemporary literature with me.

Thanks also to the anonymous readers at the University of Virginia Press, whose comments helped immensely to improve the book, and to the humanities editor, Cathie Brettschneider and her assistant, Angie Hogan, as well as to Beth Ann Ina, my wonderful copyeditor. And, finally, thanks to my parents and siblings, and to Bryan and Nina, without whom none of this would matter.

I revised the book with the help of a Women's Studies Summer Research Award from Arizona State University and a junior research release from ASU's Department of English. Research on chapter 5 was completed under the aegis of a Canadian Studies Faculty Enrichment Program Fellowship.

PARTS OF chapter 1 were previously published as "Twenty-first Century Chicana/o Border Writing" in *South Atlantic Quarterly* 105.4 (Fall 2006): 825–51, and are used with permission of Duke University Press. Parts of chapter 2 were published as "The U.S.-Mexico Borderlands Write Back" in *Arizona Quarterly* 57.1 (Spring 2001): 91–112, and are reprinted by permission of the Arizona Board of Regents. An earlier version of chapter 5 appeared as "Canada-U.S. Border Narratives and U.S. Hemispheric Studies" in *Comparative American Studies* 3.1 (March 2005): 63–77, and is reprinted by permission of Sage Publications Ltd. Copyright (© Sage Publications, 2005).

Border Fictions

Introduction

The Diverse Spaces of Border Fictions

CONTEMPORARY POPULAR U.S. discourses about the country's land borders with Mexico and Canada almost always emphasize their porosity to unwanted people.[1] While undocumented immigration via the 2,000-mile border with Mexico has long been a familiar topic, the September 11, 2001, attacks have drawn additional attention to the permeability of the southern boundary to terrorists. Since the border has been so vulnerable to undocumented immigration, the argument goes, it could also easily be overcome by terrorists using immigration as a cover.[2]

The 3,800-mile boundary with Canada has become linked to a similar rhetoric. The world's longest border between two countries is now often characterized as a potential gateway for terrorists and undocumented immigrants. These concerns draw on the widely held U.S. view of Canada as a safe haven for terrorists and a country with lax immigration laws. According to a frequently repeated newspaper story, many of the hijackers involved in the 2001 attacks on the United States entered the country via the border shared with Canada. In fact, however, all of the hijackers had been legally admitted to the United States. They arrived at U.S. airports on tourist, business, and student visas granted in third countries. And only about 3 percent of the more than one million undocumented immigrants enter the United States through Canada every year (Gillies).

Rather than seeing U.S. land borders as threats to security, discussions of U.S. borders in the humanities at the turn of the twenty-first century have focused on *one* specific border community and its opposition to U.S. empire. Gloria Anzaldúa's enormously influential book *Borderlands/La Frontera* (1987) emphasized Mexican American responses to subjugation by the U.S. nation-state. The historian Herbert Eugene Bolton has been credited with coining the term *borderlands* in the 1920s to highlight similarities in the histories of various nations in the hemisphere.[3] But Anzaldúa used the concept to symbolize Chicana opposition to exclusion from the benefits of U.S. citizenship and from the 1950s–1970s Chicano cultural nationalism movement (Chicanismo).

Vividly summarized in the concept of Aztlán, Chicanismo identifies contemporary forms of Mexican American oppression with the creation of today's border between the United States and Mexico in 1848. The imperialist absorption of Mexican territory by the United States turned native and Hispanic populations into minorities overnight. Chicanismo reconsiders this area as the Chicano ancestral homeland by declaring Mexican Americans the heirs of the Mesoamerican Aztecs. To point to the existence of a Mexican culture in the United States well before the foundation of the country, Chicanismo recuperates the Mesoamerican myth that Indians migrated to the Valley of Mexico from an area that is now the U.S. Southwest. This insistence on the myth of Aztlán emphasizes that Mexican culture existed in the United States well before the foundation of the country and that migration between Mexico and the United States follows an age-old circular pattern.

During the 1990s Anzaldúa's notion of borderlands became one of the guiding metaphors of Chicana/o studies, and it has spawned new forms of Latina/o studies. Here, borderlands symbolically evoke growing ties between Latina/os and the economic and political realities in their countries or regions of origin (Flores 195). The notion of borderlands has also come to denote how the academic study of the United States has recently moved beyond U.S. borders.[4]

As popular and academic discourses have turned U.S. borders into metaphors, a significant body of work has emerged at the turn of the twenty-first century that highlights the greater complexity of U.S. national boundaries with Mexico and Canada. The setting of these cultural productions at the seams of two nations is so closely interlinked with their subject matter that they cannot be easily moved to another place without distortion or loss of significance.[5] Border fictions are thus grounded in assumptions similar to insights articulated in scholarship by cultural geographers, such as David Harvey, Doreen Massey, and Edward Soja. Like the work of these thinkers, border fiction asserts that a particular place is as much affected by human projection and representation as people and communities are affected by the landscape. Yet fiction can, in a way different from other types of representation, draw on the power of imagination to depict alternative visions of past, current, and future developments, particularly underexplored connections among various individuals and communities that inhabit the border landscape.

Border Fictions explores a sample of the existing cultural representations that highlight such links among border territories and their diverse populations. The novels, short story collections, autobiographies, and dramas discussed here suggest that the transnational nature of borders significantly affects those who reside or travel through these areas, both their views of themselves and their relationship with these locations. At the same time, however, the specific cultural beliefs, histories, and material circumstances of individuals and communities also produce diverse conceptions of border spaces. The fiction examined in this book adds to popular and academic discourses on U.S. boundaries an attention to undocumented Asian border crossings, indigenous struggles for border crossing and land rights, the effects of changes in Mexican border cities on Mexican American communities, and deepening interdependencies among the United States and its two neighbors.

Representations of these issues also point to connections among various communities. Border literature highlights related historical and contemporary experiences with expressions of U.S. imperialism and, often, with the repressive policies of other North American nation-states as they have manifested themselves at U.S. land borders. While imperialism has traditionally been associated with the nineteenth-century European acquisition of overseas colonies, the United States' ascension to and maintenance of its hegemonic status in the world is also increasingly understood in terms of "empire."[6] Scholarship on U.S. empire locates the roots of U.S. imperial power in fifteenth-century colonization and settlement of the Americas. Colonization set the stage for the later formation of individual nation-states as successors of colonial powers. The development of the U.S. nation-state was characterized by various interlinked forms of empire. The desire for territorial expansion seamlessly connected spatial and temporal U.S. efforts at nation- and empire-building and expressed itself through geographic domination over indigenous peoples through displacement, confinement, and decimation; the movement of subjugated people through slavery and immigration inside national borders; and the articulation of desires to dominate and expand into other parts of the hemisphere (Kaplan, *Anarchy* 15).

This desire to acquire land eventually also shaped the outlines of the United States. Today's U.S. national boundaries were formalized in the wake of military and diplomatic conflicts over land masses that were *contiguous* with what was then the United States but which happened to be (partially) held by other colonial powers or their budding nations-to-be. The U.S. border with Mexico was established in the aftermath of the 1848 Mexico-U.S. War, which compelled Mexico to give up half of its territory and also created the Mexican (American) borderlander and thus a tradition of Mexican (American) writing about the border. The boundary with Canada was officially created in the Treaty of 1818 after the War of 1812 between the United States and Britain. The formalization of the border supported notions about the uniqueness of Canada vis-à-vis the United States.[7] The formation of U.S. borders paved the way for the acquisition of land geographically not contiguous with the United States, as exemplified in the 1863 Monroe Doctrine and the establishment of an overseas empire after the Spanish-American War in 1898.

In their focus on the territories where two nation-states intersect, border fictions move beyond inquiries that emphasize only the imperialistic role of the United States for developments in border areas. Border literature also points to the importance of the United States' neighboring nations—Mexico and Canada—as well as their state-sponsored nationalisms for shaping border environments and the lives of their populations. Similar to the United States government, those in the Mexican and Canadian governments and their colonial predecessors have engaged in acts of colonialism against citizens, residents, or (im)migrants that have manifested themselves at the borders of their respective nations. When the governing bodies of neighboring countries have come to differing or conflicting policy solutions in their treatment of similar border populations, those boundaries were often temporarily transformed into sanctuaries.

Particularly in the nineteenth century, U.S. borders became pathways for Chinese immigrants. Barred from legal admission to the United States for a decade, Chinese were still permitted entry into Canada, from where they could cross into the United States. Both lines of national division additionally provided (at least temporary) refuge for native people trying to escape government repression and, later, for black slaves who escaped from the United States. At the end of the twentieth century, the Canada-U.S. border also promised sanctuary for refugees from South America who were denied asylum in the United States.

In each case, each border's capacity to function as a sanctuary turned out to be short-lived, because Mexico and Canada, even before they became independent nations, ultimately supported U.S. policies or passed legislation similar to that in the United States. This fact points to the United States' incipient domination of its two neighbors as early as the nineteenth century, a development that intensified at the beginning of the next century. At the same time, however, it appears that the interests of the elites in each (emerging) nation may have been well served by collaborating with the United States in the creation and later maintenance of its empire status.

With the exception of work by Edith Eaton from the turn of the twentieth century, most of the literature examined in this book emphasizes diverse *contemporary* border communities and their attempts to articulate experiences with U.S. empire and repressive state-sponsored nationalisms. This work highlights two current manifestations of empire—free trade and the attendant increase in military might—that have had significant impact on U.S. border developments. Hemispheric free-trade agreements like the 1991 Canada-U.S. Free Trade Agreement (CUFTA) and the 1994 North American Free Trade Agreement (NAFTA) between Canada, the United States, and Mexico are informed by the neoliberal ground rules that are the defining mark of our contemporary moment, often described as "globalization." *Neoliberalism* denotes the resurgence of liberalist ideologies promoting the functioning of markets without the interference of nation-states or international regulatory entities.

As they specify the circulation of goods, services, and moneys in North America independently of most government-imposed tariffs and taxes, hemispheric free-trade agreements have drastically affected U.S. border areas and populations. NAFTA has accelerated the creation of export-producing zones in Mexican border areas. Maquiladora assembly factories dominating these zones have attracted larger numbers of people from the Mexican interior, who often become potential migrants to the United States. A combination of a stronger peso, higher wages in Mexico, the demise of some tax and tariff exemptions for imported components as inscribed in NAFTA, and a U.S. recession that dampened demand for Mexican exports has recently led to a decline in the number of Mexican maquiladoras.[8] But even as production is being moved to other countries, most notably China, Vietnam, and Guatemala, migrants from Mexico and other parts of Latin, Central, and South America keep coming to the border to cross into the United States.

The U.S. government has reacted to increased migration from Mexico by militarizing the southwestern border. Declaring the exterior boundaries of the United States an extended zone rather than a geographically delimited line has allowed the installation of checkpoints. Set up along at least thirty-five and no more than one hundred miles from the national boundary, these checkpoints function as the border's equivalent, where

Fourth Amendment rights necessitating probable cause for arrest can be suspended (Michaelson 95–96). The border itself has also been fortified with ever-stronger fences, wall-like structures that evoke comparisons with the infamous Berlin Wall, new technologies of control, and a record number of Border Patrol personnel and National Guard troops.[9] Significant border buildup began in the early 1970s; it took more dramatic forms in the 1990s to preempt the expected increase of unauthorized immigration as a result of economic liberalization under NAFTA (Purcell and Nevins). Although it has redirected would-be entrants to different, generally more dangerous parts of the border, border militarization has not diminished crossings by long-distance or long-term migrants, who now enter with the help of more costly smugglers and who also take greater risks. In fact, in the mid-1990s many more people died from exposure, particularly in the Arizona desert, than perished from drowning (mostly in the Río Grande), or from homicide and automobile-pedestrian accidents in the late 1980s (Eschbach, Hagan, and Rodriguez 11–12, 14).

Although the free-trade agreements create such negative effects on border crossers, the United States continues to pursue plans to extend them throughout the hemisphere. These plans reflect U.S. efforts to remain competitive with other powerful countries in Europe and Asia and their involvement in respective trading blocs. This ongoing triadic regionalization of the world points to the decline of the United States' hegemonic economic and political position. Immanuel Wallerstein has dated the weakening of U.S. global dominance to the 1970s, when the Vietnam War used up U.S. gold reserves and the collapse of the Bretton Woods accords opened financial markets to speculative trade in foreign currencies and other financial instruments (18). So far, the United States has managed to maintain its hegemonic status by virtue of its huge consumer market, overwhelming financial power, and reserve of unchallenged military might (Harvey, *New Imperialism* 68). But the country's increasing recourse to military power, shown in historically unprecedented border enforcement at home and increases in military action abroad, can also be read as the mark of a declining empire that compensates for economic and political losses by attempting to remain the sole superpower in the military realm.

Many of the border fictions examined in this book explore the interrelated effects of free trade and border militarization on a variety of border communities, including Chicana/os, Mexican immigrants and border residents, native people, and undocumented immigrants from Asia. In addition, border literature also draws attention to the complexities surrounding the Canada-U.S. boundary, which are rarely addressed in popular and academic discourses on U.S. borders. Just as NAFTA has had detrimental effects on the Mexico-U.S. relationship, the agreement has also deepened asymmetries in the relation between the United States and Canada, which has been the economically closest between any two nations.

Integration between the two countries is not primarily achieved in border locations, as in the Mexican case. The northernmost international boundary stretches across prairie and mountain terrains and does not cover many highly urbanized places or twin cities. With little labor mobility across the Canada-U.S. boundary and no maquilas in Canada's border towns, Canadian dependency has taken less obvious forms than Mexico's. Since the first half of the twentieth century, Canada has moved from its formal colonial status in the British Empire to a formally independent, yet actually quite dependent status as a "middle power" with a degree of direct foreign (U.S.) ownership unparalleled anywhere else on the globe (Panitch 82). Today, one third of Canada's exports to the United States are, as in Mexican maquilas, products assembled from U.S. components; in the car industry the figure is 60 percent (Hart).

In the aftermath of the September 11, 2001, attacks, the Canadian government has buckled to sustained U.S. pressure and begun to tighten its refugee law and border-enforcement policies so they more closely resemble similar U.S. measures.[10] While the Canada-U.S. boundary has not been militarized with walls or fences, it has witnessed the progressive tightening of immigration legislation and an increase in the number of U.S. border guards policing it.[11] Particularly sensitive portions like the "Seaway Corridor," which bisects Cornwall Island on the transnational Akwesasne Mohawk reservation, have been enforced with a ten-foot chain-link fence topped with barbed wire (Taliman 14). In addition, internal border checkpoints and car stops were implemented in Michigan after 9/11, especially in the Detroit-Dearborn-Toledo corridor, areas with large Arab American and Arab immigrant populations (Michaelson 100–101).

As it formulates diverse approaches to questions of empire and state-sponsored hemispheric nationalisms, border literature also articulates alternatives. This fiction envisions new forms of oppositional nationalism that take on pan-ethnic and transnational shapes and that are independent of the nation-state. Such visions draw on and place into dialogue the progressive aspects of diverse anticolonial nationalisms of the 1950s–1960s, which emerged both inside and outside U.S. borders as "(in some cases inchoate) protests against the spread of (capitalist) modernity" (Tomlinson 173), yet that had little relation to one another.

Texts about Canada and Mexico set out to separate the progressive impetus of state-sponsored nationalisms from their affinities with the nation-state. Early forms of cultural nationalism arose in Canada and Mexico in the 1920s and 1930s to articulate these countries' cultural differences from and resistance to growing manifestations of U.S. empire. At this time, both countries had become sufficiently and nominally independent as nation-states. Canada became formally independent from Britain in the 1930s and Mexico consolidated itself after its revolution in the 1920s. The two countries' subsequent attempts at nation-building reinforced the realization that their geographical proximity to the United States made them especially vulnerable to incipient forms of U.S. cultural, political, and economic domination.

Other analyses of U.S. empire became available in the 1950s–1960s in the form of dependency theory and cultural nationalism. Dependency theory argues that Latin American nations are underdeveloped not because of inherent defects or historical "backwardness" but because of their specific position in a world economic system that keeps them dependent. Models of cultural imperialism represent a variant of dependency in Latin America and the dominant framework for theorizing the Canadian relationship to its southern neighbor. Canadian cultural nationalists in particular believe that Canada is susceptible to U.S. domination primarily because it lacks a cohesive national culture and founding myth. The corollary of Canadian cultural nationalism has been extensive state intervention in economic, social, political, and cultural life, including the creation of state-sponsored cultural industries; the establishment of a strong social-democratic welfare state; and the expansion of public enterprise and public-service economies. As they became state-sponsored ideologies, however, Mexican and Canadian nationalisms were depleted of their anticolonial impetus. But in both Canada and Mexico, the association between the United States and cultural imperialism rose to renewed prominence as free-trade initiatives were negotiated in the 1990s.

Similar to the border cultural productions about Canada and Mexico, border texts from and about the United States attempt to divorce various forms of 1950s–1960s U.S. ethnic nationalisms from their less progressive manifestations. These nationalisms surged in response to (mainly) domestic expressions of U.S. imperialism. Repressed during the years of nation-building and state consolidation, diverse U.S. ethnic communities forged alternative representations of belonging to mobilize their constituents in activist civil rights struggles. But these various cultural nationalisms fell back into ethnic absolutism; they also became isolated from one another after their institutionalization in the U.S. academy in the form of ethnic and race studies. Proponents of each field felt the need to articulate highly separatist concepts of ethnic and racial autonomy as they competed for institutional recognition (Quintana 19).

Border literature revalues various tenets of these cultural nationalisms, particularly for their ability to serve as bridges in new transnational and multiethnic forms of nationalisms. Notions of American Indian pan-tribalism, Asian American pan-nationalism, and Chicanismo's assertions of interethnic and transnational solidarity with other communities figure centrally in these attempts. Chicanismo's emphasis on the indigenous roots of Chicana/os, for example, enabled collaboration among Chicana/o and Native American students in the formalization of American Indian studies programs. At the same time, Chicanismo also implied a pan-Americanism that joined Chicana/os with working-class Mexicans as *un pueblo sin fronteras* (a people without borders) ("El Plan" 1). Some border literature even builds thus far largely unthought-of connections among various U.S. ethnic, and Canadian and Mexican state-sponsored cultural nationalisms that anticipate forms of political activism with unusual methods and utopian goals.

The creation of such bridges in border fiction manifests itself through the choice of similar aesthetic devices, such as trickster figures, the composite novel format, and magical realism. All three elements are associated with the local space of the Americas and, sometimes, with resistance to U.S. empire. The common setting of the border as well as common protagonists, themes, and principles of storytelling hold together the individual parts of the short-story cycle or composite novel, a generic convention employed by several border fictions. As Mary Louise Pratt has argued, the mixing of elements from the novel and short story has become especially popular in traditionally marginalized areas, which would include most border regions.[12] As a genre with prenovelistic roots, the composite novel combines the international genre of the novel with localized forms of storytelling. The use of trickster figures accomplishes a similar purpose. Although tricksters can be found in other geographies, they are deeply rooted in the precolonial realities of the Americas, and they have become a cross-cultural trope in U.S. ethnic writing.[13] Borrowed from oral traditions, the trickster-coyote signifies the dissolution of boundaries and a state of transition and change.

Some border literature also employs magical realism, which, like the trickster figure, draws attention to and dissolves boundaries, such as those between locally grounded narrative traditions and the European realistic novel (Valdez Moses 111). Coined originally in reference to 1920s German expressionist painting, magical realism became a pan-Latin American aesthetic label in the 1920s and 1940s, and particularly in the 1960s through the fictional and critical work of the Colombian Gabriel García Márquez, the Venezuelan Arturo Uslar Pietri, the Guatemalan Miguel Ángel Asturias, and the Cuban Alejo Carpentier. Especially Carpentier insisted that what he called *"lo real maravilloso"* (marvellous realism) was a representational mode unique to the Americas. Representatives of the boom, such as Julio Cortázar, Carlos Fuentes, and Mario Vargas Llosa, later made similar pronouncements (Larsen 775).

Michael Denning has called the most famous example of magical realism, Gabriel García Márquez's *Cien años de soledad* (1967), the "literary analogue of the 1960s dependency theory of Latin American Marxists" (*Culture* 71). While its penchant for formal experimentation resembled Anglo-American forms of modernism, magical realism was also closely related to the emergence of more militant versions of Latin American nationalism that often took anti-U.S. American forms.

As "perhaps [the] most important contemporary trend in international fiction" (Faris 1), magical realism is today employed in a variety of contemporary writings, especially in work by U.S. ethnic authors and by writers from postcolonial countries.[14] Critics have, however, pointed to its less-progressive politics in comparison with 1960s magical realism. They have argued that in its contemporary usage, magical realism tends to flatten the distinct regional traditions on which it draws and that it evokes nostalgic longing for premodern local realities and communities by minimizing the burden of this past (Denning, *Culture* 51; Valdez Moses 132).

It is important to remember, however, that 1960s magical realism never constituted a politically homogeneous movement; despite a shared criticism of U.S. domination, its practitioners had diverse political orientations, ranging from socialist to liberal to conservative (Larsen 783). The contemporary border fictions that employ magical-realist aesthetics similarly exhibit significant political differences, despite their shared object of critique. Some border fictions employ magical realism to conceptualize the complexity of contemporary neoliberal realities, while others present reformist approaches, and still others call for the revolutionary overthrow of the dominant order. The choice of a certain aesthetics or political form such as nationalism thus does not also guarantee a specific ideological commitment.

In their emphasis on the diverse materiality of border locations, border fictions collectively move beyond dominant conceptualizations of who inhabits and can speak for the border. U.S. academic approaches generally equate border writing with cultural productions by Latina/os and with cultural nationalist approaches to the U.S. Southwest as Aztlán or borderlands. Because U.S. boundaries have become so closely identified with such questions, many of the texts examined in this book have been ignored or classified as examples of other ethnic or national (and sometimes regional) traditions. Their analysis has consequently been confined to separate academic fields, such as American Indian, Asian American, Latin American, and Canadian studies. As a result, diverse historical and contemporary issues affecting borders have often been relegated to the margins of individual academic disciplines and treated in isolation from one another.

A comparative study of border literature also points to hemispheric perspectives underlying various ethnic and area studies fields. American Indian studies has expanded its original pan-tribal focus on native tribes in what is now the United States to also pay attention to the treatment of indigenous peoples in Canada and, to a much smaller extent, in Latin America (Varese 138). But few comparative studies exist that take into account distinct histories of settlement, colonization, contact, and subordination in different nations of the hemisphere. Asian American studies has similarly moved beyond an original focus on the pan-national civil rights struggles of Chinese, Koreans, Japanese, and Filipinos in the United States to develop an international focus on ties between U.S. Asians and parts of Asia—which has, however, left little room for a comparative hemispheric lens on Asian-descended peoples in the Americas.

The framework of *Border Fictions* also differs from Canadian and Mexican approaches to border literature. In contrast to the neglect of U.S. borders in Asian American and American Indian studies, Canadian and Latin American studies center on strong conceptions of international boundaries. While borders figure as the basis for articulations of unique national identities in these two fields, however, the actual geographies of national boundaries and their contemporary changes could benefit from further study.[15]

In Canada, the term *borderlands* or the *border* is often used to signify the situation of the entire country in relationship to its more powerful neighbor to the south. The border concept highlights that the southern Canadian boundary has historically been the most populous and developed part of Canada. The line dividing Canada from its southern neighbor contains significant urban and industrialized centers of power and a few developed border cities, such as Buffalo-Toronto, Detroit-Windsor, and Seattle-Vancouver. Sixty percent of the Canadian population, currently thirty-two million people, live within one hundred miles of the U.S. boundary and are constantly exposed to U.S. hegemony in the cultural, political, and economic realms.

In the metaphorical approach common in Canada, the border often symbolizes Canadian efforts to resist U.S. cultural, economic, and political intrusions. The border thus functions as a bulwark for definitions of Canadian particularities, which are almost always conceptualized as differences from its southern neighbor. Public and elite support for forging a unified sense of nationhood different from U.S. national identity also provided the conditions for the emergence of a strong social-democratic welfare state in the 1960s.[16]

While the Canadian boundary with the United States has traditionally functioned as a stronghold for concepts of Canadian national identity, in Mexico, the northern border region is often singled out as the weakest link in efforts to maintain a distinct national identity vis-à-vis the more powerful United States. This view denies the border's significance for the emergence of specifically Mexican notions of national identity. Forged in the aftermath of the Mexican Revolution and in the context of increasing U.S. dominance, concepts of Mexican national identity are based on a strong dualism between the Anglo-Saxon Protestant and the Ibero-American Catholic worlds. This dualist notion was shaped by revolutionary activity in the border region and by the border experiences of *mexicanidad*'s chief architect José Vasconcelos. Vasconcelos's emphasis on Mexican identity as a form of *mestizaje,* a mixture of European and pre-Columbian cultures, set itself in direct opposition to notions of U.S. nationhood that have largely dismissed the influence of indigenous peoples. *Mexicanidad* provided the context for the consolidation of the Mexican nation-state, which was later manifested in the creation of a national infrastructure in health, education, communications, and public financing under the Lázaro Cárdenas regime (Fuentes, *A New Time* 71).

The elevation of *mexicanidad* to state-sponsored status in the 1920s marginalized the impact of the northern border region on modern notions of *mexicanidad*. Attempts to maintain a centralized identity also led to the neglect of enormous changes in the northern borderlands throughout the 1980s and 1990s and their effects on notions of national culture. As the area became the most prosperous and fastest-growing region in the context of NAFTA, the Mexican government created cultural border programs designed to include border populations into notions of *mexicanidad* (Castillo and Tabuenca Córdoba).

In this context, the term *border literature—literatura fronteriza—* emerged to denote the growing body of writing about the northern border region that was, in part, encouraged by state-sponsored border programs. Because of its emphasis on questions of location, the term *literatura fronteriza* also encompasses cultural representations of the border by Mexico City–based writers. But because this centrist output has remained privileged over that of northern Mexican authors, critics, and artists, a separate term, *literatura de la frontera,* has been coined to denote this work.[17]

While the distinction between border residents and those who do not dwell at the border carries progressive connotations in the Mexican context, it is less useful for the transnational framework developed in *Border Fictions.* Many of the authors examined in this book cannot be discussed in terms of their regional or spatial affiliation because they have led lives that cross ethnic and national frontiers. Most of the writers, in fact, engage in fascinating and complex strategies of self-identification that draw selectively on aspects of their own identities and experiences to articulate affinities with a particular group or sometimes with multiple communities. These strategies are usually elided by discussions of the authors within regional, ethnic, or national categories. More generally, this book's focus on the diversity of border areas challenges the very equation of the border space with a particular community, defined in either ethnic or regional terms.

The first part of *Border Fictions* explores texts about Chicana/o, indigenous, and Asian American border populations. Chapter 1, "Chicana/o Writing and the Mexico-U.S. Border," charts the underexamined historical tradition of writing about Chicana/os at the Mexico-U.S. boundary to open it up to comparison with literature about other border communities. Unlike most Chicana/o cultural productions with which the metaphor of the "border" has become identified, Chicana/o border literature employs the international boundary as explicit setting and theme. Miguel Méndez's work of the 1960s focuses on Mexican (im)migrants within the border region, while literature from the 1980s and 1990s, by such authors as Gloria Anzaldúa, Norma Elia Cantú, and Alberto Alvaro Ríos, examines questions of Chicana/o quotidian life, cultural traditions, and identity formation along the Mexico-U.S. line. Twenty-first-century literature by authors like Ito Romo, Richard Yañez, and Lucrecia Guerrero addresses the negative effects of U.S.-dominated neoliberalism on the majority, Mexican-descended populations of U.S. twin cities. This literature also revives Chicana/o civil rights struggles in the form of activism for border crossing rights and environmental justice.

The next two chapters examine border texts about indigenous and Asian American and Asian Canadian borderlanders. This work inserts itself firmly into the ongoing discussions about U.S. borders from which it has been largely absent, while also elevating hemispheric perspectives to a more central position within Asian American and indigenous studies. Chapter 2, "Asian Border Crossings," analyzes representations of Asian undocumented immigration across the U.S. borders with Mexico and Canada in the work of Edith Maude Eaton (Sui Sin Far) and Karen Tei Yamashita. This chapter stands out from the rest of the book and its emphasis on contemporary literature in that it examines several of Eaton's texts from the turn of the twentieth century. While her work has become integral to U.S. Asian American and U.S. regionalist canons, its border qualities continue to be overlooked. This chapter focuses on Eaton's creation of the first-known fictional representation of the undocumented U.S. border crosser across the Canadian boundary as clear precursors to later depictions of Mexican *indocumentados*.

In the chapter, I also discuss how Yamashita's novel extends the concerns of Eaton's work into the contemporary time period by fictionalizing similarities among Asian and Mexican-descended communities in their encounter with expressions of U.S. empire. Read together, the work of Eaton and Yamashita questions the near exclusive modeling of theories of "illegal" U.S. border crossings after the movement of Mexicans into the United States. The work of Eaton and Yamashita thus reveals important intersections among Asian (American), Chicana/o, and inter-American approaches.

Chapter 3, "Native Border Theory," explores indigenous perspectives on hemispheric borders in the work of Leslie Marmon Silko and Thomas King. While Silko has become well known in U.S. Native American studies, King's fiction has been much less widely discussed, even though he is a major figure in (indigenous) Canadian literature. Silko and King focus on the southwestern Yaqui and the northern Blackfoot, respectively. Their tribal identities are rooted in each community's separation by the U.S. frontiers with Mexico or Canada.

The two writers position these border tribes as paradigmatic figures for the rethinking of border and American Indian studies. Silko's and King's work adds to border studies a spatialized understanding of national boundaries that is embodied in indigenous claims to borders as ancestral homelands. Their imaginative focus on border tribes also complicates dominant notions of affiliation in American Indian studies that have been marked by artificial dichotomies between tribalism and pan-Indian activism. Work by Silko and King jointly elevates progressive elements of U.S. pan-tribal activism to a hemispheric level that also allows participation from individuals and groups of other ethnic and national communities. The fictionalized activism for land and border crossing rights, however, remains firmly grounded in the struggle for individual tribal sovereignty.

The second part of the book explores fiction from Mexico and Canada. Chapter 4, "The View from the South," could have also been placed after the discussion of Chicana/o texts of the Mexico-U.S. border. Such placement would have fit with increasingly popular Latina/o studies perspectives that bridge Chicana/o and Mexican cultural productions. But the insertion of two other chapters exploring indigenous and Asian American views on U.S. borders interrupts these by-now more-accepted notions of who resides at and can speak about the border to highlight understudied connections among Chicana/o, Asian American, and indigenous borderlanders.

Chapter 4 explores the work of the northern Mexican border writers Federico Campbell and Rosina Conde as well as the Mexico City–based writer Carlos Fuentes. This chapter places into dialogue concerns about Mexican nationalism and U.S. empire articulated in Mexican *literatura fronteriza* with Chicana/o-Latina/o views of *la frontera* as a place of opposition to U.S. nationalism. Fuentes's *The Crystal Frontier* in particular adds to Chicana/o cultural productions a focus on the role of Mexican nationalism and the Mexican state in supporting or resisting U.S. hegemony. On the one hand, Fuentes rethinks progressive, anticolonial aspects of Mexican nationalism to oppose contemporary forms of U.S. empire. On the other hand, Fuentes also critically highlights the collaboration of U.S. and Mexican governments in the ongoing deepening of Mexican dependency on the United States in the realms of labor and migration.

Chapter 5, "A Border Like No Other," analyzes border narratives in English by Clark Blaise, Guillermo Verdecchia, Jannette Turner Hospital, Kelly Rebar, and Michael V. Smith. These fictions move U.S.-based inter-American frameworks beyond their current emphasis on the Latin American–U.S. relationship. At the same time, Canada-U.S. border representations also participate in redirecting Canadian studies from its internal focus on questions of national identity toward a wider, hemispheric lens. Canadian border literature opens up the cultural nationalist emphasis on the border to other concerns. This work enlarges the border's traditional function as a metaphor for national differences to also include a more complex emphasis on Canada's position in the hemisphere in the context of the country's continuing dependence on the United States. Canadian border fiction thus articulates criticism of U.S. imperialism toward Canada while also highlighting the shortcomings of the Canadian cultural-nationalist response.

Throughout, *Border Fictions* emphasizes the hemispheric orientation of the examined border literatures. In so doing, the book articulates a North American perspective grounded in national borders that participates in ongoing efforts to internationalize the humanities through comparative and transdisciplinary dialogue.[18] One of these efforts is exemplified in the inter-American research perspective. This approach finds an important precursor in Mexico-U.S. border studies, a lens that emphasizes Chicana/o communities and sometimes their experiences with the national border. Even though *Border Fictions* focuses only on North America, that is, the territory now encompassing the United States, Canada, and Mexico, its model of study has the potential for adaptation to the larger hemispheric context that is the purview of inter-American studies.

While the origins of inter-American studies can be traced as far back as nineteenth- and early twentieth-century work by José Martí and Herbert Eugene Bolton, a host of hemispheric scholarship emerged in the mid-1980s and early 1990s.[19] Produced in comparative literature, Latin American studies, and, to a limited degree, in Chicana/o studies, this work developed topographically comparative models of the Americas that sometimes also included the Caribbean or, less often, Canada.[20]

As their influence waned throughout the 1990s, the impact of these early inter-American models on recent hemispheric perspectives seems to have remained marginal. Alongside other internationalized (post- and transnational) models, such as the Black Atlantic and the trans-Pacific, two largely unconnected versions of inter-American studies have emerged.[21] Each model positions a specific U.S racialized community at the center of a comparative field, thus privileging particular historical processes, geographical spaces, communities, regions, and languages. The linguistically and geographically comparative New World studies emphasizes the transnational African American experience of slavery as a point of intersection with plantation colonialism in the Caribbean and northern Brazil (Smith and Cohn 2).[22] Having emerged from Mexico-U.S. border studies, Literature of the Americas foregrounds the Southwest (often identified with the

Mexico-U.S. border) and its ties with Latin America through a focus on Latino-Chicana/o populations. While New World studies has developed from a fusion of Black Atlantic, African American, and Caribbean studies, Literature of the Americas is largely conceptualized as a bridge across U.S.-based Chicana/o-Latina/o scholars and Latin American studies.

Border Fictions suggests an alternative inter-American framework that focuses on North American borders and that places into dialogue hemispheric approaches to these geographies from Chicana/o, Asian American, American Indian, Latin American, and Canadian studies. Such a model shifts the focus in humanities-based border studies from a particular ethnic group, its critique of exclusive notions of U.S. citizenship, and its connections to Latin America, to a spatialized perspective that acknowledges the internal diversity of border areas and its linkage to theories of nationalism and U.S. imperialism.

While all the disciplines that could potentially contribute to inter-American studies have much to gain from interdisciplinarity, any such model needs to address the divergent histories of the individual academic fields involved, especially differences in their institutional power. In their current form all of the disciplines are, like work in the humanities in general, under attack. Since their inception in the aftermath of civil rights activism, U.S. ethnic studies have had a tenuous foothold in U.S. academia, and their envisioned partial convergence with area studies may further endanger their existence.

U.S. area studies, such as Latin American studies, are also under siege, both in the United States and in Latin American countries. The field's political identification with the Left in the United States, galvanized by the rise of dependency and cultural imperialism paradigms in Latin America, diverges from its originally intended function in support of U.S. foreign cold war policies. In Latin America, academic inquiry is generally threatened as a result of shrinking funding under neoliberal conditions. A field with origins outside U.S. borders, Canadian studies is also in decline, both in the United States and in Canada. Canadian studies was institutionalized in only a few U.S. universities, without significant federal or foundational support (Alper and Monahan 173). The general disinterest in all issues Canadian within the United States has further diminished the importance of this field, despite the fact that some programs have expanded to become North American studies. And even though Canadian fiction and scholarship are moving toward a larger comparative framework on the Americas, the decline in cultural nationalism may signal the end of the Canadian studies tradition in Canada.[23]

In attending to differences among these fields, *Border Fictions* hopes to dispel some of the current suspicions toward hemispheric paradigms based on their potential association with U.S. economic, political, and cultural domination of the Americas. I do not propose an institutionalized form of collaboration among the fields under discussion. While the boundaries between these academic disciplines need to be bridged on an intellectual level, such crossings do not also need to lead to the establishment of inter-American programs or departments at the cost of weakening already embattled fields. Instead, I envision interdisciplinary partnerships that would begin with the discovery of mutual interests, proceed to an acknowledgement of compatibility between methods and intellectual focus, and culminate in the production of intellectual offspring with a character all of its own.[24]

As is the case with any partnership, models of interdisciplinarity always threaten to place one discipline in a position of subordination to another. This possibility looms especially large since the various fields under discussion are afforded differential institutional power in the U.S. academy. They often appear to have to compete with one another for ever-shrinking resources and funding.[25] Moreover, there exists understandable anxiety that an inter-American studies perspective will reinforce the hegemony of monolingual and monocultural American studies scholarship that has mirrored, albeit inadvertently, the United States' role as a global empire.

Like other inter- and North American studies work, the model of study developed in this book limits itself to texts written in or translated into English. This limitation can partially be explained by the institutional location of much recent inter-American studies (like my own) within English departments, which require the use of English-language texts in the classroom. But my work does not preclude the eventual development of a multilingual inter-American studies that would encompass Spanish, Portuguese, French, English, indigenous languages, and the many other languages of the immigrant Americas.

Since it will be impossible to have equal command of all these languages, the work of translation needs to become a focal point of inter-American studies. Kirsten Silva Gruesz has recently emphasized the importance of translating other languages into English; as she notes, in the current moment, translation mainly works to transport concepts from English into other languages so that monolingual English speakers receive fewer and fewer nondomestic ideas ("Translation" 88). Yet the mere availability of translations does not also ensure the mobility of fictional texts or the ideas they represent. In addition, as *Border Fictions* is at pains to show, alternative, non-U.S.-based concepts can be found as well in fiction written in English. The border fiction from English Canada and by U.S. ethnic writers that is the subject of this book, for example, severely complicates the few available U.S. discourses on North American border locations today.

Equally valid is the objection that as a geographically limited model, inter-American studies excludes a variety of other possible locations that could be the basis for transnational work. Gretchen Murphy has argued that a limited focus on the Americas merely extends the exceptionalist view of the United States onto the hemispheric plane as articulated in policies like the Monroe Doctrine. As she notes, the ideology underlying the doctrine "impelled and concealed U.S. imperialism inside the imagined confines of the Western Hemisphere and beyond" (26).

Yet, precisely because the academic study of the United States, as "American studies," has long uncritically appropriated the name of the entire hemisphere for one particular country, its first obligation is to engage in a comparative study of the Americas. Contemporary scholarship in particular also needs to address the ongoing regionalization of this world, which finds one expression in the formation of the hemisphere as an economic and political unit under agreements like NAFTA. Such a focus on the Americas will always constitute just one form of or a starting point for intersections with other geographical models and international orientations. The development of cross-regional comparative frameworks on borders can also counter the theoretical problem of closely attaching theories of culture to territory (McClennen 408). A hemispheric perspective thus understood will enable much-needed connections among the humanities-based use of borders as sites for the critique of U.S. nationalism and the social-science emphasis on international boundaries as new scales of importance in the global economy.

Besides its interest in questions of academic reorganization, this book's comparative reading of border fictions also chronicles some ongoing and possible future developments toward more inclusive forms of political alliance-building. *Border Fictions* aims to participate in the construction of common languages that facilitate communication among various border communities about questions of U.S. empire and differential forms of nationalism—both repressive and progressive—in the hemisphere. The resulting alliances will allow individual groups to retain their distinctiveness and incommensurability rather than resolve them into the unitary and separatist logic of their cultural nationalist precursors. Writing in a different context, Amitava Kumar has argued that such "collective communities of which we have only partial intimations . . . are already part of our world" (xxxi). My hope is that the emphasis on the diverse spatialities of U.S. border areas and their connection to complex global developments developed in this book will contribute to move debates about U.S. borders beyond their current association with either one community or with public discussions of undocumented immigration and Middle Eastern terrorism. Hopefully, the book will contribute to renewed interest in work on U.S. land borders within inter-American frameworks.

1 Chicana/o Writing and the Mexico-U.S. Border

ITO ROMO's recent novel *El Puente = The Bridge* (2000) begins with the lament of Tomasita, a housewife from the Mexican border city of Nuevo Laredo, who has lost her husband to cancer. He worked as an industrial waste disposal superintendent for a U.S.-owned maquiladora assembly plant that releases waste into the stream behind their house. Tomasita grinds up dried mulberries and the shards of her favorite cooking pot into a very fine powder. She then "emptie[s] her washtub and the sorrows of her soul" (3) into the Río Grande/Río Bravo. When the river turns bright red, the change attracts the attention of residents from Laredo and Nuevo Laredo. They assemble at the international bridge between Mexico and the United States where their individual stories also come to intersect.

In its focus on the bridge separating the twin cities of Laredo, *El Puente* sets itself in the somewhat underexplored tradition of Chicana/o writing about the border between Mexico and the United States.[1] As Justo S. Alarcón wrote in 1992, a surprisingly small number of Chicana/o literary works deal explicitly with this location (65). These works include texts by authors like Gloria Anzaldúa, Aristeo Brito, Norma Elia Cantú, Oscar Casares, Dagoberto Gilb, Rolando Hinojosa, Arturo Islas, Miguel Méndez, Américo Paredes, John Rechy, Alberto Ríos, Sergio Troncoso, and Helena María Viramontes.[2] Their writing employs the border as theme and setting while also contributing to the area's long-standing symbolic value as a signifier of the mythic Chicano homeland Aztlán, Chicana/o identity, and Chicana/o literary experimentation.

Yet these texts also reveal significant changes in the usage of the border concept that largely correspond to generational divisions. Miguel Méndez's work of the 1970s, for example, examines the international boundary from the perspective of the (im)migrant, who has also become a general symbol in Chicana/o writing for displacement, oppression, and rebellion. The larger group of border writing from the 1980s and 1990s, most famously exemplified in Anzaldúa's work, employs the border as a starting point for discussions of Chicana/o quotidian life, culture, and identity. This literature recognizes deepening divisions between Mexico and the United States, manifested, for example, in intensified U.S. border militarization. But border writing ultimately emphasizes the openness of the southwestern boundary as crucial to processes of Chicana/o identity and cultural formation. Such a focus engenders representations of alternative conceptions of belonging outside of national borders.

More recent Chicana/o border literature that has appeared at the turn of the twenty-first century places Chicana/o communities in the context of U.S.-driven neoliberal developments and their regional expression along the Mexico-U.S. line. The work by Romo that I cited at the beginning of this chapter, Richard Yañez's *El Paso del Norte* (2003), and Lucrecia Guerrero's *Chasing Shadows* (2000) engage the negative effects of contemporary forms of U.S. empire on Mexican border towns and on the majority, Mexican-descended population in U.S. twin cities. This fiction highlights how intensified maquila industrialization in the context of binational agreements like the 1994 North American Free Trade Agreement (NAFTA) has contributed to environmental pollution and created conditions for increased labor migration from Mexico's interior. Neither development stops at the Mexico-U.S. border. While the U.S. government has been slow to respond to environmental degradation, it has, throughout the 1990s, reacted to increased migration by taking border enforcement to historically unprecedented levels. As cultural productions by Romo, Yañez, and Guerrero show, these developments affect not only immigrants from Mexico but also Mexican-descended populations on the U.S. side.

Their writing further suggests that the deepening of divisions between Mexicans and Mexican Americans embodied in border militarization is mirrored in spatialized gendered, class, and political differences *within* U.S. Mexican communities. Ongoing migration from Mexico tends to exacerbate these divisions as it continually (re-)creates economic, cultural, and political distinctions among newcomers and older generations of Mexican Americans. Aside from emphasizing the spatiality of the Mexico-U.S. border, then, new Chicana/o literature stresses hitherto largely underexamined internal distinctions within Mexican American communities.

Recent writing also revives the commitment to political struggles that originally shaped 1950s–1970s Chicanismo in the form of resistance to neoliberal expressions of globalization. In this fiction, U.S. borders become places where Chicana/o civil rights struggles reemerge as individual and collective activism for border crossing rights and environmental justice. Because of its spatial focus, twenty-first-century Chicana/o border fiction thus demonstrates, as Doreen B. Massey puts it in *For Space,* that space is integral to the formation of latent political subjectivities that highlight the openness of the future (9–11).

Aztlán and the Mexico-U.S. Border

Chicana/o literature has often been characterized in terms of its connections to two interrelated factors associated with "the border": an interest in formal innovation, theorized as a form of symbolic border crossing, and a local grounding in the U.S. Southwest, understood as border territory. Héctor Calderón and José David Saldívar have described Chicana/o cultural production as "an expression of a social group that has given *the* distinctive cultural feature to the American West and Southwest" (Calderón and Saldívar 2). They emphasize that Mexican Americans as an ethnicized group were, like the Southwest itself, created by the redrawing of the international boundary in the aftermath of the 1848 Mexico-U.S. War.

While early cultural production from or about the absorbed territory by authors like Jovita Gonzáles, María Amparo Ruiz de Burton, and Américo Paredes exist, border art began to flourish primarily in the context of 1950s–1970s Chicano activist and cultural-nationalist struggles for full U.S. citizenship rights.[3] These struggles further consolidated the territorial link between Chicana/os and the Southwest. The Chicano movement was shaped by the activism of Mexican-descended residents of the Southwest, many from families who have lived in the United States for generations but who have had little to no voice in local decision making. Activist struggles for labor, education, and land rights largely took place in the border states of California, Texas, Arizona, and New Mexico.[4]

The cultural nationalist version of Chicanismo was also firmly grounded in the U.S. Southwest, designating this geography both as the origin of Mexican civilization and former Mexican territory. Chicanismo articulated land claims to the Southwest in the idea of the Chicana/o homeland Aztlán located in this area. In the founding document of Chicanismo, "El Plan Espiritual," its purported author, Alurista, supported such territorial claims by declaring Chicana/os to be the descendants of the Aztecs, the aboriginal inhabitants of (parts of) the Southwest before they migrated to today's Mexico.[5]

Even though the Chicano movement was never homogeneous, the myth of Aztlán gained ascendance in activist struggles and also in attempts to institutionalize Chicana/o studies in the U.S. academy. Cultural nationalism influenced the so-called 1960s–1970s Chicano renaissance in the arts, shaping the themes of this literature long after Aztlán had ceased to function as an effective organizing tool for political activism (Aranda 22). Tomás Rivera's *Y no se lo tragó la tierra/And the Earth Did Not Devour Him* (1971) and Miguel Méndez's *Peregrinos de Aztlán* (1974, trans. as *Pilgrims in Aztlán* 1992) exemplify the general thrust of the literary renaissance and, perhaps more important, its immediate conflation with the notion of border literature. Both works describe collective experiences of Mexican (descended) people in the United States in terms that are reminiscent of Chicanismo's attempt to create a unifying ideology. *Tierra* stresses the emergence of a group consciousness among migrant populations. Referring to the notion of Aztlán in its title, *Peregrinos/Pilgrims* includes a short utopian dream sequence in which Chicana/os and undocumented immigrants establish a homeland in the desert.[6] The novel also showcases the transnational Southwest as a place where the poorest inhabitants of both Mexico and the United States are exploited and marginalized.

Peregrinos/Pilgrims and *Tierra* have both been labeled border literature.[7] This designation acknowledges that the two novels draw on the border lives of each author to represent Mexican (descended) populations and that they experiment with orality-influenced and fragmented narrative structures. But the two works' designation as border writing also highlights the ready conflation of Chicana/o literature with border writing and omits significant differences between the two novels. A consideration of *Tierra* as border literature especially neglects the novel's actual setting. While *Tierra* begins in the border area of south Texas where Rivera grew up, the majority of the novel focuses on the placelessness of migrant life that he experienced accompanying his parents on their quest for farm work and laboring himself as a migrant worker. Rather than being based in the border territory, *Tierra* predominantly narrates the *movement* of migrants throughout the southwestern and midwestern United States in the 1940s and 1950s within an experimental, "border crossing" aesthetics that includes shifts in narrative voice, time frames, and locations.

Labeling *Tierra* border literature reaffirms the novel's central position in the Chicana/o literary canon, which has only uncomfortably accommodated *Peregrinos/Pilgrims* (Castillo, "Pesadillas" 53), the first novel of a border crossing novelist that is set on both sides of Mexico-U.S. border locations. Born in Bisbee, Arizona, Méndez had to relocate with his family to El Claro, Sonora, after his father lost his job in the mines during the Great Depression. At age fifteen, Miguel Méndez returned to Arizona by himself to work as a farm and construction laborer. An autodidact who never obtained more than a sixth-grade education, Méndez eventually became a professor of Spanish at the University of Arizona. In the preface to *Pilgrims in Aztlán*, Méndez expresses his multilayered border crossing identity, which is conceptualized differently on each side of the international boundary when he identifies as a "Mexican Indian, wetback, and a Chicano" (2).

In addition to differences in their life experiences (and the fact that Méndez highlights his indigenous roots), Rivera and Méndez also encountered divergent contexts for the production of their work that significantly influenced its reception. While *Tierra* was originally published in bilingual format by the Chicano publishing house Quinto Sol, *Peregrinos* was published solely in Spanish by Editorial Peregrinos, an independent press that Méndez and his friend Aristeo Brito established in Tucson in 1974. The novel did not became available in English until 1992, when it was commissioned for translation by Bilingual Press and published as *Pilgrims in Aztlán*. As Teresa McKenna writes, the fact that *Peregrinos* was originally composed in Spanish (and was not available in English translation until the early 1990s) has largely excluded it from the Chicano literature classes that are dominated by the English-language requirement of most English departments (McKenna 34).

The explicitly transnational border life examined in *Peregrinos* also appears not to have been as easily assimilable to the Chicana/o canon as the migrant experience described in *Tierra*. *Peregrinos/Pilgrims* is unabashedly "local." It is set in Tijuana and in the Californian and Arizona portions of the U.S. Southwest near Yuma and Sonora. All of these settings play important roles in the novel. In a recent reevaluation of Méndez's work, Gary Keller has called the author a "master of place" with regard to the Sonoran Desert. José Pablo Villalobos has similarly praised *Peregrinos* because it provides "an unrivaled depiction of a border reality" (Villalobos 133). The novel depicts its border locations in explicit transnational terms. As Méndez writes in the preface of *Pilgrims,* the book presents "the thoughts and feelings of those who suffered the most on both sides of the border" (2). *Peregrinos/Pilgrims* fictionalizes both Mexican-descended people in the U.S. Southwest and the toils of Mexicans in the northern borderlands during a period of approximately fifty years. This time period covers the realignments brought on by the Mexican revolution of 1910 and the enormous demographic growth of the U.S. Southwest and northern Mexican border cities throughout the 1960s.

The novel thus adds to the Chicana/o myth of Aztlán an attention to the transnational character of the Mexico-U.S. borderlands. Méndez designates "the vast stretches of Arizona, New Mexico, and Texas" as "Chicano lands" (173), a place where "Chicano people [are] reduced to the worst of humiliations, enslaved in the fields, the mines, the cities, denied their rights and dignity because they were dark and weak" (173). The novel also focuses on the perils facing Mexican (im)migrants who have to cross the Arizona desert and perform hard manual labor upon arrival.

At the same time, *Peregrinos/Pilgrims* represents life on the other side of the border, specifically in Tijuana, Baja California. In addition to treating such well-known themes as prostitution, street children, and nightlife, *Peregrinos/Pilgrims* fictionalizes migrants in Nogales who live transborder lives between Mexico and the United States, always on the verge of crossing the border or returning from it. Given Méndez's more intimate familiarity with Mexican border towns like Nogales, Sonora (which is located in close proximity to Bisbee, Douglas, and Tucson, where the author grew up and later resided), it is interesting that he chose to focus on Tijuana, a city he visited only once. Debra Castillo has suggested that *Peregrinos/Pilgrims* largely recuperates stereotypes about Tijuana because the city offered Méndez "an organizing image and a metaphor for all that is wrong with those aspects of border culture forged in the pressures from the United States" ("Pesadillas" 47). But perhaps Méndez's choice of Tijuana was also prophetic, because some Arizona border cities grew into larger urbanized areas somewhat similar to Tijuana in the context of 1990s neoliberal globalization.

In addition to drawing on the border experiences of its author, *Peregrinos/Pilgrims* experiments with orality and fragmented narrative structures, an aesthetics often represented in the metaphor of border crossing. Formally less unified than *Tierra*, *Peregrinos/Pilgrims* presents "the whole spectrum of the border reality," "a physical and psychological reality fragmented even in its components, a reality that is contradictory, perverse, and arbitrary" (del Pino 90). Individual narrative segments are not bound together by plot and do not progress in time. Only some of the stories are narrated through the consciousness of a central character, Loreto Maldonado, an eighty-year-old Yaqui and former general of the Mexican Revolution who makes a living washing cars and doing odd jobs on the Mexican side of the border. *Peregrinos/Pilgrims* also employs elements of orality. Mostly presented through the mind of Loreto, oral versions of the lives of the oppressed are contrasted with the falsifying written version of official records, particularly about the Mexican Revolution (Bruce-Novoa, "Righting" 79). As Bruce-Novoa argues, when Maldonado dies at the end of *Peregrinos/Pilgrims,* the reader is expected to take his place as the keeper of these oral histories ("Righting" 79).

Héctor Calderón's discussion of fragmented storytelling and orality in Rivera's *Tierra* illuminates an important function of Chicana/o experimentation with narrative. Calderón posits that *Tierra* brings together elements of realism and modernism with localized forms of storytelling to represent what should be judged a third-world experience in the first world (113). *Peregrinos*'s combination of what Castillo has called high-modernist fragmentation with old-fashioned social realism ("Pesadillas" 53) similarly chronicles the transformation of a peasant, rural, or agricultural world by new economic realities that provided the context for the creation of a Mexican (American) migrant culture. Despite its quite contemporary view of the border area as a transnational location marked by deep inequities among and within border populations, however, *Peregrinos/Pilgrims* has received little attention as a work of border fiction. Other critical paradigms have prevailed that continue to associate "the border" with more symbolic questions of Mexican American culture and aesthetics.

Borderlands Writing

These critical approaches linking Chicana/o identity and aesthetics with terms like *borders, borderlands,* and *border crossings* rose to prominence throughout the 1980s and 1990s. This period also witnessed the publication of creative work about the Mexico-U.S. border by authors like Gloria Anzaldúa, Norma Elia Cantú, Dagoberto Gilb, Alberto Ríos, Sergio Troncoso, and Helena María Viramontes. While these writers continue the aesthetic experimentalism of earlier Chicana/o border fiction, they also diverge from its focus on the Southwest as a context for examinations of Mexican (American) migrant lives. Frontera writing largely disposes of Aztlán in favor of borderlands, an imaginary that is related to but separate from the everyday Mexico-U.S. border, which functions as the starting point for examinations of Chicana/o culture and identity formation. Rather than migration, frontera writing stresses the *result* of a shifted border and of (im)migration, the formation of hybrid cultures and *identities* that complicate dominant U.S. notions of citizenship.

Directing itself to mixed audiences that include Anglo readers, border-lands writing insists that the folklore, traditions, and cultures of Mexican Americans have developed *in spite of* the Mexico-U.S. border. Such binationalism provides a model of belonging other than that of national citizenship. While frontera work recognizes the geopolitical hardening of the border and deepening divisions between Mexico and the United States, it focuses on cultural acts of border crossing, including bi- and multilingualism, for the formation of Chicana/o culture. This literature expresses the view of many Chicana/os that the Mexico-U.S. border constitutes an entirely arbitrary divide that has separated *one* people since the 1848 Treaty of Guadalupe Hidalgo.

The most famous border text from this period, Gloria Anzaldúa's *Borderlands/La Frontera* (1987), has given poetic voice to this opinion, stating that the Mexico-U.S. border represents a "1,950 mile-long open wound dividing a *pueblo*, a culture" (2, emphasis in original). *Borderlands/La Frontera* refigures the Southwest and its designation as Aztlán in the explicitly transnational notion of *la frontera*, which has become the guiding metaphor of Latina/o studies (Flores 198). Even though other writers were also engaged in displacing Aztlán from the center of Chicana/o studies, Anzaldúa's work has had the largest cultural impact.[8]

Borderlands/La Frontera opens with a geographical focus on the Texas-Chihuahua borderlands, the place where Anzaldúa grew up, and whose division by the Treaty of Guadalupe Hidalgo served as the model for narratives of Aztlán. Her book articulates spatialized concerns with border developments at the time of her writing that include intensified U.S. border militarization, the growth of maquila industries in Mexican border cities, violence against undocumented border crossers, and the transformation of U.S. ranching into large-scale agribusiness with negative effects on the environment.[9] But already at the end of the first chapter, *Borderlands/La Frontera* moves from observations of border realities to questions of Anzaldúa's identity as someone affected by exclusion from the U.S. nation and by the masculinism and heterosexism of the Chicano movement. Anzaldúa's emphasis on geopolitical changes at the international boundary thus quickly gives way to her attempts to identify the border fence with questions of identity. She describes the fence as "running down the length of my body, / staking rods in my flesh, / splits me splits me / *me raja me raja* / This is my home / this thin edge of barbwire" (2–3).

To theorize a space in which these divisions can be overcome, *Borderlands/La Frontera* forges the now famous notion of a mestiza borderlands consciousness that comprises white (Anglo), Mexican, and Indian elements as well as multiple languages. Mixing historical, theoretical, and poetic genres, the book replaces the male Aztec mythology that has been central to Chicanismo with *female* Mesoamerican myths of empowered femininity in order to make room for Chicanas. Like the work of Lorna Dee Cervantes, Denise Chávez, Sandra Cisneros, and Cherríe Moraga, Anzaldúa's text has contributed to conceptualizing neo-indigenous and feminist versions of Aztlán. Theorizing questions of mixed identity of Chicanas like herself, Anzaldúa's book extends the metaphorical use of the border as a designation of Chicana/o empowerment to notions of hybrid identity formation. This hybridity can function as an alternative to essentialist notions of belonging and citizenship in a nation or culture.

Other frontera work from the 1980s and 1990s by Alberto Ríos and Norma Cantú continues the tradition of merging a thematic focus on the Mexico-U.S. border territory with aesthetic experimentation to examine the notion of multiple boundaries. The author of various books and chapbooks of poetry, a memoir, and three collections of short stories, Ríos has seen his work included in scores of national and international literary anthologies, such as the *Norton Anthology of Modern Poetry*. While *Pig Cookies and Other Stories* (1995) is set entirely in a small town in Mexico, much of Rios's poetry; his other two short story collections, *The Curtain of Trees* (1999) and *The Iguana Killers* (1984); and his memoir, *Capirotada: A Nogales Memoir* (1999), are located in southern Arizona and include periodic border crossings into Mexico.

Ríos's work focuses on Nogales, where the author grew up. Even though he sometimes ventures north and south of this location, the Arizona side of the twin cities serves as the primary setting for examinations of the everyday lives and cultures of Mexican American border dwellers. The opening section of his memoir *Capirotada* begins with a description of Nogales, its history, and its natural and built landscape. The author stresses the undivided nature of the border territory as the "stretch of land reaching from Guyamas, Mexico, on the Sea of Cortés, to Tucson, Arizona, compris[ing] an ancient region known as the Pimería Alta," located along an "old trading route." As he writes, "people who had families in one part of this region also had relatives in the other parts" (2). *Capirotada* emphasizes mutual transnational influences in the border area, expressed in metric signposts, cross-border shopping, the coexistence of Spanish and English, and the constant border crossings from Mexico that, along with tourist visits, make up what he calls the actual, yet secret, population of Nogales, Arizona. Ríos also briefly addresses the transborder effect of maquilas in Nogales, Sonora, on the water and air quality along the U.S. portion of the border, and he recounts the historical openings of border fences in downtown Nogales for special holidays and parades.

The author describes the hardening of the international boundary, the replacement of fences with concrete, the ending of cross-border parades, and the closings of border crossings at times of national crisis since the 1970s. But the emphasis of the memoir remains on the permeability of the border, especially in the cultural and mental realms. Ríos writes, for example, that "[p]eople always talk about the border as that fence between people there in those towns. That's not the border. It's something else, something underscoring the difference between danger and grace, which is not something that separates people. It's something that joins them, as they face the same border" (49). Rather than develop a collective notion of Chicana/o culture and identity, throughout *Capirotada* Ríos traces the myriad layers of his individual border life. This includes his upbringing in Nogales, Arizona, by parents of different cultures and languages who were displaced to the area from the lands of their birth. Having grown up in Chiapas, Mexico, Ríos's father crossed the border as an undocumented immigrant, joined the military, and acquired citizenship through military service in World War II, where he also met his future wife, a British nurse.

Two of Ríos's collections of short stories are also set in Nogales, Arizona, but they comment less on geopolitical border developments than the opening segments of *Capirotada*. A recipient of the Western States Book Award in Fiction, *Iguana Killer* consists mainly of coming-of-age stories in which the young male protagonists, othered in some ways, seek their way in the world of 1950s and 1960s Nogales. "The Child" constitutes an exception. This story focuses on the politically charged issue of drug smuggling across the Mexico-U.S. border, featuring fictionalized smugglers who use the hollowed-out body of a dead child as a means to illegally transport drugs.

Perhaps the most widely discussed story among Chicana/o critics, "The Child" has often been associated with magical realism as an oppositional aesthetic strategy.[10] In *Border Matters,* José David Saldívar has described Rios's work, including "The Child," as mixing "the social realism of the border corrido" with "*lo barroco* of the Américas to create a Chicano phantasmatic" (67). He reads Rios's oeuvre as engaging in "magical realist storytelling" (68), highlighting how this form mixes seemingly incompatible genres. Mary Pat Brady, however, has considered the magical-realist qualities of "The Child" as an expression of "the impossibility of adequately fictionalizing such an atrocity in the first place" (184). She has posited that "The Child" highlights the extent to which the drug economy has transformed everyday practices in the border area (187). These differing evaluations of Ríos's magical realism point to the complexity of this aesthetic strategy and to the kind of research that is still necessary to fully understand its status in the contemporary period.

Ríos's second collection of short stories, *The Curtain of Trees,* recounts stories of everyday life in Nogales in the 1930s and 1940s that, as Ríos states in his author's note, he "imagine[d] and . . . remembered and as they have been told to [him]" (xi). As David King Dunaway and Sara L. Spurgeon write, *Curtain* describes "a 1950s world hovering on the brink of the twentieth century yet still resolutely clinging to a nineteenth-century way of life" (171). The collection's namesake as well as the short story "Nogales and the Bombs" address the impact of the Mexican Revolution on the relationship between the two Nogaleses. The other pieces portray the notion of "the middle," the realm taken for granted, which Ríos associates with the geographical border space with which he is most familiar. In his author's note, Ríos writes that the stories "are about the Arizona border with Mexico at the middle of this century . . . from a time-between-times about people who inhabit what is a place-between-places, physically, emotionally, and historically. The crude, ten-foot, pseudo-Berlin wall that separates the two countries now in Nogales is a good bookmark for these stories" (xi). In a recent interview, Ríos has similarly identified this middle space with notions of daily routine, stating that he searches for "the edge, the epiphany, the fingersnap, that exists in the middle, which is where we least expect to find these things and never think to look" (Wootten 57).

Despite the fact that Ríos never claims representative status by emphasizing his family's uniqueness vis-à-vis other border residents, critics like Richard Vela have discussed Ríos's texts within frameworks that focus on *collective* Chicana/o identity formation. Vela has argued that Ríos employs the realities of the border as a lens through which to explore "the hybrid identities that develop in border situations" (115). Norma Cantú's book *Canícula,* which she calls a "fictional autobioethnography," has received critical treatment similar to that of *Capirotada.* Winner of the Premio Aztlán, *Canícula* experiments with form to signal the author's self-conscious use of the memoir as a genre, focusing more overtly than Ríos's work on questions of collective Chicana/o identity formation and culture. The book is an account of Cantú's upbringing in the late 1940s to mid-1960s along the south Texas–Nuevo León border space, particularly in the twin cities of Laredo and Nuevo Laredo. A collage of eighty-five vignettes and twenty-three interspersed photos, *Canícula* blends several genres—fiction and autobiography, the novel and the short story, ethnography and creative writing—to trace the border-crossing family traditions that provided the context for Cantú's upbringing. In the introduction to the book, Cantú, an anthropologist by training, describes her work as the second part of a nonexisting trilogy. She also deliberately mismatches photographs and narratives, and she omits and retouches pictures. These strategies not only question the notion of truthfulness that is still often associated with autobiography and memoir but they also continue the tradition of linking writing about the border to aesthetic experimentation with genre.

Cantú's book focuses on the customs and traditions of her family that straddle the geopolitical boundary. The map at the beginning of *Canícula* indicates a Laredo metropolitan territory without division. For Cantú, this border region primarily serves as a space that allows the author to examine issues of Mexican American identity formation and to play with expectations about genre. Ellen McCracken has argued that in *Canícula* the border functions as "the complicated unitary space of [Cantú's] family's history and evolving identity on both sides of the border." McCracken also highlights how this geography is linked to the book's border crossings, manifested in "genre hybridity, visual/verbal hybridity, and the intersection of competing critical, linguistic, and other cultural codes" (262).

The Laredo border thus serves primarily as a metaphor of Chicana/o identity and aesthetics, while *Canícula* refers only twice to historical and geopolitical events along the border as they affected the narrator's family. The book touches on her grandparents' repatriation to Mexico during the Great Depression (which parallels that of Miguel Méndez and his parents) and her father's immigration to the United States. In a brief interlude that does not provide deep historical context, the narrator's grandmother remembers how her whole family was deported from San Antonio in 1935: "she and Marilio, my Texas-born grandfather, and their two young daughters packed all their belongings and drove their pickup truck down from San Antonio" (5).

The narrator here refers to Mexican (American) repatriation during the late 1920s and early 1930s in response to concerns about competition with native-born workers and alleged overrepresentation among the unemployed ranks and the nation's relief programs. Even though repatriation has a longer history that dates back to the declaration of Texas as an independent republic, it took more massive forms in the context of the Great Depression. Mexicans and their U.S.-born children left voluntarily or were deported by the Immigration Service. These deportations resulted in widespread violations of civil and human rights, an instance of which is exemplified in the deportation of the narrator's grandparents and their children, even though the grandfather had been born in the United States. Other violations included illegally imprisoning immigrants and not permitting returnees to dispose of their property or to collect their wages, separating families, and deporting the infirm (McKay).[11] Unlike most deportees, who were sent to the border in packed trains, the narrator's grandparents returned to Mexico in their own vehicle, a Ford pickup truck laden with their belongings. Yet at the border crossing "from one Laredo to the other," the family lost everything to corrupt custom officials (5).

Canícula's narrator also relates how in 1948 she, her father, mother, and her grandmother crossed "the bridge on foot from one Laredo to the other" in a sort of "coming home, but not quite" (5). The father had used the money he had made from working in Indiana to move the family from Mexico to the United States, "but not too far north, not too far away from family" (29). This time the crossing is legal; everyone's papers are in order.

While the works of Ríos and Cantú showcase the intricacy of connections among border reality and metaphor, critical evaluations of work by perhaps the most famous Chicana writer, Sandra Cisneros, as an instance of border literature exemplify how the conflation of the border space with issues of Chicana/o identity and formal experimentation divorces symbolic concepts from the literal territory of the national boundary. In her reading of Cisneros's second book of fiction, *Woman Hollering Creek*, Katherine Payant, for example, has pointed to the work's use of border tropes—its focus on Chicana/os' origins in Mexico and their continuing linkage with Mexico through immigration, the stress on shared pre-Columbian or mestizo myths and legends, and the depiction of Chicano/as as straddling "two or three cultures" (95). As Payant puts this last point, borrowing language from Anzaldúa, Cisneros's characters, many of whom struggle to transcend culturally dictated gender roles, live lives "on the borderlands" (96); that is, they constantly cross several linguistic and cultural barriers.

While Cisneros certainly uses these border tropes and the genre-crossing aesthetics of the short-story cycle, none of her work is explicitly located along the Mexico-U.S. boundary. Instead, all of her fiction centers on female narrators who have a Mexican father and a Mexican American mother and who frequently visit their father's family in Mexico. Winner of the National Book Award, *The House on Mango Street* takes place in two locations: Chicago, where both the author and the narrator grew up, and Mexico City, where the author and narrator spent some time visiting family. *Woman Hollering Creek* (1991) is largely located in San Antonio and at times fictionalizes the narrator's border crossings into Mexico to visit family. Cisneros's most recent novel, *Caramelo* (2002), draws on all three locations. While the novel contains a scene where the narrator and her family cross the Mexico-U.S. border, *Caramelo* predominantly performs the narrator's search for her Mexican roots, embodied in her attempts to construct and creatively invent the lives of her grandparents in Mexico and of her parents in the United States.

Just as readings of Rivera's *Tierra* have established the novel as an instance of border writing even though it is largely set elsewhere, Cisneros's work is considered border literature within a framework that permits the use of "the border" in its symbolic meaning as a designation for questions of Chicana/o identity and aesthetics. In this sense, the border tropes Payant identifies in Cisneros's work could theoretically be found in much if not all Chicana/o literary texts, independently of their actual spatial or local focus.

Some critics have even argued that the "image of the border has become fully meaningful not only when we consider it as a physical line, but when we decenter it and liberate it from the notion of space to encompass notions of sex, class, gender, ethnicity, identity, and community" (Benito and Manzanas 3). But one of the more troubling aspects of "liberating" the border from its spatial referent to denote Chicana/o concerns with homeland, migration, identity, and aesthetics is that the voices of other border communities become muted.[12] In fact, the metaphorical linkage between Chicana/os and the U.S. southwestern border perpetuates the potential exclusion of other borderlanders already embodied in Aztlán. In its definition of Mexican Americans as mestizos, Aztlán selectively draws on the modern Mexican philosophy of *indigenismo*. While this philosophy elevates parts of Mexico's indigenous past to official versions of nationhood, it overlooks the long history of the suppression of Mexican Indians. Stressing possession of the Southwest, Aztlán also neglects indigenous claims to aboriginality in this region. In addition, the myth of Aztlán is grounded in events along the Texan border, where the Treaty of Guadalupe Hidalgo divided pre-1848 settlements so that their residents became citizens of two different countries (Kaup 12). This focus on regional developments, which involved relatively small populations, marginalizes the disproportionately much larger impact of continuing Mexican migration (and conditions in Mexico) for contemporary Mexican American communities.

As the term *borderlands* has displaced the dominance of Aztlán, this symbolic approach to the international border area similarly threatens to erase the historical record of native tribes who were, as Daniel Cooper Alarcón and José Aranda Jr. have reminded us, harassed, killed, converted to Catholicism, forced into slavery, dispossessed of their tribal lands, and forcibly inducted into European systems of socialization. Bypassing the border's spatial referent also silences U.S. Native Americans' nationalist struggles for sovereignty based in aboriginal land claims, and it fails to recognize the concerns of northern Mexican borderland residents.

Twenty-first-Century Chicana/o Border Fiction

While many of the 1980s–1990s border writers, including Alberto Ríos, have continued publishing, writing on the Mexico-U.S. border by emerging authors, such as Romo's *El Puente = The Bridge,* Yañez's *El Paso del Norte,* and Guerrero's *Chasing Shadows,* has also appeared. Even though the generational distinction between this work and its predecessors is not always clear-cut, the newer texts articulate different understandings of connections between Chicana/os and border geography. Literature from the early twenty-first century focuses on the effect that changes in Mexican border towns have on U.S. communities of Mexican descent in U.S. border cities. The authors thus consider expressions of globalization in both border and urban areas. These are two locations where new networks of global organizations and new types of political actors have become more clearly visible than in other sites (Sassen, "Nation States"). To use García Canclini's description of Latin American cities, border and urban areas can "serve as laboratories for degraded multicultural encounters and simultaneously develop as strategic centers for commercial, informational, and financial innovation, dynamizing the local market as it is incorporated into transnational circuits" (*Consumers* 7). As they highlight such changes in border cities, the newer Chicana/literature also shifts from the Spanish-inflected bilingualism of borderlands literature to near-complete English monolingualism, perhaps indicating that the authors imagine themselves writing to U.S. and global audiences that include non-Spanish speakers.

Like Cantú, Romo sets his work in Laredo, which is also his hometown. While he never refers to the setting by name, the novel mentions a "little city by the river" (85), which sports "the largest inland port of the United States" (29). Laredo's proximity to Nuevo Laredo and the two cities' connection by a bridge are described thus: "Looking toward the bridge, Convent [street] ran right onto the bridge, and the bridge ran right onto Guerrero. Guerrero became Convent. Convent became Guerrero. Two different streets. Two different countries. Two different worlds. Hot black pavement separating them. That's all" (48–49). Romo has said that he chose the bridge as his setting because "Laredo and Nuevo Laredo are really one community. The bridge itself is the only thing that separates one side from the other. I wanted to focus on the bridge itself, let people see that it really was a passage, plain and simple, from one country to another. I wanted readers to see that over the bridge passed real people who felt pain and sadness and happiness and all those things that real people feel, not aliens, not wetbacks, real people" (Becerra).

In his choice of setting, Romo stresses the arbitrary division of the two cities. The 1848 Treaty of Guadalupe Hidalgo set the two towns on separate yet interlinked paths of development. As Laredo officially became part of Texas, Mexicans who wanted to retain their Mexican citizenship moved across the river to what was later named Nuevo Laredo, but many also stayed. Today, three-quarters of Laredo's residents are of Mexican descent. In the context of globalization, Nuevo Laredo has grown in numbers and industrial importance. While manufacturing jobs have declined in Laredo, Nuevo Laredo has become a strong industrial center, with the maquiladora industry constituting the city's second-largest economic sector. By 2000, Nuevo Laredo's population had grown to almost three times the size of its U.S. counterpart.[13]

El Puente depicts the river's color transformation in magical-realist terms that also draw on the originary anticolonial impetus of Latin American "boom" writing. As Romo describes the river's change, "[T]he waters of the Rio Grande had begun to turn a dark, dark red, like the Nile turning into blood in Cecil B. DeMille's *The Ten Commandments,* like magic" (130). Explanations of this color change range from religious miracle or industrial waste poisoning to government conspiracy. As in much magical realism, however, the river's transformation is also attributable to realistic events. Motivated by her husband's death, Tomasita, the novel's protagonist, pours a mixture of ground clay shards and dried mulberries into the stream where the maquila's "big-mouthed pipe com[ing] out of the factory wall . . . emptied into the river" (130). Tomasita's protest against the environmental pollution that is responsible for her husband's death is not a spontaneous act of outrage and grief. It is the outgrowth of a long, deliberate process of morning and introspection carried out over months of collecting mulberries and grinding them with clay into a very fine powder that is capable of being absorbed by the river.

As she spreads the powder in the stream that feeds the Río Grande via the pipe heading out of the maquila to the mouth of the river, Tomasita commits an act that underscores one of the disastrous side effects of U.S.-led border industrialization. Binational agreements that culminated in NAFTA have enabled corporations to systematically take advantage of lower labor and operating costs, tariff and value-added tax differentials, and the limited enforcement of weak environmental and labor regulations in Mexico. The creation of maquila assembly factories and the subsequent population growth in Mexican border towns in the absence of adequate public infrastructures have worsened existing environmental problems, such as the pollution of air, water, and land; and the overconsumption of water and other natural resources (Spalding 113). In the context of lax environmental laws, waste produced by maquilas, especially industrial solvents suspected of causing growing rates of cancer in the border region, is improperly treated or simply dumped on land and in the water.

The environments where poor residents live or work are disproportionately affected by degradation, which has drastic consequences for their health. After her husband José's death, Tomasita's health also fails; she goes deaf and loses her sense of smell. Asked to leave the company rental house, Tomasita moves into a two-room shack in a *colonia*. Lacking paved roads and sanitary water and sewer systems, this low-income housing development exemplifies the unplanned and unregulated nature of growth in Mexican border cities. Tomasita's *colonia* is located by the international river, which functions as her backyard, toilet, and bathroom. She is exposed to water that is, like the water in border towns more generally, polluted by untreated sewage, agricultural chemicals, and pesticide runoff, as well as by extensive dumping of industrial byproducts like heavy metals and toxic chemicals (Spalding 114). In addition to José's cancer, *El Puente* also fictionalizes other effects of environmental pollution that are related to contaminated water. A child is born with a spinal deformity, which is traced to the mother having drunk Mexican tap water, and a dentist in Juárez recommends purified rather than public water to avoid the risk of infection after dental work.

As a public manifestation of Tomasita's protest, the river's color change sparks collective responses. The book's individual vignettes explore the lives of fourteen women from both sides of the border, who become part of a crowd that gathers at the bridge to watch the river. In the tradition of the short-story cycle or composite novel, their individually complete stories are interlinked through the common setting, theme, and principles of storytelling. *El Puente*'s protagonists visit the international bridge at roughly the same moment: when an eighteen-wheeler honks; when Soledad from Nuevo Laredo gives birth; when Pura, a retired Laredo resident, dies of a heart attack; and when Rosa, a fifteen-year old Mexican American, attempts suicide by jumping off the bridge. Just as life emerges from death, these events bring together people whose lives might otherwise not have crossed.

On her way across the bridge to Laredo, Tomasita miraculously regains her sense of hearing and is thus able to listen to the newborn's cry. Tomasita places her hands on the child's head, leaving a red stain in the center. She performs the same gesture of benediction when a Mexican guard posted at her house does not follow his orders to shoot her. As she tries to cross the bridge back to Nuevo Laredo a few days later, a U.S. soldier recognizes Tomasita from wanted flyers and shoots her. Tomasita dies with a bullet hole in the middle of her forehead. The circumstances of Tomasita's Christlike death on the bridge articulate a strong critique of U.S. border militarization that has, by all accounts, failed to deter growing numbers of immigrants. The prevalence of military might and violence at the national boundary has created an environment in which border deaths have become commonplace. Besides the growing number of people who die trying to cross the border, immigrants are routinely mistreated by smugglers, thugs, and the Border Patrol. Recent decisions to place the U.S. National Guard along the border in support of the Border Patrol may lead to a resurgence of past accidental shootings of immigrants and U.S. residents in border locations.[14] While Tomasita is just another border casualty, she also becomes their most visible representative, dying in the spotlight the U.S. media has cast on the bridge.

Her association with Christlike martyrdom and the proximity of her death to water also suggest the possibility of redemption and rebirth.[15] At Tomasita's burial, her bullet wound is covered by an enormous sparkling emerald donated by "a wealthy Mexican housewife" (148) who has volunteered to take care of Tomasita's body. In one of his many cameo appearances throughout the novel, the NBC anchorman Tom Brokaw tells the audience that Tomasita's death sparked grief within this otherwise "typically quiet border community" (148–49). *El Puente* leaves us with the image of rebirth in the figure of another Mexican housewife taking care of Tomasita's remains (and perhaps continuing her mission). The book also gestures to the possibility that the border community's grief may transform into other forms of protest against the manifestations of U.S. neoliberal politics at the border that contributed to Tomasita's violent death.

In contrast to *El Puente*'s attention to the international bridge, Richard Yañez's *El Paso del Norte,* a finalist for the Texas Institute of Letters Award for Best Work of First Fiction, focuses on his hometown, El Paso, and its connection to Ciudad Juárez. El Paso has become one of the foremost U.S. centers of cultural production along the Mexico-U.S. border. The title of Yañez's collection points to the sixteenth-century collective designation of the two border cities as El Paso del Norte. As a result of the 1848 Treaty of Guadalupe Hidalgo, the area that today encompasses El Paso became U.S. territory. In 1888 the city of El Paso del Río del Norte changed its name to Ciudad Juárez in honor of Benito Juárez, hero of the revolution against France. El Paso was the first U.S. border city with urban concentrations of Mexicans (García 235), and currently two-thirds of its residents are of Mexican descent. El Paso's economy exemplifies neoliberal growth without prosperity, which is characterized by the prevalence of labor-intensive, low-value-added jobs (Simcox). The population of Ciudad Juárez is at least three times the size of El Paso's; the economy of its twin is dominated by maquila production with similar features.[16]

While all of Yañez's short stories can stand on their own, some contain interrelated characters and themes that connect Chicana/o communities to changes at the border. Most of the short stories are set in El Paso's working-class neighborhood Ysleta. They take place in a residential street, pretentiously called Nottingham Drive, and in several convenience stores. Ysleta is located less than a mile from the Zaragoza International Bridge. In Yañez's book, the transnational geography of Ysleta not only marks divisions between Mexico and the United States but also signifies internal differences among the Mexican majority population of El Paso. These economic, gendered, and political divisions become spatialized in residential segregation or, as Raymond A. Rocco has conceptualized this phenomenon, in the *multiplication* of Latina/o-Chicana/o communities. In his study of Latina/o communities in Los Angeles, Rocco argues that their diversification somewhat supersedes developments that have historically segregated Mexican Americans into a relatively cohesive group separated from other communities.

Yañez's opening story, "Desert Vista," focuses on Raul Luis, a junior high school student, whose family moved to Nottingham Drive a year ago. Here Raul Luis has to renegotiate the boundaries between his family's tenuous middle-class status and his new working-class neighborhood. Its schools are marked with graffiti, and its common language is Spanish, which Raul Luis does not really speak. The neighborhood is internally divided along even more complex class lines, spatialized through a barrier of wooden posts and metal rails with a "No Passing" sign (5). The barrier marks off the poorer parts of the street where houses have "[n]o basketball courts. No birdbaths. No mulberry trees" (16). The house of a classmate Raul Luis tries to befriend is described thus: "One side of the roof was missing shingles and appeared ready to cave in. The front door was more rust than any color of paint. [One] couldn't tell where the cement driveway ended and the grassless yard began. Trash and tumbleweeds clenched the chainlink fence" (17). Boys from the other side of the barrier often express their disapproval of the street's division by draping Raul Luis's house in toilet paper and covering it with mudballs.

"Rio Grande," the last story in the collection, is set in both El Paso and Ciudad Juárez. The story directly addresses the effects of border militarization on Mexican American residents. Throughout the collection, El Paso has been portrayed as a place where manifestations of border enforcement are ever present. Intoxicated Mexican American teenagers are afraid to be "mistaken for wetback smugglers or drug runners" (85); they are constantly aware of the "helicopters above—the ever-present migra- . . . busy watching for mules or coyotes, drug and wetback smuggling" (23).

"Rio Grande" fictionalizes responses to these developments. The story opens as the teenage narrator José and his Anglo friend Steve drive around in their truck, drinking. José's association with Steve and his desire to be called "Joe" indicate his degree of assimilation to white U.S. society. The two adolescents witness how the Border Patrol arrests undocumented immigrants in front of the local Kmart. When a teenage girl slips away, a Chicano agent named Roberto Duran pursues her, threatens her with his gun, and beats her so severely with his baton that his Anglo colleague John Wayne eventually intervenes. A fight ensues, in which a "mass of green uniform rolled around in the oil stains and gravel of Kmart's parking lot. . . . If their Stetsons hadn't been knocked off, it would have been hard to tell exactly who was who. . . . The illegals jailed in the Suburban rocked it back and forth, making all kinds of noise, presumably rooting for the gringo. A first, I'm sure" (82). As both agents are eventually carried away in an ambulance, the girl sets all the other undocumented migrants free.

These events initially do not seem to have an effect on José; there is no clear evidence that he feels solidarity with the Mexican nationals who are mistreated by a Border Patrol agent of Mexican descent. Instead, the two friends cross into Juárez to get drunk in one of the bars that caters to "mostly El Paso high school students and Fort Bliss GI's" (85). As it juxtaposes the two forms of border crossing, *El Paso del Norte* points to the irony that while undocumented immigrants are prevented from entering the United States in pursuit of work that keeps the U.S. economy afloat, underage U.S. citizens are able to pursue illegal activities on the other side of the border.

Upon his return home, José observes a Border Rights Coalition demonstration against proposed projects to replace the chain-link border fence with a steel wall. The forty to fifty protesters pass around petitions against the building of the wall, carrying signs that read "2 Cities = 1 People," "No More Fences," and "Free Bridge" (89). Border Patrol agents dressed in riot gear use tear gas to break up the demonstration. Even though he tries to remain detached from what he sees as "none of [his] business" (90), José is knocked down, beaten, kicked, and arrested. He then experiences, in attenuated form, the treatment of undocumented border crossers that he observed that morning in front of the Kmart. The INS detention cell he spends the night in "smelled worse than the infested Rio" (91), but he knows that it is much better than the other, collective holding cells where hundreds of undocumented immigrants are held. José's experience spawns a newfound awareness about the effects of border developments on his own life that may translate into activism. After he is released, he recounts that "yesterday's numbness is gone" (92).

Like Yañez's book, the eleven stories in Lucrecia Guerrero's *Chasing Shadows,* the recipient of a Pushcart Prize nomination, are held together by a geographical focus on a border town. Mesquite is characterized by internal divisions among Mexican American communities and their separation from residents of Mexico. Unlike Yañez, who explicitly names his border setting, and Romo, who gestures toward it, Guerrero creates a fictive location that evokes the twin border city of Nogales, Arizona, where the author grew up. However, in an interview Guerrero has stated that while the border setting was "crucial" for her work, "Mesquite is not Nogales. It can be all that is Nogales and more—all that I make it" (Caldwell).

Thus, although it is loosely based on Nogales, *Chasing Shadows* can be read as a collection of fiction about any larger border city. Even though the two towns of Nogales evolved from separate settlements, for a long time their developments were interlinked. In the early 1920s, for example, Mexicans of relative means lived on the U.S. side of the boundary, while most working-class Mexicans employed on the U.S. side lived in Mexico. It was difficult to distinguish between the two national territories in any meaningful sense (Nevins 45). Since the 1980s, the Sonoran Nogales has evolved from a small town to a booming industrialized city, its growth fueled by maquiladora factories. The population of Nogales, Sonora, has increased to about ten times the number of Nogales, Arizona, whose population has remained relatively stable. Eighty-one percent of its residents are of Mexican descent.[17]

Like Romo, Guerrero emphasizes gender as an important variable in border issues, but hers is the only text that also evokes some of the indigenous Mexican mythology underlying Chicanismo and its feminist transformation by writers like Anzaldúa to depict developments along the border.[18] Not as cohesive as *El Puente,* the individual short stories in *Chasing Shadows* are nevertheless more clearly interrelated than the various narrative pieces in *El Paso del Norte.* Connections among Guerrero's stories unfold chronologically. Guerrero has said that publishers encouraged her to interlink the various stories, some of which had already appeared separately, to make them even more marketable (Caldwell).

Most of the characters' lives intersect in the impoverished U.S. neighborhood of Frontera Street or in other public spaces in Mesquite, such as its elementary school and its bus depot. Located literally on the border, Frontera Street represents one of two sites where the internal division of the border town is visibly delineated by a "tall chain-link that separates Mesquite into two cities" (110), the fifteen-foot fence that replaced less sturdy barriers in 1995. While one fence "center-cuts the length of the street, separat[ing] Mesquite from Mexico" (11), another is located near the downtown business area "where uniformed immigration officials keep the perimeters well-defined" (110).

In "The Curse," inhabitants of the Mexican Mesquite wait by the fence to ask U.S. residents for water. Except for the collection's central protagonist, a young girl named Tonantzin Salazar, no one wants to help because, as one character puts it, "our water level is low, too, so nobody can expect us to share with the Mexicans" (32–33). Tonantzin is named after the Virgin of Guadalupe, a connection reinforced by her only valuable belonging, a pendant featuring the Virgin and the Hummingbird. This association highlights her suffering and marginalization; Tonantzin is even poorer than the majority of the residents of Frontera Street's apartment complex, and her father's persistent absence exposes her to threats of male violence and potential pedophilic abuse. But Tonantzin's linkage to indigenous mythology also emphasizes her empathy and solidarity with those less fortunate than herself. The novel connects Tonantzin's attempts to help Mexicans from the other side with the Chicana/o myth of a unified Southwest, the "land of [la] raza, now in Arizona, once Mexico, and before, when it simply was" (152–53).

Chasing Shadows also highlights political differences within Mexican American communities that often intersect with class. More established and often more well-to-do residents in the United States fear the competition of newcomers who are at the bottom of the U.S. socioeconomic ladder. Cookie McDonald, a Mexican immigrant who has lived in the United States for twenty years, exemplifies successful assimilation to U.S. society, despite her initially unlawful entry into the United States. Cookie's undocumented immigration and her subsequent marriage to an Anglo afforded her class mobility from housemaid and peasant in Mexico to homeowner and member of what she believes is the U.S. middle class. In the book's only passage about Mexico, Cookie remembers how her class status in that country was further reinforced by her dark skin. Her story highlights the sheer impossibility of overcoming these barriers, partially because of the belief that pure blood traceable to the Spanish aristocracy could be damaged by marrying someone of lower class and racial status.

Rather than reject the racially inflected class ideology that oppressed her in Mexico, however, Cookie affirms its U.S. variant. She constantly reminds her daughter of the importance of maintaining her light skin color and keeps herself apart from the poorer residents of the apartment complex in Frontera Street that she sees from her house on the hill. Cookie even physically inscribes the economic and political divisions between herself and the residents of the apartment building by asking her husband to put barbed wire around the fence of their own house, "[l]ike the taller one at the border," and to plant a hedge so high that "she won't be able to see the street below" (24). As the unnamed narrator of this story asks, "Doesn't she have a right to protect her position?" (19). When approached by a Border Patrol agent, Cookie agrees to spy on Frontera Street families and to report undocumented border crossings. She is especially interested in Joaquín de la Torre, a cotton-field laborer, border-rights activist, and poet who is politically involved with students and migrant workers and helps to bring undocumented people across the desert. His name evokes Joaquín Murrieta, a colorful early California bandit with Robin Hood charisma, who has become a larger-than-life myth. As Guerrero states, this myth continues to give "people hope and courage" (Caldwell). Cookie's diligent reports to the Border Patrol place Joaquín under surveillance. He almost gets arrested on trips across the border, and one night Joaquín does not return home at all.

While his fate remains unclear by the end of the collection, it is intimated that he may have died in the desert at the hands of U.S. authorities. His mother has a vision of Joaquín's "death-limp body left on the desert floor, his face so pale it seemed as though his tan were only fading paint, translucent in the glow of the ghostly white moon" (168). Even though his is yet another border death conditioned by the intersecting forces of border industrialization and militarization, the collection ends on a hopeful note. Flaco Valencia, a longtime friend of Joaquín's, arrives to comfort Joaquín's mother. Throughout the collection, Flaco has shown compassion for members of the community weaker than he. As Flaco comes to speak to Joaquín's mother, "it is as though—for just a moment—all the dreams she passed on to Joaquín return, pulse back into her heart" (175). Perhaps, the story tells us, Flaco will continue Joaquín's mission, a form of individualized political activism for border crossing rights and against U.S. border militarization.

The Multiplicities of Chicana/o Border Writing

The texts by Romo, Yañez, and Guerrero continue the political struggles that underlie Chicanismo and have informed early border literature. But the newer fiction moves beyond the 1980s–1990s emphasis on Chicana/o culture and identity formation to highlight the effects of contemporary forms of U.S. empire on Mexican American communities in U.S. border areas. Because it is less interested in symbolic questions of homeland or cultural and identity formation, this literature thus creates fewer opportunities for the persistent conflation of symbolic and literal meanings of the border.

El Puente, El Paso del Norte, and *Chasing Shadows* connect Chicana/o communities to neoliberal change in Mexican border towns. While Romo emphasizes the environmental consequences of U.S.-led maquiladorization, his work, like that of Yañez and Guerrero, also explores the effects of U.S. border militarization, purportedly directed at Mexican "illegals," on Mexican American communities. The three texts fictionalize spatialized divisions among border cities' majority populations as mirrors of a national boundary that reinforces economic and social differences between residents of Mexico and the United States. The authors also depict U.S. border cities as spaces where Chicana/o civil rights struggles, originally directed against exclusion from the benefits of U.S. citizenship, may re-emerge in the form of individual and collective transnational activism for border crossing rights and environmental justice.

While *El Puente, El Paso del Norte,* and *Chasing Shadows* are not completely free of metaphorical imaginings about the region and continue to favor U.S. towns and their majority populations, the three texts remind us of the spatial nature of the Mexico-U.S. boundary, which has been somewhat relegated to the margins of Chicana/o and humanities understandings of "borders." In its emphasis on Chicana/o populations and their connections to the Mexico-U.S. border space, the tradition of Chicana/o border writing examined in this chapter also intersects with the fiction about other borderlanders that is the subject of this book. Like Chicana/o cultural productions, literature about Asian-descended, indigenous, Mexican, and Canadian border dwellers focuses on U.S. boundaries, engages in literary experimentation, and examines questions of U.S. empire and its intersection with the repressive nationalisms of neighboring countries. But, unlike writing by Chicana/o authors, this work, for the most part, has not also been associated with symbolic notions of "the border." A comparative study of border fiction links U.S. boundaries to a wider range of issues than those hitherto imagined in the metaphor of the border.[19] Such a framework places Chicana/o-Latina/o studies at the intersection of other area and ethnic studies fields within inter-American studies.

2   Asian Border Crossings

AFTER RELATIVE silence throughout the twentieth century (with the exception of the Great Depression and Operation Wetback in the 1950s), borders again surged into the limelight as entryways for undocumented immigrants in the early 1990s. Manifestations of economic recession in California contributed to a profusion of nativist discourses that focused on immigrants from south of the Mexico-U.S. border. The quest to illegalize undocumented entry was, however, also significantly energized by the 1993 discovery of the Golden Venture, a ship carrying undocumented Chinese immigrants (Rotella, *Twilight* 72).

For a brief period at the end of the twentieth century, coverage of U.S. borders began to include reports about an increase in border crossings by Chinese immigrants. A *Newsweek* feature article from March 1999, for example, characterized the Mexico-U.S. border as a prime location for undocumented Chinese immigration into the United States. And the discovery in 2000 of the "largest global alien smuggling ring" between the United States and Canada demonstrated that the other, often forgotten northern border with Canada was becoming another major transit corridor linking China to the United States ("Huge" A1). Many of the estimated 100,000 undocumented Chinese who have come to the United States every year since the late 1980s (P. Smith x) use the northernmost U.S. border as their point of entry. That fewer Chinese crossers are caught by U.S. authorities as compared to people from Mexico and Latin, Central, and South America is, in part, also a result of much higher smuggling fees and more sophisticated networks, which, in the words of one journalist, "buy better odds" (Rotella, *Twilight* 72).

Destined for New York's Chinatown, most of the undocumented immigrants travel across a Mohawk reservation on the St. Lawrence Seaway, which straddles New York, Ontario, and Québec. Jurisdiction over the territory is assumed by several local, regional, and national institutions, and immigration or custom controls on border crossings no longer exists (Gibbins 160). Smuggling networks alternatively use a variety of other Canada-U.S. gateways, including Ontario's Walpole Island First Nation reservation, which is separated from Michigan's Harsen's Island by a narrow channel off the St. Clair River. When the river freezes, immigrants turn to Detroit's Ambassador Bridge and to the train tunnel connecting Port Huron, Michigan, and Sarnia, Ontario ("Island").

The link between U.S. borders and Chinese immigration has a much longer history not considered in these journalistic accounts. Several short stories published at the turn of the twentieth century by Edith Maude Eaton (1865–1914), the first fiction writer of Asian descent in North America, imaginatively depict earlier "illegal" U.S. border crossings.[1] These were not undertaken by Mexicans across the Mexico-U.S. border but by Chinese traversing the then largely uncharted and unguarded boundary with Canada. Just as Chinese border crossings have only recently moved to the foreground of U.S. immigration history, Edith Eaton's work was rediscovered in the context of the Asian American Renaissance when U.S. Asian American studies became formalized as a field in the mid-1970s and 1980s.[2]

Penned under the name Sui Sin Far, Eaton's journalistic and fictional work appeared between 1888 and 1913 in various U.S., Caribbean, and Canadian periodicals and newspapers. Thirty-eight of Eaton's stories, only some of which had previously appeared, were published in 1912 as *Mrs. Spring Fragrance*.[3] Like many other writers residing in Canada at the turn of the century, Eaton first sent her stories to U.S. outlets and later physically moved to the United States because of the dearth of publishing opportunities in Canada.[4] The decision to publish in the United States or to move there had enormous consequences for the content and the critical reception of Canadian writers' work (Thacker 132). In Eaton's case, when her early stories about Montréal Chinese began to appear in small U.S. journals that often bore a regionalist focus, their Canadian settings became muted. And when Eaton moved from her home in Canada to other parts of the hemisphere in search of more lucrative work, her work shifted more clearly in thematic focus to comply with U.S. expectations.

The institutionalization of Eaton's work in the U.S. Asian American canon and, throughout the 1990s, its inclusion in the body of "American" literature through regionalist frameworks highlights her later preoccupations with questions of identity formation. But these critical lenses obscure the focus of much of Eaton's earlier work, both her stories and nonfiction, on the relationship between Chinese immigrants and the Canadian border. An analysis of this writing emphasizes the largely overlooked relevance of national boundaries and national politics to the formation of today's Chinese diaspora in North America. In her work, Eaton created the first-known fictional representations of the undocumented U.S. border crosser forged in the intersection of divergent and conflicting state policies in North America.

Differences among early forms of U.S. empire and Canadian immigration policies manifested themselves at the shared border and transformed it into a gateway for Chinese immigrants. The 1882 passage of U.S. exclusion legislation barred most Chinese from legal entrance into the United States. Many Chinese began entering Canada, which did not pass its own version of an exclusion act until 1923, mainly under pressure from the United States. In the meantime, Canada's 1885 Chinese Immigration Act simply imposed head taxes on Chinese immigrants that made entry into Canada more difficult but not illegal. After the passage of each subsequent U.S. exclusion act, larger numbers of Chinese would be admitted into Canada, many of whom would then cross the border into the United States "illegally." It was believed that 99 percent of those arriving in Canada intended to cross the border into the United States. Canadian law, in fact, allowed those Chinese destined for the United States to remain in the dominion for ninety days without paying the required head tax (E. Lee, *America's Gates* 153).

At the time, this boundary had not yet been firmly established in multilateral agreements or supervised by custom and immigration officials (McIlwraith 54). While immigrants took advantage of lax enforcement all along the border, its northeastern portion, the setting of Eaton's border crossing stories, was even less well guarded (E. Lee, *America's Gates* 154). According to U.S. immigration estimates, between the 1880s and the early 1900s at least a few thousand Chinese entered the country every year via the Canada-U.S. boundary (E. Lee, *America's Gates* 153).

In 1997, almost one hundred years after Eaton's stories originally appeared, the Japanese American writer Karen Tei Yamashita published *Tropic of Orange*, a novel that takes up some of the issues raised in Eaton's work. Yamashita's work focuses on Chinese undocumented immigration via the Mexico-U.S. boundary and, more generally, on increasing intersections among Asian American and Latino communities along the border. A comparative analysis of the two writers suggests new and fruitful connections between Asian American perspectives, border and

Latina/o studies, and inter-American approaches. Yamashita's novelistic account of contemporary undocumented Chinese border crossings across the Mexico-U.S. line participates in ongoing debates about the Mexico-U.S. border and U.S. empire in the Americas, a discussion from which Asian American studies has so far been largely absent. *Tropic* also develops new inter-American lenses by articulating a pan-ethnic and transnational counterideology that inflects 1950s–1970s Chicanismo and its geographical association with the U.S. Southwest with the progressive politics of pan-Asian civil rights struggles.

The Chinese *Indocumentado* at the Canada-U.S. Border

Edith Eaton was the first Chinese-descended author in North America to fictionalize the struggles of Chinese immigrants at a time of strong bias against them.[5] The daughter of an English father and a Chinese mother who grew up in England, Eaton lived in Montréal from the time she was about eight until the age of thirty-two.[6] The Eaton family's move from England in 1872 coincided with the increase in emigration from mainland China that had occurred since the mid-nineteenth century. Predominantly men migrated to several destinations, including Canada, the United States, the Caribbean, and other parts of the Americas. These outflows took place in a context of increased market and border liberalization. The opening of Chinese ports to commerce and the liberalization of anti-emigration laws, as well as labor demands in U.S. and Canadian railroad expansion projects and in Caribbean plantations, converged to create conditions for emigration. While many women stayed home, some left China as sex workers and as wives or daughters of (usually wealthier) Chinese men.

A mixed-race, middle-class merchant family, the Eatons arrived in Canada under very different circumstances than the majority of Chinese men who came alone as temporary working-class laborers. Yet Edith Eaton became fascinated with the Chinese emigrants she encountered through her missionary work and, later, through her journalism. While her younger sister, Winifred Eaton (1875–1954), claimed that her ancestry was Japanese and published mainly romantic stories with Japanese settings under the name Onoto Watanna, Edith Eaton consistently stressed her similarities with the Montréal Chinese.[7] She identified with this group despite the fact that she did not speak Chinese, was rooted in English Victorian middle-class culture, and could pass as white, both culturally and racially. Eaton emphasized common exposure to racialization but also acknowledged similarities between the impoverishment her own family encountered once settled in Canada and the class status of the majority of Chinese immigrants in Montréal.

Eaton's autobiographical sketch "Leaves from the Mental Portfolio of a Eurasian," which originally appeared in the *Independent* in 1909, recounted several incidents of racism against her family, first in England and then in Canada. In addition, Eaton repeatedly stressed her family's descent from the merchant class to the working class in Montréal, which exposed her to poverty so severe that Eaton had to leave school before adolescence. In a 1912 letter to the *Boston Globe,* Eaton acknowledged that her family's economic status worsened the racism leveled against her and her siblings. About the nexus between class and race, she wrote that "[s]ome Eurasians may affect that no slur is cast upon them because of their nationality. . . . Wealth, of course, ameliorates certain conditions. We children, however, had no wealth" (Far 289). Eaton recognized the same factors at work in the treatment of other Chinese in Montréal. In an 1894 piece in the *Montréal Daily Witness,* for which she was a correspondent, she wrote that the Chinese who lived in Montréal at that time "are by no means aristocrats . . . [but] belong to the very lowest class of Chinese" (Far 183). Eaton also acknowledged that many Chinese immigrants lost their upper-class status after arrival in North America. In a 1913 letter to the *Independent,* she stated that "[m]any of the Chinese laundrymen I know are not laundrymen only, but artists and poets, often the sons of good families" (Far 232).

The thirty-eight pieces in *Mrs. Spring Fragrance* share a common thematic focus on diverse Chinese communities in Canada and the United States in various stages of their development. Rediscovered when Asian American studies became institutionalized in the United States, *Mrs. Spring Fragrance* has been classified as an early example of Asian American writing, and, more recently, it has been included in the canon of U.S. literature as a regionalist work. These two instances of canonization point to the close nexus between categories of ethnicity and region as markers of marginalized forms of identity.

Because much of it is set in the Chinatowns of Seattle and San Francisco, Eaton's work is usually considered an example of regionalist or local color writing, but such approaches neglect her early texts, which were mostly set in Montréal and along the eastern portion of the border with the United States.[8] Eaton's work may have garnered a regionalist designation not only because of its emphasis on Chinatowns but also because her writing appears starkly individualist when compared to more established literary models of the time.[9] Her stories often read like personal tales or anecdotes, and as extensions of her journalistic or autobiographical work. As Judith Fetterley and Marjorie Pryse have emphasized, aesthetics play a major role in the assignation of the regionalist label. These two critics show that the categories of regionalism or local color writing have been assigned to nineteenth-century work, produced mainly by U.S. women authors, which employs idiosyncratic styles that do not fit into the other, more dominant literary movements of the time, such as realism and naturalism.

In similar fashion to those who claim Eaton's early work for regionalism, Asian American studies scholars have placed Eaton squarely in the Asian American canon by focusing only on her later, U.S.-based work. Frank Chin's 1975 anthology *Aiieeee!*—which was among the key works of the Asian American Renaissance—credited Eaton as "one of the first to speak for an Asian-American sensibility that was neither Asian nor white American" (Chin et al. xxi). While the collection did not include samples of her work, Chin accused Eaton of using Chinese stereotypes available in the "yellow peril," zealous missionary, and "Chinatown" literature of the time (Chin et al. xxi). Eaton's institutionalization in the 1980s and 1990s as a pioneer of Chinese North American writing was similarly characterized by discussions about her usage of clichés about the Chinese because of her ambiguous status within emerging Chinese communities. Critics agree that Eaton lapses into occasional orientalism, evident in her frequent feminization of Chinese men, her focus on Chinese families to the exclusion of the problems of the bachelor society, and her depiction of the Chinese as a community poised for assimilation.[10]

A discussion of Eaton's work within these U.S.-based concerns about authenticity and writerly authority might be expected from the regionalist framework, which has historically emphasized relations of a particular region to a nation, but it is surprising coming from Asian American studies given the ongoing transformation of the field into an international discipline. In its early form, Asian American studies, which had grown out of civil rights struggles, highlighted expressions of U.S. empire, as evident in the denial of citizenship and land ownership as a result of exclusion, forced relocation during World War II, and racial segregation. This critique of U.S. imperialism distinguished itself from the focus of other U.S. civil rights movements through its emphasis on a pan-nationalism that included Chinese, Japanese, Korean, and Filipino Americans (Espiritu 32).[11]

Today, Asian American studies has shifted in two ways. The field now accounts for changes in the internal composition of the U.S. Asian

American community, and it has developed a global lens that focuses on U.S. Asian American–Asian relations. The first reconfiguration responds to transformations in the demographic makeup of U.S. immigrants. Japanese no longer immigrate in a significant way, while Chinese and Filipinos continue to arrive in large numbers, and South Asian and Southeast Asian immigration is on the rise.

The second framework highlights what Sau-Ling C. Wong terms the "denationalization" between Asian and Asian American studies, that is, the growing permeability between U.S. racialized groups and inhabitants of their respective countries or areas of origin. This internationalized perspective comprises comparative approaches to multiethnicity in the United States and in Asian countries, and comparative understandings of Asian immigration. Within this approach, the study of constituents of pan-ethnic Asian America, such as the Chinese, has become reoriented to a diasporic framework. At the same time, the internationalized lens also increasingly focuses on nations whose histories have helped generate the recent rise of postcolonial Asian populations in the United States, including Filipinos, Pacific Islanders, South Asians, and Southeast Asians.[12] Critics have noted, however, that a focus on regions and communities in Asia with ties to the United States merely acknowledges *vertical* connections between various U.S. racialized groups and their respective third-world countries or areas of origin. Rachel Lee, for example, has argued that these paradigms "establish new boundaries around their subjects by evoking reformulated regions that might be substituted as the proper domain of Asian-American studies" (108).

If it pays attention to the hemisphere at all, globalized Asian American studies has limited itself to imagining comparative histories of U.S. imperialism and colonialism in Mexico, Hawaii, and the Philippines (Nguyen and Chen).[13] Such perspectives leave no room for the distinctive histories and identities of Asian Canadian communities. They cannot account for the specificities of Canadian forms of suppression, such as Chinese exploitation and exclusion during the nineteenth and early twentieth century, the internment and repatriation of Japanese Canadians during World War II, and the exclusion of immigrants from Korea until 1943 and from India between 1908 and 1951 (Goellnicht 6). Current Asian American studies efforts to comparatively address other geographies like those of Mexico, Hawaii, and the Philippines need to take note of the marginalization of Canadian Asian issues to prevent a similar extension of existing U.S. frameworks and theories into these territories.

The institutionalization of Eaton's work within U.S. ethnic and region-alist paradigms has above all obscured the stress she placed on the speci-ficity of her Canadian settings and the treatment of Chinese in Canada, in addition to neglecting to inquire into the effect of the material circum-stances that surrounded the publication of her work. While the Montréal Chinese community was initially limited to a few sailors, merchants, and domestics, who were exoticized, it grew rapidly in the 1890s in the con-text of U.S. exclusion acts. In fact, Montréal assumed a central role for the distribution of Chinese labor to the Americas as many of the Chinese were travelers to the United States (White-Parks, *Sui* 28–29). The declin-ing need for Chinese labor after the 1885 completion of the Canadian transcontinental railroad expansion and the end of the Canadian gold rush, along with the arrival of larger numbers of Chinese immigrants, in turn produced more virulent forms of racism and exclusionary legislation like the head tax.

In her early journalism and in letters to Montréal newspapers, Eaton courageously spoke out on the interlaced issues of racism and state-sponsored violence against Chinese, such as travel and immigration restrictions, head taxes, and harassment by government officials. In an 1896 letter to the *Montreal Daily Star,* for example, Eaton protested plans to raise the head tax for Chinese desiring to come to Canada. She questioned official justifications for the passage of the new legislation, such as notions of Chinese as unfair competitors, carriers of disease, and subjects of public assistance, all of which are reminiscent of contempo-rary arguments in the United States against undocumented Mexican im-migration. Eaton deconstructs these arguments, positing that "Chinese labor is needed and wanted in Canada" (Far 196), that Chinese tend to be exploited by white Canadians, and that, when in need, they take care of each other rather than become public charges. Especially her argu-ments for the labor function of the Chinese differ significantly from the missionary defense of the existence of Chinese in the United States.

In her work, Eaton thus moved beyond the more superficial under-standings of the roots of racism in cultural differences or phenotypes to also acknowledge economic and political factors. In an 1890 article in the *Montréal Daily Witness,* Eaton reveals how narratives of exclusion have subsumed class differences under categories of race. She showed that even well-to-do Chinese merchants usually exempted from the U.S. Exclusion Act were forced to travel from Boston to Vancouver (on their way back to China) "in bond"—that is, in locked, guarded train compartments, "like a Saratoga trunk" (Far 180)—and were at the mercy of corrupt Canadian customs officials.

Two extant widely known and anthologized short stories by Eaton focus on undocumented border crossings and specify the northeastern Canada-U.S. border as their setting. "The Smuggling of Tie Co" and "Tian Shan's Kindred Spirits" imaginatively chronicle the emergence of the undocumented border crosser at the Canada-U.S. national boundary. These crossers are represented as tricksters who move across boundaries of gender and nationality to escape personal or social restrictions or to solve complex dilemmas.[14] In "The Smuggling of Tie Co," a Chinese laundry worker hires the Canadian border smuggler Jack Fabian to help him enter the United States via the St. Lawrence River, which separates today's Canadian provinces of Ontario and Québec from New York State.

In her journalistic work, Eaton discussed how the surge in undocumented immigration *created* the occupation of the border smuggler, which was usually chosen by Canadians, U.S. Americans, and a few Chinese. In her letter to the *Star,* Eaton characterized border smugglers as individuals "contaminated by white men and American lawyers . . . [to] bleed the poor Chinese laborers who are desirous of passing into the States . . . from which by a disgraceful law they are barred out" (Far 193–94). Jack Fabian engages in this profession for financial reasons and because "there is a certain pleasure to be derived from getting ahead of the Government" (Far 105). Having just escaped from a U.S. jail where he was held for people smuggling, he is confronted with the newly established "paper son system" that is undermining his business. A nonfictional passage in the short story describes how this system allowed male Chinese to falsely claim parental lineage through a U.S.-born Chinese American as "a scheme by which any young Chinaman on payment of a couple of hundred dollars could procure a father which father would swear the young Chinaman was born in America" (Far 105). In addition, some Chinese and whites started producing false crossing papers, which allowed the passage of "large batches" of immigrants (105).

Despite these changes, one of the workers in the laundry business, Tie Co, hires Fabian to help him cross the border. Fabian assumes that Tie Co is like most other "Chinamen who intend being smuggled [and who] always make arrangements with some Chinese firm in the States to receive them" (106). During their clandestine trip into upstate New York, Tie Co makes what, at this point, seems a strange admission when he confesses that the only reason he chose Fabian is because he likes him. Upon their imminent discovery by U.S. immigration officials, Tie Co flings himself into the river, ostensibly to eliminate any evidence of Fabian's illegal activities. Only after Tie Co has committed suicide does Fabian find out that the Chinese immigrant had been a woman in disguise.

Eaton's second story about border crossings from Canada, "Tian Shan's Kindred Spirit," begins with a description of Tian Shan's prowess for evading detection by U.S. authorities during his repeated border crossings, but then shifts its focus to the female protagonist Fin Fan, Tian Shan's "Kindred Spirit." Like many other Chinese laborers, including the fictional Tie Co, Tian Shan entered New York State clandestinely to find more profitable employment. But he keeps coming back into Canada to see Fin Fan, the daughter of a merchant who is awaiting arranged marriage. In one of his most daring trips, Tian Shan uses an "Indian war canoe" to cross the St. Lawrence River (Far 121). The story refers to frequent connections between Chinese immigrants and indigenous people living in the Canada-U.S. borderlands. Some native people worked as people smugglers, and Chinese were sometimes also disguised as Indians when crossing the border (E. Lee, *America's Gates* 161). Such cross-ethnic meetings continue into the present when Chinese traverse the Canada-U.S. boundary via reservation land.

During one of his visits to Canada, Tian Shan nearly kills the man to whom Fin Fan has been promised in an arranged marriage. To escape Canadian prison, Tian Shan crosses back into the United States, but he is discovered by U.S. immigration authorities, jailed, and told that he will be sent back to China. The story ends when Fin Fan joins Tian Shan in his prison cell, thus defying her parents' plans for her marriage. Disguised as a male border crosser, she intentionally seeks detection by authorities so that she can be "repatriated" with Tian Shan. That both the recent Chinese immigrant and the Canadian resident of Chinese background are deported to China rather than to Canada indicates that, as in the United States, the rights and benefits of residency were not accorded to those of Chinese background in Canada. Further, the decision to send the fictionalized characters to China also reflects changing U.S. immigration law; only after 1892 were Chinese returned to China rather than to the country from which they came, partially to avoid repeated attempts at undocumented border crossing. Like Fin Fan, however, some Chinese manipulated this legislation to their advantage, crossing the border in hopes of securing free passage to China (Ryo 132).

It is of interest that the two stories focus on laundry workers and laborers rather than the merchants or middle-class Chinese who were the subject of most of Eaton's work, especially her later oeuvre, and who were treated as separate categories from laborers in exclusionary laws. The stories also employ some of the generic conventions of melodrama that focus on love and marriage by attributing Tie Co's and Fin Fan's crossings of national and gender boundaries entirely to their desire to be with the men they love. In addition, Fabian's failure to appreciate Tie Co's sacrifice renders the story part of a fictional tradition that presents unhappy endings to interracial relationships. Like most of the Chinese protagonists in Eaton's early stories, these two heroines die in North America or return to China.

But the stories also use the geopolitical border between Canada and the United States as a location that enables or even requires gender transgression. Eaton's work thus gestures toward the persistent slippage between the crossing of national lines and gender boundaries. The two border crossing stories fictionalize women who do not conform to the nineteenth-century popular stereotype of the Chinese prostitute. They are laborers or daughters of merchants, and they cross the border in pursuit of love. Tie Co is shown to have used "gender-bending" to gain employment in a Canadian laundry and to obtain a certain degree of personal safety from the Canadian border smuggler. The daughter of a shopkeeper, Tie Fan disguises herself as a man to cross the border with the intention of surrendering to authorities so she can be together with her incarcerated sweetheart.

Eaton's focus on the predicament of undocumented women immigrants points to persistent gender bias in the making of nineteenth-century immigration legislation that would be enacted at the border. The scarcity of Chinese women in North America is often explained by reference to the patriarchal nature of Chinese society, which encourages women to stay home; or, it is attributed to the fact that the Chinese did not want to settle permanently in the United States and bring their families. Recent scholarship has, however, emphasized that U.S. immigration law specifically targeted Chinese women. Mechanisms for limiting the immigration of Chinese women were put in place well before the first U.S. Chinese Exclusion Act was passed in 1882. The 1875 Page Law prohibited the entry of Chinese women for the purpose of prostitution and continued to be enforced even after Chinese exclusion laws went into effect (Chan 95, 108). Because Chinese women were often equated with prostitutes, the Page Law also affected many other groups of Chinese women, including female students and the wives and daughters of merchants, who were actually exempt from exclusion laws (Chan 109).

The establishment of the "paper son system" that Eaton's story references at length provided primarily Chinese *men* with access to less dangerous means of entering the U.S. and gaining citizenship there, thus contributing to an overall decline in undocumented border crossings. In the 1950s most of the undocumented Chinese American immigrants were made up of paper sons (Ngai 204). While exact numbers remain unknown, there were far fewer "paper daughters." Sucheng Chan has shown that paper daughters first received judicial attention in 1925 after the U.S. Supreme Court had ruled that the wives of U.S. citizens could no longer be admitted. Perhaps, Chan speculates, using paper daughters became a new method of bringing women into the country. Compared to the success the paper son system usually promised to Chinese men, however, in virtually all reported cases, immigration officials and judges found many reasons to reject women's applications as paper daughters (Chan 129–30).

Owing to a lack of publishing opportunities in Canada, Eaton sent all of her early stories about the Montréal Chinese, including "The Smuggling of Tie Co," to publishing outlets in the United States, particularly little magazines (Ferens 61).[15] While no publication reference exists for "Tian Shan," "The Smuggling of Tie Co" originally appeared in 1900 in the *Land of Sunshine,* a journal founded by the Los Angeles Chamber of Commerce to promote southern California real estate. Mainly interested in depictions of the native and Mexican American populations of the Southwest, *Land of Sunshine* also included work on Chinese immigrant themes as Los Angeles's Chinatown continued to grow (White-Parks, *Sui* 86). Once Eaton was published in the *Land of Sunshine,* the Canadian settings and concerns of her stories disappeared. In introducing her work, the editor Charles Lummis described the protagonists of Eaton's stories, some of which were postmarked in Montréal, as "Chinese characters in California or on the Pacific Coast" (qtd. in Chin et al. xxi). Some critics have claimed that Eaton was complicit in this because her stories written in Montréal implied or claimed the U.S. West Coast as their setting (Ferens 67). But both of Eaton's border crossing stories insist on the geographical specificity of their settings along the Canada-U.S. boundary. "The Smuggling of Tie Co" begins by describing Jack Fabian as someone who is "contrabanding Chinese from Canada to the U.S." (107), and at one point in his trip across the border, Fabian says to his charge, "We are in New York state now" (107). And "Tian Shan's Kindred Spirit" opens with a portrayal of Fin Fan as the "daughter of a Canadian Chinese storekeeper" (120), and the protagonists' border crossings are associated with specific localities, such as the St. Lawrence River, the Lachine Rapids, and Rowe's Point (124).

After working for a Canadian newspaper in Jamaica, Eaton followed the trajectory of her work and became part of a larger exodus of women writers from Canada, who moved to the United States at the turn of the twentieth century to work in the expanding publishing and journalism industries. Until the establishment of international copyright guidelines with the Berne Convention (which took effect in the British Empire in 1887) and the U.S. Copyright Law of 1891, even the most well-known authors residing in Canada had little hope of making a living from their writing (Gerson 110). As one women writer wrote, "Alas! Canada has, as yet, failed to provide a market for her writers; and writers must live—at least we *think* we must" (qtd. in Gerson 109). Residing in the United States also provided Eaton with greater access to major U.S. publishing venues (Ferens 108).

Eaton initially moved to the West Coast of the United States, to Seattle and San Francisco, but she kept returning to Montréal, where she ultimately died. Seattle's Asian American community was similar in size to that of Montréal when Eaton first arrived on the West Coast, but in San Francisco she found an older, larger, and more established Chinatown. Just as the *reception* of her work as U.S. American was influenced by its publication in Californian venues, after her move to the United States, Eaton's writing itself became shaped by U.S. conventions.

Her exposure to racialization and economic marginalization in the early part of her life continued to mark all of Eaton's work and shaped her awareness of economic differences among Chinese in North America that were often subsumed under the category of race in discourses of exclusion. While she satirized the notion that any immigrant can become nobility in the United States (Far 23), however, Eaton began to focus on privileged sectors of the Chinese and their attempts at assimilation, issues she did not generally pursue in her earlier work. While in her early stories from Montréal most of the Chinese protagonists die or return to China, in her later work Eaton asserted the possibility of survival and settlement (Ferens 9). Most of Eaton's characters in these stories are middle-class and carry sophisticated names that suggest their educated backgrounds, which in part explains why they are less imbued with clan and regional loyalties and more willing to adopt mainstream U.S. values (Yin 92). In her later work, Eaton fictionalized several U.S.-style stories of success, such as that of Lu Seek, who owns shares in a Mexican railway and operates an employment agency to supply wealthy San Franciscans with houseboys, gardeners, and cooks.

Written in the United States, her autobiography, "Leaves from the

Mental Portfolio of a Eurasian," also marks Eaton's newfound emphasis on her Eurasian or "cosmopolitan" identity. Dominica Ferens has argued that this shift in identification was largely influenced by Eaton's experiences with racialized communities in Jamaica and the United States. She posits that Eaton's encounter with Jamaican society, which was marked by rigid race stratification, made her more conscious of her own racial identity so that Eaton began to identify herself in her autobiography as one of the "brown people of the earth" (Ferens 70).

But Eaton's emphasis on her Eurasian identity also appears to have enabled her to identify with the more privileged sectors of the U.S. Asian American community. This identification obscured important differences between their situation and hers. Even the most economically successful Asian Americans were perpetually threatened by policies of racialization that treated all people of a specific national (ethnicized) background in the same way. But Eaton was able to exempt herself from this treatment because she could pass as white. By all evidence, she freely entered the United States sixteen years after the 1882 passage of the U.S. Chinese Exclusion Act to achieve the kind of higher class status she admired of other U.S. Chinese. Yet, nowhere in her writings does Eaton acknowledge this fact. The muting of her own privileges within mixed-race identity paradigms also accompanied her overall shift away from an emphasis on the politics of exclusion in her early focus on Chinese communities in Canada. It is significant that Eaton's collected work does not contain outright criticism of the U.S. Exclusion Act, while her writing from Canada is characterized by overt rejection of similar legislation.[16] Her newfound U.S.-inflected ideas of assimilation and biculturalism thus do not seem to have engendered the same kind of political commitment in journalism and fiction that she exhibited in her earlier work.

Contemporary Asian Mexico-U.S. Border Crossings

Like Eaton's work, Karen Tei Yamashita's *Tropic of Orange* emphasizes undocumented border crossings. Set in Baja California, Mazatlan, Mexico, and in Los Angeles, Yamashita's novel addresses underrepresented forms of contemporary Asian immigration and its intersection with other forms of border crossing. The novel depicts growing parallels among various communities in the border region and in Los Angeles, a city whose urban sprawl reaches and is shaped by the border.

Tropic particularly focuses on important similarities between Asian Americans and Latinos. In the 1960s, Asian Americans were frequently evoked alongside other U.S. racialized groups in the United States in the framework of comparative internal colonialism theories. But today Asian Americans are often omitted from cross-ethnic considerations. Their general economic ascension has enabled assumptions of their full social, cultural, and political integration. Yet Asian American racial difference is, whenever politically exigent, still available for racist activation and mobilization (Palumbo-Liu 4–5). In addition, the community itself is internally splintered by political issues that affect Asian Americans, such as discussions of undocumented immigration from mainland China and other Asian countries as well as debates over affirmative action and bilingual education (Palumbo-Liu 4).

Important historical and contemporary interconnections between Asians–Asian Americans and other communities clearly exist. During the Oxnard Strike of 1903, for example, Japanese and Mexican laborers formed the Japanese-Mexican Labor Association to fight against the Western Agricultural Contracting Company.[17] And César Chávez's United Farm Workers joined laborers of Mexican and Filipino descent. In her 1996 *Immigrant Acts,* Lisa Lowe also emphasizes the deepening of affinities between Asian and Mexican emigrants in the United States in contemporary garment production. Yamashita employs fiction's imaginative license to emphasize other overlapping concerns of both groups. She has said that fiction, unlike the anthropological approaches in which she was trained, allows her to cross disciplines because she does not have to "prove everything" and can focus on the "entire world" rather than one history or story at a time (Gier and Tejada).

Yamashita's grandparents on both sides emigrated from Japan to California around the beginning of the twentieth century, a time of intense migration that provides the context for Eaton's work (White-Parks, *Sui* 28–29). Yamashita grew up in California and spent some time tracing her genealogy in Japan and researching the immigration of Japanese to Brazil. Despite the fact that her first novel, *Through the Arc of the Rain Forest* (1990), about Japanese in Brazil, won the Kafka Prize and the Before Columbus Foundation Award, her work has generally received little critical attention. *Through the Arc* has primarily been reviewed as fiction with an environmental message and was marketed with other works about the Amazon when it first appeared (Gier and Tejada). Yamashita has said that she had immense trouble getting the novel published because it did not fit into any niche: "It wasn't Asian American feminist literature; it wasn't magic realism; it wasn't science fiction" (Murashige, "Karen Tei Yamashita" 323). Yamashita has also speculated that the book was too experimental and political (Gier and Tejada).

King-Kok Cheung notes that *Through the Arc* has been "elided in both ethnic studies and multicultural studies" because it does not "dwell on being Asian American" (Cheung 19), the kind of subject matter that is expected of an Asian American contemporary writer. And Rachel Lee argues that because *Through the Arc* focuses on Japanese immigration to Brazil, it "makes it an uneasy fit with traditional definitions of Asian American literature, which . . . places too much emphasis on U.S. nationalist politics" (107). Lee also points out that within U.S.-centered definitions of Asian American fiction, the novel's main character is too different from the immigrant profile developed in other Asian American cultural productions (113). In the framework of the ongoing shifts in the internationalization of Asian American studies, *Through the Arc* has recently been rediscovered for its emphasis on global approaches to Asian populations. Viet Thanh Nguyen and Tina Chen, for example, briefly mention Yamashita's work because it expresses a "new world vision [that] is not so much about Asian Americans, but about the hybrid populations of the Americas—of which Asians are a part—that developed as result of American and European colonization" (Nguyen and Chen). Similarly, Kandice Chuh has recently discussed Yamashita's work about Brazil, including *Through the Arc,* as an example of fictional work that opens fruitful inter-American approaches within Asian American studies.

Tropic's focus on the colonial history and neocolonial present of the Americas has apparently also not lent itself well to emerging internationalized Asian American studies frameworks that have paid little attention to the hemisphere.[18] In Yamashita's novel, Japanese and Chinese Americans are not necessarily the most important protagonists, but they are associated with tenets of Asian American pan-ethnicity—its emphasis on similarities across Japanese, Chinese, and Filipino Americans—as well as the symbolism of the 1960s Chicanismo movement. *Tropic* also represents alternative post-NAFTA realities in the form of magical realism, an experimental strategy popularized by 1960s Latin American boom fiction. The novel's use of magical realism is announced on the cover, and Yamashita herself has acknowledged the influence of writers like Gabriel García Márquez, Mario Vargas Llosa, Jorge Luis Borges, and the Brazilian Moacyr Scliar (Murashige "Interview" 52).

As it is focused on Los Angeles, Yamashita's novel participates in discourses about the Mexican-U.S. boundary and in debates about the postmodern city. Yamashita has described Los Angeles as "one of the great centers of the Pacific Rim, to be compared with Mexico City and Tokyo—great urban cosmopolitan experiments of enormous energy and fomenting change" ("Purely Japanese").[19] The novel complements existing representations of LA by focusing on the city's multiracial nature, in Yamashita's words, "bring[ing] in those who have been invisible in the literature of Los Angeles" (Murashige, "Karen Tei Yamashita" 340).

Like twenty-first-century Chicana/o border writing (discussed in chapter 1), Yamashita's novel thus brings together the two kinds of locations—borderlands and urban areas—where conditions of globalization manifest themselves most clearly. Edward Soja's theories of the "postmetropolis" have characterized global cities as places marked by the emergence of new urban forms, a greater diversity of urban residents, and a surge in social inequalities among these populations. Drawing from Mike Davis's work on Los Angeles in *City of Quartz,* among other sources, Soja's analysis also advances explanatory models for the continuing coherence of cities, such as the reconsolidation of state power within a proliferating number of carceral institutions. In *Tropic,* Yamashita addresses the resurgence of other military forms of empire. She fictionalizes the 1992 Los Angeles riots by depicting an "army of homeless" that takes over cars abandoned as a result of a traffic accident shutting down the freeway. Various representatives of the state, like the LAPD and the National Guard, soon break up the "homeless experiment" with military force.

Tropic's central preoccupation with increasing intersections between Asian and Latin American borderlanders as a result of U.S. empire is signaled in the figure of what Yamashita has called her "pan-Asian" protagonist Bobby Ngu, a "Chinese from Singapore with a Vietnam [*sic*] name speaking like a Mexican living in Koreatown" (15). Bobby literalizes the pan-ethnic politics of Asian American civil rights struggles and its potential intersections with *Chicanismo.* Bobby left Singapore because his father's bicycle-producing company could no longer compete with a similar U.S.-owned business, and the family became impoverished. They certainly could not afford to send Bobby overseas, so he immigrates under the guise of a Vietnamese refugee and ends up in Los Angeles, where he is socialized among growing Latina/o populations.

Yamashita has said that Bobby is based on a real-life acquaintance, a Chinese who was raised in a Mexican–Central American area of Los Angeles and had a strong Chinese accent in English mixed with Spanish (Murashige, "Karen Tei Yamashita" 340). Even though Bobby would not be considered one of the 12,000 people of Asian descent who were born or grew up in Latin America and now live in Los Angeles (Ropp 220), his identity could similarly be described as "Asian Latino" because it challenges the existence of discrete cultural identities, such as "Latino" and "Asian American." Throughout the various chapters in the novel that are devoted to Bobby, he asserts both aspects of his identity. He speaks a Latino street slang, for example, while also visiting Chinatown to get herbal remedies for several ailments.

Bobby's wife, Rafaela, exemplifies the migrants from Mexico and other Latin American countries who tend to be proletarian in origin. Like many of her fellow Mexicans, who migrate north in search of work, Rafaela moved from Mexico's interior toward its border where the internationalization of U.S. (and other Asian and Western European) capital has created abundant opportunities for women to work in maquiladoras. Like women workers in these sites, Rafaela engages in low-wage service industries both in Mexico and, after her immigration, in the United States. Despite their differing socioeconomic backgrounds, once in the United States Bobby and Rafaela encounter similar difficulties when attempting to gain upward mobility, which birth in the United States can open up for some members of racialized communities. Bobby's longer-term residency in the United States allows him to start up his own janitorial business and to sponsor the immigration of his Mexican wife. But despite Bobby's hard work at two different jobs and Rafaela's pursuit of a college education, they remain at the bottom of the U.S. socioeconomic hierarchy.

Tropic depicts another interracial relationship between an upper-middle-class Chicano reporter, Gabriel, and his Japanese American girlfriend, Emi, that draws attention to socioeconomic differences between and among Latino and Asian American diasporic groups. In contrast to Bobby and Rafaela, who are recent immigrants, Gabriel and Emi are U.S.-born third-generation Americans who have assimilated to the U.S. ideal of upward class mobility and define themselves more in relationship to their jobs in the mass media than in terms of their ethnic identities. Emi is described as being so "distant from the Asian female stereotype . . . [that] it was questionable if she even had an identity" (19). As a journalist, Gabriel strives to become like his role model, the journalist-activist Rubén Salazar, who was allegedly killed by police during the Chicano civil rights movement. Like Salazar, Gabriel attempts to give voice to those who have not been represented, such as the homeless of Los Angeles and displaced indigenous communities in Mexico. Gabriel thus sets himself in the tradition of the civil rights movement; as Yamashita has said, "he has affinities to a past that is similar to my past, with the Asian-American movement or the Chicano movement" (Gier and Tejada).

But Gabriel's activism is always somewhat undercut by his unexamined attachment to Chicanismo's highly idealized notions of Chicano culture and its relationship to Mexico. He develops a crush on Rafaela as the incarnation of a supposedly purer Mexican culture. He also buys a house in Mazatlan, the home of his grandparents, even though he never really intends to live there As they trouble the narrative of a culturally and ethnically homogeneous U.S. nation, the protagonists Emi and Gabriel epitomize values of upward mobility that have been integral to ideals of U.S. nationhood.

Despite their differing class background, Emi and Rafaela eventually become linked as women of color. Emi's graphic death at the hands of police during the homeless riots and Rafaela's rape by the drug and organ smuggler Hernando in Mexico symbolize the kinds of violence that women often face in the global economy. Bobby's twelve-year-old cousin Xiayue, who has been smuggled from mainland China into Tijuana, Mexico, is threatened with similar kinds of bodily violence. Her arrival in North America exemplifies underrepresented forms of contemporary Asian immigration and their intersection with immigration from Mexico and Latin, Central, and South America. Although the majority of Asian immigrants (often ethnically Chinese members of professional and elite backgrounds from Taiwan, Singapore, and Hong Kong) today enter the United States legally, up to 100,000 undocumented Chinese, most of whom are from the Fuzhou area in the northeast coast of Fujian Province and from economically poorer backgrounds, come "illegally" every year (P. Smith x).

After the capture of several Chinese ships by U.S. authorities in the early 1990s, Chinese cartels began to employ more indirect routes from China to the United States that involved passage through Mexico (and sometimes other Latin, Central, and South American countries) and required travel across the Mexico-U.S. border. As a result of cooperation between human cargo smugglers—Chinese "snakeheads" and Mexican "coyotes"—the border has, in fact, become one of the major transit points for Chinese immigration (Rotella, *Twilight* 72–73). The new centrality that organized people-smugglers play in this movement shows that the once relatively simple act of Chinese border crossing fictionalized in Eaton's short stories has become associated with a much more complex system of illegal practices, which also continue to thrive on the persistence of gender dichotomies. Male Chinese undocumented immigrants pay for their passage either up front or once they arrive at their destination. Female border crossers, however, are often transported "for free," to become prostitutes or domestics in the United States. This gender difference in immigration becomes manifest in *Tropic* through the story of Bobby's cousin. Once they find Bobby, the snakeheads threaten to force

Xiayne, who has just arrived in Tijuana on board a ship, into prostitution unless he pays off her transportation costs. To lower the price, Bobby decides to drive from Los Angeles down to Tijuana to smuggle Xiayne across the border himself.

While the comparison between Bobby and his cousin reveals further internal differences among segments of the Chinese diaspora today, Yamashita also draws attention to growing intersections among undocumented Chinese and "illegals" from other countries. Bobby's cousin's immigration story demonstrates that, in response to expressions of U.S. empire, Chinese immigrants converge spatially at U.S. land borders with immigrants from Mexico and Latin America. In *Globalization and Its Discontents*, Saskia Sassen has identified the transnationalization of U.S. investment as the most decisive factor in transforming out-migration from certain countries into large-scale immigration. With regard to Mexico, intensified U.S. investment in labor-extensive maquila production has acted as a catalyst for massive immigration into the United States. Similar to post-NAFTA developments in Mexico, since China opened itself up to international trade and foreign capital moved there in the 1980s, Chinese out-migration has been on the rise. U.S. and other foreign investment in export-oriented sectors have encouraged the establishment of special economic zones along the Chinese coast, where, as in maquiladoras, many young women are employed. The deepening of economic, political, and cultural ties with countries like China and Mexico has thus produced the necessary conditions for large-scale waves of out-migration that take both documented and undocumented forms.

Once attracted to the United States as a result of economic forms of U.S. empire, undocumented immigrants are now faced with the violence at U.S. borders that has come to replace U.S. state involvement in other areas. In response, immigrants from Mexico and China employ similar border crossing methods, such as passing themselves off as U.S. citizens of Latino or Asian descent. To trick the Border Patrol, Bobby makes sure that his cousin gets rid of her "Chinagirl look" (204). He takes her to a beauty salon where she gets a haircut like that of his Mexican wife Rafaela and buys her new American clothes and toys. After that, they cross the Tijuana-Isidro border without problem: the "[o]fficial eyeballs Bobby's passport and waves them through . . . [They] [d]rag themselves through the slit jus' like any Americanos" (205).

Another of *Tropic*'s protagonists, the performer-laborer Arcangel, is the composite figure of an undocumented border crosser. Bridging various ethnic and national communities, he articulates a political ethics that challenges contemporary forms of U.S. empire. An "actor and prankster, mimic and comic, freak, a one man circus act" (47), Arcangel draws on indigenous Aztec mythologies, Mexican performance art, and the tradition of the trickster figure common in Asian American, American Indian, and African American cultures. Modeled after the well-known Latino performance artist Guillermo Gómez-Peña, Arcangel functions as the voice of the colonized in Latin America.[20] He connects various histories of European colonization in the hemisphere to globalization in the Americas. In one of his performances, Arcangel becomes the Mayan prophet Chilam Quetzal, foretelling the end of the world exactly fifty-two years after the European "discovery" of various parts of the Americas.

Arcangel also represents undocumented immigration through the metaphor of shifts in geography and time. In another of his performances, he pulls the Tropic of Cancer, the line dividing northern from southern Mexico, across the Mexico-U.S. border. Represented as a north and south post-NAFTA divide, the Tropic of Cancer's movement north changes realities in both countries: days become longer, geographical expanses stretch, and various cultural influences begin to merge.

Toward the conclusion of the novel, Arcangel turns into another incarnation, "El Gran Mojado" (The Big Wetback), so that he can fight SUPERNAFTA in a wrestling match called "El Contrato Con América." Whereas SUPERNAFTA represents the "Norte-Americanization" of Mexico, The Big Wetback's immigration signifies the movement of Mexico's culture into the United States. Wearing "a ski mask of camouflage nylon, [a] blue cape with the magic image of Guadalupe in an aura of gold feathers and blood roses, leopard bicycle tights, and blue boots" (260), Arcangel reminds his audience of the Mexican tradition of masked superheroes (*enmascerados*). This tradition includes Zorro and the 1940s' El Santo, who set the style for a generation of masked wrestlers; it also invokes the ski-masked *"hombros sin rostos"* (men without faces) of the Zapatista Army of National Liberation (EZLN), especially their most well-known representative of national liberation, Subcomandante Marcos. Arcangel's semblance to Marcos places this latest revolutionary in the tradition of other Mexican heroes, also celebrated in Chicanismo, to suggest that the EZLN struggle continues progressive tenets of Mexican revolution into the contemporary time period.

In Arcangel, Yamashita thus disentangles precolonial mythologies and Mexican national traditions from their use in narratives of *mexicanidad* and Chicanismo. Arcangel's form of discourse, which he calls "political poetry," integrates italicized poetic or mythic passages about instances of Latin American oppositional history into the narrative. This merging of mythic poetry and narrative can be considered another expression of magical realism, an attempt to incorporate alternative—transnational and cross-ethnic—accounts of empire into the novel so as to intervene in currently dominant representations of a neoliberal continental future.

As El Gran Mojado, Arcangel deconstructs SUPERNAFTA's promise of freedom and progress through the uninhibited flow of U.S. capital. Recounting five hundred years of indigenous Latin American history, he links colonialism in the southern hemisphere to processes of globalization by showing that the new economic agreement further reinforces Mexico's subservient position in the global economy. One of Yamashita's characters refutes the assertion that, with the passage of NAFTA, Mexico will become part of the "North, too." He argues, "If Martians landed here, they would know. They would swim nude in Acapulco, buy sombreros, ride burros, take pictures of the pyramids, build a maquiladora, hire us, and leave" (132).

As a symbol of ongoing struggles over the representation of the post-NAFTA Americas, the wrestling match between SUPERNAFTA and The Big Wetback ends undecided: SUPERNAFTA implodes after sending a missile launcher into Arcangel's heart. The simultaneous deaths of these two characters represent more than the increasing degree of hemispheric interdependence; they also symbolize the possibility that when the signifiers of first-world imperialism and third-world underdevelopment destroy each other and the borders they represent, new ways for imagining a different kind of continental future may emerge.

Bobby and Rafaela magically reunite at the wrestling match. Still located in Mazatlan, Rafaela pulls on her end of the Tropic of Cancer to get to Los Angeles. Once there, she feeds the orange that connects the Tropic—the north-south hemispheric division—to the dying El Gran Mojado. Rafaela's actions allow for the possibility that Arcangel may return in yet another incarnation. Once the orange is cut free from the hemispheric line, Bobby strains to hold on to its two—suddenly meaningless—ends. As the most explicitly multiracial character in the novel, Bobby comes to signal the hope that the dichotomous thinking represented in the wrestling match will be replaced with new myths that can cross what we now perceive to be national, racial, and ethnic divides. Bobby asks himself, "What are these goddamn lines anyway? What do they connect? What do they divide? What's he holding on to?" (270).

Asian Americas and Inter-American Studies

As revisionist historiographic representations of undocumented border crossings, the works by Eaton and Yamashita place Asian Americans firmly within the geography of the North American hemisphere and point creatively to important similarities between two temporally distinct moments of immigration from Asia, particularly that of the Chinese. An analysis of works by Eaton and Yamashita thus complicates theories of border crossing gleaned primarily from Mexican immigration. Eaton strove to depict exclusionary policies aimed at Chinese immigrants in Canada and the United States. Their struggles to cross hemispheric borders at the turn of the twentieth century, declared "illegal" by U.S. and later Canadian legislation, preceded the contemporary Mexican *indocumentado*. Yamashita's focus on the undocumented who make up an important part of growing diasporic populations in the United States opens up more explicitly the study of Asian Americans to comparative approaches with other populations. In her spatial emphasis on national boundaries as locations for new, as yet unformalized transnational and pan-ethnic alliances, Yamashita combines tenets of Chicanismo with the pan-Asianism of Asian American civil rights struggles.

Besides complicating theories of border crossing, the work of Eaton and Yamashita also brings hemispheric perspectives to the dominant diasporic framework in Asian American studies. This framework is in danger of simply expanding U.S.-based models of analysis to the global plane. The mere inclusion of Canadian texts into already existing, U.S.-based frameworks, as occurred with the canonization of Eaton's work, ignores the importance of national differences and national borders. This approach also marginalizes the importance of the material inequities in publishing industries that forced Eaton and other Canadian writers to send their work to the United States or to move there themselves, with significant consequences for their oeuvre. When U.S. approaches foreground Eaton's work about U.S. Chinatowns in the U.S. West, they marginalize Eaton's Canadian issues and settings. In fact, they perpetuate a process that was initiated when Eaton published much of her fictional work about Canada in *The Land of Sunshine,* a journal with an explicit regionalist focus on the U.S. West. Similarly, appeals to existing categories of Asian American identity formation have caused critics to gloss over the fictional work of a writer like Yamashita. She freely draws from a wide range of diverse national and ethnic aesthetic and conceptual traditions associated with the Americas, such as Chicanismo and Latin American "boom" magical realism, which are usually not considered her "own."

The work of Eaton and Yamashita also highlights the necessity of studying not only manifestations of U.S. empire but also other nation-states and their nationalisms to understand developments along national boundaries and in the hemisphere. Throughout the history of U.S. borders, Mexican immigration was not the only or even the decisive factor in the enforcement of these geographies. Immigration from the south first had to be linked to other types of "illegal" flows embodying dominant fears of a particular period—Chinese exclusion at the turn of the twentieth century, alcohol during Prohibition, drugs and increased Chinese undocumented immigration in the 1980s and 1990s, and threat of terrorism in the twenty-first century—to become elevated to the center of U.S. national attention.

Shortly after Eaton published her short stories about Canada-U.S. border crossings, tightened controls at the Canadian border shifted Chinese immigration to the southern border, where at least several hundred a year entered in the early 1900s (E. Lee, *America's Gates* 158).[21] Canada eventually gave in to U.S. pressure and, in 1923, passed its own Exclusion Act that banned all immigration from China except for merchants, students, and children born in Canada. The Mexican government, in contrast, was initially reluctant to accommodate U.S. requests for cooperation in the enforcement of U.S. exclusion laws. Mexico was more interested in attracting immigrants and did not want to violate international agreements with China or damage U.S. economic investments in northern Mexico that, to an extent, also relied on Chinese labor. In marked contrast to U.S. and Canadian policies, Mexican civil law at the turn of the twentieth century also accorded several thousand Cantonese immigrants resident status and thereby provided them with rights equal to those of Mexican citizens (Peña-Delgado 184).

Reactions against Chinese immigration took local and regional forms. Mob violence, public-health regulations, segregation provisions, and bans on interracial marriage in various municipalities during the 1910s and 1920s were designed to harass the Chinese into leaving Mexico. These measures intensified in the context of the Great Depression, when vigilante groups began to take Chinese to the Mexico-U.S. border and when the Sonoran governor Rodolfo Calles ordered Chinese residents to evacuate their businesses (E. Lee "Orientalisms," 248). Because of lacking binational cooperation, Chinese exclusion at the Mexico-U.S. border came to be enforced by means of policing, and the nature of the hitherto perfunctory international line between the United States and Mexico began to change. The Immigration Service posted "Chinese Inspectors" along the border in the early 1890s to curb the unauthorized entry of Chinese.

Up to this time, crossers only needed to report to a United States Port of Entry for inspection by the Customs Service, whose so-called line riders also patrolled the boundary and controlled undocumented immigration. While focusing its attention on curbing the immigration of an estimated 60,000 undocumented Chinese from 1882 to 1920, the Immigration Service showed no interest in the much larger number of Mexicans (an estimated 1.4 million) entering the United States via the Southwestern border (E. Lee, *America's Gates* 171). Inspection of Mexican border crossers did not begin until after the passage of the Immigration Act of 1907 because they were seen as temporary labor rather than excludable "aliens" like the Chinese ("Early Immigrant"). Mexicans were not required to show proof of citizenship when crossing into the United States, whereas Chinese were always stopped under the assumption that they were "aliens." But whenever Chinese border crossers were able to claim Mexican citizenship, they were allowed to cross freely (Peña-Delgado 188).

Once created with respect to the Chinese, the trope of the *indocumentado* could easily be applied to other groups, and border enforcement soon shifted to address Mexican undocumented immigration. According to the memoir of the former Border Patrol officer Clifford Perkins, the Border Patrol took over the duties of the Immigration Service officers in the Chinese division as well as those of the former Customs Patrol at the Mexico-U.S. border. The Border Patrol also drew on U.S. and Canadian law-enforcement experiences in controlling the Canada-U.S. boundary. Only three years after the creation of the Border Patrol, its operations were officially extended from the U.S.-Mexico border to also cover Florida and the Canadian border. Throughout the 1920s and 1930s a roughly equal number of agents worked on both borders. Only the repeal of Prohibition allowed the Border Patrol to shift its efforts from preventing the smuggling of alcohol across both boundaries to preventing entry of unauthorized immigrants (Nevins 29).

As Erika Lee argues in *At America's Gates*, the extent to which the governments of each U.S. neighboring nation supported U.S. politics of Chinese exclusion also influenced the degree to which U.S. borders became militarized. The multilayered nature of border developments is missed by dominant paradigms that tend to focus only on Mexican immigration or the Mexico-U.S. relationship.

That hemispheric work in Asian American studies may be emerging as a complement to the focus on Asia-U.S. connections is evident in recent calls from within the field. Erika Lee has emphasized the comparative analysis of Asian migration in the Americas as one way of situating the history of Asians within local, regional, national, and global contexts ("Orientalisms," 235). Such a focus, she argues, moves beyond the geographical confines of both the United States *and* the Pacific, while highlighting the transnational dimensions of racial formations to forge connections with other perspectives, such as work on the Atlantic world and on the African diaspora. My reading of Eaton's and Yamashita's work similarly stresses how it lends itself to comparative analyses of undocumented migration to North America that could bridge Latina/o, Asian American, Latin American, and East Asian area studies. As a complement to the focus on the Asian American–Asian connection, such comparative transnational and pan-ethnic models can also include the views of other border communities, such as those of indigenous peoples, which I discuss in the next chapter.

3   Native Border Theory

U.S. BORDERS and transnational Indian reservations have been more than potential gateways for undocumented immigrants, as discussed in the previous chapter. They have also provided a home to native people whose perspectives on hemispheric borders between the United States, Mexico, and Canada have remained largely unknown in U.S. border studies and are cited only incidentally in American Indian scholarship.[1]

Recent border literature by the native authors Leslie Marmon Silko and Thomas King addresses this oversight. These writers focus on the transnational Yaquis and Blackfoot, whose tribal identities are rooted in each community's separation by U.S. frontiers with either Mexico or Canada.[2]

In their fictional work, Silko and King show that border tribes have been central to the historical and contemporary pan-tribal alliances that emerged in response to manifestations of U.S. empire and subjugation by other nation-states in the hemisphere. The two authors also remind us of historical precursors to expressions of empire that include the creation of national borders and their sometime transformation into sanctuaries. Finally, Silko and King stress how contemporary manifestations of U.S. empire and the repressive policies of other North American nations reinforce these historical challenges to native notions of sovereignty. Border militarization and economic agreements like NAFTA, which formalize the ongoing commodification of nature and its resources, have further undermined border tribes' struggles for independence from hemispheric nation-states and their boundaries.

As longtime residents of the U.S. border territories to which they were displaced, Silko and King transform U.S. boundaries into sites of hemispheric pan-Indianism. Silko grew up of mixed Laguna Pueblo, Mexican, and Anglo heritage on the fringes of the Laguna Pueblo reservation in New Mexico. In her novel *Almanac of the Dead* (1991), she inscribes cultural material gathered from tribes throughout the Americas, including the Laguna Pueblo and the Mexican Maya, onto the Arizona-Sonora border territory where she now lives. This geography is also home to the Yaquis, a federally recognized U.S. tribe whose members left Mexico to escape violent government repression during the early twentieth century. Of Greek, German, and Cherokee descent, King similarly places Cherokee, Shawnee, and Apache traditions in the landscape of the transnational Blackfoot who live along the Alberta-Montana border, where King resided for several years.

Silko's and King's emphasis on specific border tribes moves indigenous conceptions of empire and nationalism at U.S. boundaries to the forefront of border and American Indian studies. This fictional work thus asks for a reconsideration of the central tenets underlying both fields. On the one hand, Silko and King emphasize tribal claims to border areas as ancestral homelands. Like indigenous peoples more generally, border tribes consider the places where they reside as geographies that are sacred, home to deities, ceremonial sites, and generations of ancestors, even when histories of displacement or the loss of the homelands may be part of a particular tribal or national experience. This spatialized understanding of nationhood generates tribal struggles for self-government, unimpeded cross-border passage, and the right to exercise jurisdiction over land and its resources.

On the other hand, Silko's and King's work also positions border tribes as central figures for rethinking questions of attachment within American Indian studies. Work in the field, particularly by historians and anthropologists, is currently dominated by analyses of a specific nation-state, tribe, or chiefdom (Meyer and Klein 198).[3] Often linked to debates about authenticity, in the United States this focus emerged partially in response to the initial pan-tribal emphasis of American Indian civil rights struggles, which tended to marginalize the specificities of individual tribal cultures and histories. The resulting dichotomy between tribalism and pan-tribalism has inhibited the emergence of other possible trajectories for American Indian studies, including an attention to the hemisphere. Even though some American Indian studies perspectives already address the existence of indigenous peoples in Canada, and to a much smaller extent in Latin America, few comparative studies exist that take into account different histories of settlement, colonization, contact, and repression in various nations of the hemisphere.[4]

While they differ from each other in form and level of political radicalism, the works of Silko and King highlight the centrality of border tribes in historical pan-tribal alliances as precursors of contemporary and imagined future forms of pan-Indian activism. Recent activism has already taken transnational forms that center on struggles for land and border crossing rights. The 1999 joint declaration of the Assembly of First Nations and the National Congress of American Indians, "Declaration of Kinship and Cooperation among the Indigenous Peoples and Nations of North America," for example, identified the maintenance of border crossing rights and the full recognition of indigenous cultures as concerns common to native people in the United States and Canada.[5] A more recent statement passed on the occasion of the Third Summit of the Americas in Québec City responded to the proposed extension of the North American Free Trade Agreement (NAFTA) into the hemisphere. Entitled "Indigenous Peoples and the Free Trade Area of the Americas," the 2002 statement characterized the Free Trade Area of the Americas (FTAA) as another instrument for the redrawing of maps since the colonization of the Americas. These events resulted in the founding of various nation-states based on the absorption of Indian lands. The summit stressed that any free-trade agreement must first recognize land claims and self-governance as the fundamental human rights of indigenous people as well as address earlier treaty violations and the genocide committed against indigenous and mixed-race peoples.

Like this contemporary activism, the fiction by Silko and King shifts the pan-tribal impetus of Native American civil rights struggles to the hemispheric level. The two writers imaginatively employ U.S. border sites (with Mexico or Canada) to either reaffirm or establish new connections among tribal nations throughout the hemisphere. Their fiction develops an expansive and inclusive hemispheric vision that is nevertheless rooted in the pursuit of an individual nation's or tribe's sovereignty from national borders in North America. Silko and King thus reaffirm the historical and contemporary role of border areas as, at the same time, homelands of specific tribal nations and locations of pan-tribal hemispheric activism against U.S. empire and repressive government policies throughout North America. Their works also suggest that a broad political focus on land rights and the free passage of people across national borders can potentially include other ethnic and national border communities.

Mexico-U.S. Border Indigeneity

Leslie Silko's *Almanac of the Dead* sets out to enlarge definitions of indigeneity to a hemispheric and global level. The novel imagines a transnational activism for land and border crossing rights that is grounded in the specific histories and cultures of tribal nations populating Mexico and the United States. *Almanac* thus dismantles the divisions among native peoples established by the Mexico-U.S. border. The Five Hundred Year Map at the beginning of the novel, which does not acknowledge national boundaries, already signals this intent. As Bernie Harder writes, *Almanac* explores indigenous people's power to exercise their rights as sovereign nations if they were united across the colonial borders that fragment and oppress them (104).

Almanac spans five hundred years and several locations in the United States and Mexico, including the border states of Arizona, Texas, California, New Mexico, Baja California, and Chiapas. The novel's title refers to ancient Mayan codices that correctly predicted the arrival of the Spanish conquistador Hernán Cortés as the beginning of the fifth Mayan sun and foresaw the disappearance of all things European from the Americas in the sixth. *Almanac* presents itself as a fictional fifth folding book that, as Silko suggests, may have survived destruction by the Spaniards in 1540 along with the other fragments, which are today housed in Madrid, Mexico City, Dresden, and Paris.

As its central focal point, *Almanac* imagines mass border crossings by Mexican Indians and landless war refugees from Guatemala and El Salvador into Tucson, Arizona. This movement is led by the Mayan "Army for Redistribution and Justice" and demands the return of indigenous land and the free passage of people across national borders. Perhaps more drastically, it also draws on the prediction that European culture will disappear in the Americas. Once arrived in Tucson, the movement gains support from a variety of U.S. and Canadian communities and individuals.

The demands articulated by the movement continue many of the tenets Silko developed in *Ceremony*. Silko's first novel is considered part of the so-called Native American Renaissance, whose beginning is symbolized in N. Scott Momaday's winning of the 1969 Pulitzer Prize for fiction.[6] While *Ceremony* has become one of the most widely taught texts in U.S. college classrooms, it took almost a decade for *Almanac* to receive wide critical attention. This delay in recognition has two reasons: the radical nature of the novel and its defiance of the established categories of identity (including those shaped by region or ethnicity) that continue to guide the reception, production, and marketing of literary texts in the United States.

In addition, *Ceremony* ends with a sense of reconciliation and hope that appears to reiterate conventions expected of Native American literature. In contrast, *Almanac* presents prophecies of violence, unrest, and revolution caused by growing inequities within and among communities and nations throughout the hemisphere. Following a tendency to conflate race and class hierarchies, early reviewers characterized the novel's overall message as "anti-white." Janet St. Clair, for example, highlighted one of the more shocking elements of *Almanac,* its depiction of decadence among wealthy, white or mestizo men, by reading the novel as an indictment of U.S. culture and a condemnation of "savage white men, each with his own horrific aberrations" ("Death" 142).[7]

Almanac is also not easily legible within the identity-based discourses that still dominate the reception of contemporary U.S. literature and the organization of American Indian Studies (and thus detract from more productive directions the field could take) (Peterson 3).[8]

Almanac questions the dichotomy between individual tribal nationalism and pan-tribal activism, collectively termed "Red Power," that has characterized indigenous thought in the United States since the civil rights struggles. Organizations like the National Congress of American Indians (NCAI), "Indians of all Tribes," and the American Indian Movement (AIM) were dominated by urbanized Indians interested in forging a pan-tribal identity that highlighted common concerns with the violation of treaties and the loss of land.[9] In an effort to include more reservation Indians, these movements, however, eventually shifted their focus from supratribal civil rights to tribe-specific issues.

Reading in this tradition, Elizabeth Cook-Lynn has characterized *Almanac* as "the foremost Indian novel in which we see the clear and unmistakable attempt to describe Indian nationalism in . . . modern terms" because it focuses on the retrieval of stolen land (90). Yet, Cook-Lynn argues that *Almanac*'s nationalism ultimately fails since it does not take into account the specificity of the tribal or national status of the original occupants of the Americas that is often codified in individual treaties.

Cook-Lynn observes that the novel's pan-tribalism does not allow "the tribally specific treaty-status paradigm to be realized" (93). She characterizes notions of tribalism as the recognition that "the very origins of a people are specifically tribal (nationalistic) and rooted in a specific geography (place), that mythology (soul) and geography (land) are inseparable, that even language is rooted in a specific place" (88). In her reading of *Almanac,* Cook-Lynn thus also reiterates her long-standing criticism of Native American literature for failing to contribute to the nationalist struggles of particular tribes she promotes in the concept of "tribal realism."[10]

But *Almanac* moves beyond the entrenched dichotomy between tribalism and pan-tribalism evoked in Cook-Lynn's remarks by taking the pan-tribal focus of U.S. civil rights struggles to a hemispheric level. The novel engages conceptual and aesthetic models drawn from a wide range of pre-Columbian cultures from what is now the United States and Mexico, and it employs indigenous humor, trickster figures, and other Mesoamerican myths of origins and prophetic returns as they have survived in contemporary Mexico and the United States.[11] While all of these elements are specific to particular tribes, they also have parallels in other cultures. In the novel, the border region becomes the site of a pan-Indian activism rooted in the specific cultural and historical traditions of individual tribes populating the border area.

Upon its arrival in Tucson, the Mayan uprising gains support from the Hopi, Navajo, Yaqui, and Tohono O'odham, U.S. tribes who reside in the transnational Southwest. Silko suggests that these tribes sympathize with the Mayan uprising because they have faced similar historical and contemporary challenges in the form of repressive government policies and expressions of U.S. empire. Silko is particularly interested in the transnational Yaqui, who left Mexico to escape the violent repression that took place during the presidential reign of Porfirio Díaz as a result of clashes with Mexican government troops. These conflicts lasted until 1926, when the Yaquis were massacred at the behest of Alvaro Obregón, whom they had supported during the Mexican Revolution.

The first modern Yaqui settlements were located near Nogales and south Tucson, as recognized in the official bequest of land in the Arizona desert and the U.S. federal recognition of the tribe in 1978.[12] Yaquis are the most widely dispersed native people of North America; they cover a 3,500-mile expanse from southern Mexico to southern California (Hu-DeHart, *Yaqui* 172, 202). Silko has said that after her move from Albuquerque to Tucson, she acquainted herself with the Yaqui to "understand how the Yaqui people felt, because they had taken refuge in Tucson after the Mexican army began the genocide of the 1900s and 1920s; of course the Yaqui people had always ranged this far north, so the land here is not so different than the land they fled" (Coltelli 123).

Because Yaquis are mestizos, with a distinct identity both as an ethnic group and a tribal nation, they represent a paradigmatic case for Silko's attempt to expand definitions of indigeneity.[13] Several of *Almanac*'s protagonists are Yaquis who move between northern Sonora and Tucson, where they both manipulate a corrupt border system and are affected by recent changes under the regime of neoliberalism. The twins Zeta and Lecha as well as their business partner Calabazas are tricksterlike figures who smuggle artifacts, drugs, and guns across the border, particularly through portions of the Tohono O'odham reservation, while some of their relatives in Mexico work as coyotes.

Zeta and Calabazas claim that their illegal activities exemplify their refusal to recognize the legitimacy of the Mexico-U.S. border. The denial of this border represents their protest against the U.S. and Mexican governments' histories of indigenous repression. Border smuggling, they assert, reaffirms the traditions of tribal people, particularly the Yaqui, who have historically either ignored national boundaries or manipulated them to their advantage in escaping state repression in Mexico. Remembering her grandmother Yoeme, Zeta, for example, thinks that the

> people had been free to go traveling north and south for a thousand years, traveling as they pleased, then suddenly white priests had announced smuggling as a mortal sin because smuggling was stealing from the government. Zeta wondered if the priests who told the people smuggling was stealing had also told them how they were to feed themselves now that all the fertile land along the rivers had been stolen by white men. Where were the priest and his Catholic church when the federal soldiers used Yaqui babies for target practice? Stealing from the "government"? What "government" was that? Mexico City? . . . Washington, D.C.? How could one steal if the government itself was the worst thief? (133)

Almanac's Yaqui protagonists are also negatively affected by border militarization. As Silko has said elsewhere, "[T]he U.S. government . . . is trying to sell off Mexico from the United States. . . . But [those they are selling off] are Indians, Native Americans, American Indians, original possessors of this continent" (Arnold 143). Crossing tales recounted by Lecha and Calabazas show that intensified border enforcement, ostensibly directed at immigrants from the south, also impedes efforts to preserve Yaqui culture and to maintain tribal unity. Calabazas reports on the difficulties of border crossing on All Souls Day, also called the Day of the Dead, which has its roots in the confluence of Mexican Indian and Spanish colonist traditions with the teachings of mission-era Jesuits and Franciscans. On that day, Calabazas recounts that "hundreds of Yaquis crossed" into Mexico and the Mexican guards did not care. But the U.S. guards suspect a link among Yaqui crossings and illegal activities; as Calabazas says, they "were on the alert for brothers and uncles hiding under firewood" (217). Calabazas's story highlights how border militarization, intended to prevent the entry of immigrants, hinders Arizona Yaquis' attempts at maintaining ties with their sister community in Sonora, where the Yaqui language and cultural traditions, including traditional ceremonies, have been better preserved.

Recent changes outside the world of the novel have further restricted such attempts. For years, the Border Patrol informally accepted tribal identification cards from border tribes like the Yaqui and Tohono O'odham, and the ninety-mile border that the Tohono O'odham share with Mexico featured gates and holes for free access to relatives on the other side. But now, passing through these gates is viewed as a violation of U.S. federal law, and tribal peoples entering the United States are required to have crossing cards or other documents showing their intent to return (Taliman 12). The same smuggling routes that Zeta and Calabazas used on the Tohono O'odham territory have recently become major gateways for undocumented immigrants from south of the border. The enforcement of large stretches of the Mexico-U.S. boundary with walls, other barriers, and additional Border Patrol personnel has funnelled migrants to portions of the Tohono O'odham reservation where the border is, at least for the time being, only marked by barbed wire.

To protect their right to free cross-border passage, some Yaqui leaders have recently formed the Indigenous Alliance without Borders, whose annual regional summits have included the Tohono O'odham and other border tribes like the Kickapoo, the Cocopah, and the Kumeyaay as well as the Gila River and Yavapai Apache. The Alliance has supported a Tohono O'odham proposal to grant U.S. citizenship to Indians in Mexico who are members of recognized U.S. tribes (Taliman 12). During the 2006 Border Summit of the Americas, native peoples assembled to protest the U.S. "Secure Fence Act" stipulating the erection of a Mexico-U.S. border wall by 2008. Participants argued that such a wall would divide the ancestral lands of many indigeneous tribes, including the Kumeyaay in California, the Cocopah and Tohono O'odham in Arizona, and the Kickapoo in Texas (Norrell).

Like everyone else who does not look white, Yaquis are hassled at official border crossings. *Almanac* recounts that when Lecha returns from a trip to Mexico, the "U.S. border agents had refused to believe Lecha and [the Laguna Pueblo Indian] Sterling were American citizens" (591). Silko's well-known piece "The Border Patrol" (collected in *Yellow Woman*) describes a personal encounter with the border patrol on Interstate highway checkpoints located north of the actual national boundary. En route to a book reading in Albuquerque, Silko and a friend were stopped and searched, while other vehicles manned by white passengers were waved through. Silko emphasizes that the Border Patrol does not need to follow rules of evidence or probable cause to detain people they deem suspicious. She argues that the effects of border militarization have transformed the U.S. Southwest into a police state where the border patrol "interfere[s] with the rights of U.S. citizens to travel freely within our borders" (344).

Besides pointing to border militarization as one potential point of intersection between the Yaqui and other communities, Silko also stresses Yaquis' central role in historical alliances with tribes of the greater Southwest, like the U.S. Apache and the Mexican Maya. For the Apache, as for the Yaqui, the Mexico-U.S. border embodied the promise of escape from nineteenth-century repressive government policies that engendered (if only temporary) alliances among otherwise unconnected tribes or among traditional enemies.

Several, often contradictory, stories of Geronimo attain a central place in these narratives. Passed on to Zeta and Lecha by their grandmother Yoeme and to Calabazas by his aunt Old Mahalawas, Yaqui narratives of Geronimo stress that Sonoran Yaquis hid him in the Sierra Madre to protect him from both the U.S. Army and Mexican forces. In its attempts to resist confinement to reservation land in the United States, the Geronimo band of the Apaches often crossed over into Mexico. Brigadier General Nelson A. Miles believed the border to be so significant to his efforts to capture Geronimo that he attempted, in 1885, to build an elaborate system of communications using a telephone system and a heliograph to police the border crossing activities of the Apache (Brady 69). Rather than finding sanctuary south of the border, however, Geronimo's band became involved in frequent conflicts with Mexican government forces. The band eventually surrendered in 1886 to General Miles and was moved to several prison camps, ending up in Fort Sill, Oklahoma. After 1907 the remaining survivors were given the option of either staying in Oklahoma or moving to the Apache Mescalero Reservation in New Mexico. Geronimo eventually died in 1909 in the Fort Sill's military hospital.

Several fictional Yaqui oral traditions presented in *Almanac* place the historical Geronimo in the context of trickster narratives, where he functions not as a tragic individual but as a communal sign for the dissolution of national borders. These stories question the official historiography of Geronimo's capture as a symbol of the end of hostilities between native people and the U.S. Army. The Yaqui narratives in the novel always reimagine these official accounts and multiply Geronimo's appearances and fates, suggesting, for example, that a warrior named Geronimo never existed, that several Apaches were mistaken for Geronimo, that another man sacrificed himself for Geronimo by letting himself be captured, or that Geronimo took on the guises of different Apaches who were at one time believed to be him. None of these versions is privileged in the novel or presented as a singular and authoritative counteraccount of Geronimo. According to the stories, differences among existing pictures of Geronimo suggest that the U.S. Army captured, photographed, and catalogued at least four different Apache raiders who were all thought to be the U.S. government's most feared enemy. Some Yaqui narratives also explain the likeness that showed through the different faces by the presence of an ancestor, "the soul of one long dead who knew the plight of the 'Geronimos'" (232).

Another interpretative possibility allows that even though an Apache warrior of great importance who was sought by the U.S. Army may have existed, he went by different names, none of which was Geronimo. Known as Wide Ledge to Yaquis, this warrior, who may have been a medicine man, enabled Apaches to move without being heard by the U.S. Army or their native scouts. Some versions of the Yaqui stories also posit that the existence of an Apache threat named Geronimo may have been completely misconstrued from Mexican soldiers' battlefield prayers to St. Jerome. They also account for Geronimo's surrender to General Miles as the work of an imposter, Old Pancakes, who later becomes a caricature of the Apache warrior in Buffalo Bill's Wild West shows. In addition, Silko's novel associates Geronimo with several contemporary indigenous characters in the novel, including Calabazas, Zeta, and Sterling, who are thus imbued with the potential to continue Geronimo's mission. As John Muthyala writes, these ambiguous Yaqui accounts of Geronimo complicate the official U.S. narratives of Indian removal and elevate Yaqui mythology to the center of pan-tribal border struggles (Muthyala, "*Almanac*" 367–68). By placing the narrative of Geronimo's capture in a novel about hemispheric pan-tribalism, Silko also enlarges the U.S.-centric lens on indigeneity. She suggests that, as she has written elsewhere, the so-called Indian Wars between native people and nation-states have been ongoing in other parts of the Americas (Silko, *Yellow* 347).

Almanac further emphasizes the historical roots of ongoing struggles by evoking Yaquis' historical ties with indigenous peoples of Mexico. Yaqui repression under the regime of the Mexican president Porfirio Díaz included deportation to the Yucatán Peninsula, the home of the Maya, where Yaquis were enslaved in chain gangs on large estates, plantations, and in silver mines. Some Yaquis escaped to Sonora or further northward to the United States. In *Almanac,* Silko fictionalizes the escape of Mayan children. They search for members of their own tribe who may have already fled with other Yaquis. The children are given an almanac for safekeeping that, because of the alliances between the two indigenous groups, chronicles both Mayan and Yaqui history (Adamson, *Middle* 142). The almanac ends up in the hands of Yoeme, who adds accounts of historical events and newspaper articles detailing crime, atrocities, and indigenous uprisings all over the world before passing it on to her granddaughters Zeta and Lecha. Like the oral narratives of Geronimo, the almanac and other texts associated with indigenous peoples of the Americas, including dreams, myths, and rumors, become alternative means of history making and identity formation.

Silko also works with Mayan notions of time as recurring and recycling rather than a progressive march of history. *Almanac* presents present, past, and future as a continuum, connecting Yaquis' historical contacts with tribes on both sides of the Mexico-U.S. boundary to present-day manifestations of resistance. The novel speculatively places the Yaqui in pivotal positions within imagined alliances between various indigenous groups. The Yaqui protagonists eventually come to support the Mayan-led "Army for Redistribution and Justice" at the International Holistic Healer's Convention in Tucson, which constitutes the cumulative highpoint of the novel. Zeta's and Calabazas's views of border smuggling as a subversive act change through contact with like-minded individuals. They recognize that rather than being isolated individuals carrying out acts of subversion, they are part of a larger, hemispheric movement with demands for tribal sovereignty from nation-states, the free passage of indigenous peoples, and the return of Indian land.

The idea of a hemispheric pan-tribalism rooted in the tribal cultures of border areas is further symbolized in one of *Almanac*'s many protagonists, the American Indian Sterling. A Laguna Pueblo from New Mexico with a vexed relationship to his tribe, his fictional persona exemplifies Silko's sometimes complicated ties to the community where she grew up. Sterling works as a gardener for Lecha and her sister Zeta. He is thus indirectly involved in their illegal border dealings, and he grapples with the idea of crime and its construction in popular narratives of Western criminals throughout the novel. At the end of *Almanac*, Sterling leaves Tucson to return to the Laguna Pueblo reservation from which he was earlier expelled by tribal elders for allowing Hollywood filmmakers access to sacred sites.

In the figure of Sterling, *Almanac* takes to a hemispheric level the individualistic story of "homing," as William Bevis has famously called the Native American narrative in which the hero returns home to his tribe rather than "lights out for the territory." Bevis writes that "[w]hat looks so often to whites like individual regression to some secure Eden may be in Native American novels an enlargement of individuality to society, place, and past" (597). Sterling's return to New Mexico coincides with the emergence of a sandstone snake formation in his community. As it points south—toward the origin of the Army for Redistribution and Justice—the snake symbolizes belief in the upcoming repossession of the Americas by indigenous people. Sterling's homecoming thus not only reaffirms his own tribal identity, which hinges on notions of kinship and its relationship to a specific place in New Mexico, but also symbolizes important intersections between his tribe and emerging hemispheric pan-Indian activism.

Aside from an envisioned revolution from the south, the novel also predicts the return of the buffalo. These predictions are reminiscent of modern projects for the restoration of the Great Plains, such as Frank and Deborah Popper's notion of a Buffalo Commons (Norden 105). The two scholars have argued that the return of the buffalo to the Great Plains will enable the restoration of health to the land, to the people that inhabit it, and to the economy of the region. The arrival of a revolutionary movement and the return of the buffalo to the transnational Southwest bolster *Almanac*'s predictions that some day all "ideas and beliefs of the Europeans would gradually wither and drop away" (511). These predictions reiterate the main ideas of 1890s American Indian millenarian movements, which opposed confinement in reservations by forecasting the disappearance of white people and the return to pre-Columbian ways of life.

But *Almanac* foresees the disappearance of whites on a spiritual rather than a literal level. The revolutionary movement thus proceeds from a more inclusive perspective than American Indian nationalism in its definition of who constitutes an indigenous person and who will benefit from upcoming change. Silko's revolution welcomes white supporters who have disclaimed their European heritage, any "convert" who would "walk with the people and let go of all the greed and selfishness in one's heart . . . [and] of a great many comforts and all things European" (710). At the same time, the revolution is also grounded in tribally specific cultural traditions, such as those of the Yaqui, and their historical or geographical contact with other tribal nations like the Apache, Maya, and Laguna Pueblo. *Almanac* expresses this expansive and inclusive sense of community as pan-tribal struggles for land and border crossing rights that encompass rather than supersede the pursuit of each individual nation's or tribe's sovereignty.

By predicting an uprising of indigenous peoples in Mexico, Silko's novel continues the prophetic power of the Mayan almanacs, as she herself has often pointed out. The novel foresaw, at least three years into the future, the 1994 uprising in Chiapas by the Zapatista Army of National Liberation (EZLN) in support of Mexican Indians, some of whom are the present-day descendants of the Maya.[14] Situated at the margins of society, Mexican Indians have been present in every Mexican uprising; the Mexican Revolution itself began as an insurrection of landless Indian campesinos under Emiliano Zapata, a Nahua Indian. He was executed by the Mexican government in 1919 because he refused to lay down the arms he had taken up to regain his village's communal lands from European settlers. The EZLN took its name from Zapata after it transformed itself from the Emiliano Zapata National Alliance of Independent Farmers, a militant campesino group formed to protect farmers against attacks by the local elites and their secret police. Silko's 1996 collection of essays *Yellow Woman* has contextualized the EZLN uprising historically, noting that it "has a five-hundred-year history; this is the same war of resistance that indigenous people of the Americas have never ceased to fight" (153).

Her vision of a "network of tribal coalitions" parallels ideas articulated in the recent Mexican Indian uprising in Chiapas under the leadership of the Zapatistas. Starting on the day that NAFTA was implemented, their putative leader, Subcommandante Marcos, declared the uprising to be a "revolution against capitalism." He predicted that the elimination of agricultural tariffs against cheap U.S. and Canadian grains would provide for the likely return to an agricultural system based on large landowner control. Just as the EZLN recognizes that any opposition movement today needs to construct its local struggles in global terms, *Almanac* stresses the necessity of pan-ethnic and transnational affiliations that draw on struggles for the reclamation of individual tribal sovereignty and for the free movement of people across international borders.

Indigenous Canada-U.S. Border Crossings

In contrast to Silko's focus on the U.S. southwestern boundary, Thomas King has, since the early 1990s, emphasized indigenous peoples' relationship to the national border between Canada and the United States. Some of King's short fiction and his border trilogy—*Medicine River* (1991), *Green Grass, Running Water* (1993), and *Truth and Bright Water* (2000)—are set on or near a Blackfoot reservation located on the border between Alberta and Montana. King's third installment of the trilogy, *Truth and Bright Water*, in particular, depicts border areas as both homes of a specific tribal nation and, at the same time, locations of potential hemispheric pan-tribalism.

The title of King's first novel, *Medicine River*, which was made into a CBC television movie and a three-part CBC radio play, alludes to the native understanding of the forty-ninth parallel as a medicine line promising sanctuary from repressive national policies. Set in the fictional town of Blossom in southwest Alberta near the Canada-U.S. border, the novel has many connections to Silko's work, which King has acknowledged as one of the main influences on his oeuvre.[15] Native people coined the term *medicine line* in the nineteenth century when differences in U.S. and Canadian policies toward indigenous peoples transformed the shared border into a site of potential refuge. In contrast to the Chinese, who circumvented exclusivist U.S. immigration law by entering the United States through Canada's border at about the same time, indigenous people viewed this location as a means of escape from the destructive policies of either nation-state. While more American Indians fled to Canada, reverse border crossings were also commonplace. Just as native people manipulated internal competition among various colonial powers throughout the eighteenth and nineteenth centuries, they also employed to their advantage differential national politics toward them that transformed the shared border.[16]

Canada and the United States were equally implicated in the decimation of native North American populations. While official constructions of Canadian national identity as more benign toward its indigenous populations tend to exaggerate some of these distinctions, different policy solutions toward native people existed and manifested themselves at the site of the national border. England's policies toward Canada's native population set the context for differences from similar U.S. measures. The 1763 Royal Proclamation recognized aboriginal land rights and the sovereignty of Indian nations, which afforded Canada's First Nations greater cultural persistence and integrity than many tribes now located in the United States. Native people in Canada were spared from outright genocide; they were not wholesale moved away from their homelands but generally settled on (much smaller parcels of) land where they lived (Miller 373).

Nineteenth-century Canadian policies of advancing Indian assimilation through confinement in reservations were also more gradually enforced by the Mounted Police and the Canadian Department of Indian Affairs. In comparison to the U.S. government's motto of "reservation or extermination," the Canadian North-West Mounted Police symbolized the relative benevolence of Canadian authority in its regulation of westward movement (Ladow, "Sanctuary" 32–33). These national distinctions in the treatment of aboriginal people are partially a consequence of less intense pressure from the westward movement of European-descendent settlers in Canada as opposed to the rapid and violent expansion of settlement into the U.S. West. To this day, native people represent a much higher proportion of Canada's total population than they do in the United States. Many live on reserves (the Canadian term for what in the United States are called "reservations"). Yet indigenous people continue to occupy a position of complexity within Canadian society. They are usually excluded from considerations within Canada's multicultural mosaic and are approached either within postcolonial theory or within Native or First Nations studies that are institutionalized in many Canadian institutions of higher learning.[17]

Named for its seemingly magical potential to correct wrongs and reverse fortunes, in nineteenth-century native use, the Canada-U.S. border became a "medicine line." The understanding of the border as sanctuary united various indigenous groups on both sides of the border. The U.S. Sioux, U.S. Nez Perce, and the Métis, a border-straddling community of white and multitribal native ancestry, for example, conferred with one another, fought the same enemies, and sought refuge with one another (Ladow, "Sanctuary" 28).[18] Most famously, Sitting Bull, leader of the Hunkpapa Sioux, found temporary refuge in Canada after defeating General Custer's forces at the battle of Little Bighorn in 1876. Insufficient support by the Canadian government and failed alliances with other borderland tribes, however, eventually forced the Sioux back into the United States, where Sitting Bull surrendered to the U.S. government in 1881 (Ladow, "Sanctuary" 31–32).

King employed the setting of the medicine line, particularly the boundary along the Blackfoot reserve, in two later novels, *Green Grass, Running Water* and *Truth and Bright Water*. Just as *Almanac* has received less attention than Silko's earlier work, the final installment of King's border trilogy, *Truth,* has garnered less interest than King's earlier bestsellers *Green Grass* and *Medicine River*.[19] Like *Almanac*, *Truth* mixes elements of indigenous nationalism with tricksterism, creation stories, and other discursive conventions common to native oral storytelling. King's oeuvre stands out for its use of native humor, which, as Vine Deloria Jr. has argued, often functions to address desperate problems facing indigenous people and to unite them around activist pan-tribal causes. King has said that "[y]ou have to be funny enough to get them laughing so they really don't feel how hard you hit them. And the best kind of comedy is where you start off laughing and end up crying, because you realize just what is happening halfway through the emotion" ("Coyote" 97).

King self-identifies as native Canadian, despite his very loose connection to his Cherokee father, his longtime residence in the United States, and the fact that he holds dual Canadian and U.S. citizenship. King's father was largely absent during most of his upbringing and eventually disappeared when he was five. It was his Greek Orthodox mother who kept her two sons' sense of being Cherokee alive by taking them back to Oklahoma and seeing relatives. King only became acquainted with other native people as a teenager and made Indian American studies his subject matter during his master's and Ph.D. studies at the University of Utah (Weaver, *That* 146–47). Today, he has no close ties to any one tribe. In 1980 King moved to Canada for an academic appointment at the University of Lethbridge. He left Canada in 1990 for the University of Minnesota but returned in the 1990s to take an academic position at the University of Guelph.

King's self-identification as aboriginal Canadian complicates notions of authentic American Indian identity even more severely than Silko's emphasis on her mixed-blood descent as a "half-breed Laguna" (Bruchac 167). In addition to notions of status within a particular tribe, King's pronouncements also question tribal and national affiliations. As Jennifer Andrews and Priscilla L. Walton have recently written, "as an 'American' Cherokee who moved to Canada, [King] can be a Canadian writer and a Native writer, but he cannot be a Canadian Native writer because the Cherokees are not 'native' to Canada" (605). But King sees himself and his work as Canadian because of its geographical setting and subject matter (Andrews 161).[20] That King's identification is largely accepted is manifested in the marketing of his two early novels, *Medicine River* and *Green Grass, Running Water*, as Canadian classics.

Perhaps because of similar border crossing experiences in their own lives, Silko and King develop utopian visions of pan-tribalism that focus on the site of a national border. Silko inscribes cultural material from tribes throughout the Americas onto the geography of the Arizona Yaquis. King similarly places Cherokee, Shawnee, and Apache traditions in the landscape of the Blackfoot with whom he became familiar when he taught at the University of Lethbridge. The university is located near

Canada's largest native reserve, a reservation of approximately 2,500 Blood/Kainai with a central business area in Standoff. King has described this reserve as his imagined home, saying, "I'm a Cherokee from Oklahoma, but I don't think of Oklahoma as home. If I think of any place as home it's the Alberta prairies, where I spent ten years with the Blackfoot people. I'm not Blackfoot, but that feels like the place I want to go back to" (King, "Coyote Lives" 92). King acknowledges his distance from the reservation experience, saying that he instead focuses on "the experience that contemporary Indians have in trying to manage living in the more contemporary world while maintaining a relationship with that more traditional world" (King, "Coyote Lives" 92).

All of King's work on the Blackfoot reveals his keen understanding of connections between attempts to preserve tribal sovereignty and notions of aboriginal residence in border areas. In his introduction to his edition of native Canadian fiction, *All My Relations,* King has emphasized parallels between the two perhaps most well-known Canada-U.S. border tribes, the Iroquois and Blackfoot, and their relationship to the international boundary. He writes that "contemporary tribes such as the Iroquois confederacy in the east and the Blackfoot confederacy in the west, [hold that] the forty-ninth parallel is a figment of someone else's imagination" (King, "Introduction" 10).[21]

The Iroquois Confederacy, which consists of the Mohawk, Oneida, Onondaga, Cayuga, Seneca, and Tuscarora Nations, connects communities with similar languages and relationships to a specific place—the land and region encompassing Lake Ontario and Lake Erie. The Iroquois were separated by events of the American Revolution. As a reward for their support of the British, the Iroquois received lands along the Grand River in Ontario, where their cultural traditions continued to thrive to a greater extent than in the New York homeland (Miller 374). Because of ongoing, significant cross-border movements of people, the Iroquois on both sides of the border have not developed into two separate cultures, as have, for example, the Yaqui fictionalized in *Almanac.* Struggles for sovereignty have found expression in efforts to maintain Iroquois border crossing rights, which include the right to work, hunt, fish, and trap on either side; to carry sacred objects and personal goods without paying duties; and to engage in commerce within tribal territories without interference of laws and regulations (Taliman 14).[22]

Unlike the Iroquois Confederacy, which consists of various groups with relatively separate national identities, the Blackfoot King fictionalizes were once a single nation who inhabited a territory stretching from the

North Saskatchewan River in Canada to the Missouri River in Montana. In the nineteenth century, three interdependent nations or tribes were created that today live on reservations in Alberta and Montana: the Siksika (or Blackfoot proper), the Kaina (or Blood), and the Piegan (or Pikini).

Despite their internal separation by a national border, the Blackfoot have maintained their collective identity, manifested in a common language, extended family ties, shared traditions like Sun Dance ceremonies, and transborder activism. Subsequent to issuing the "Proclamation Restoring the Independence of the Sovereign Nation State of Blackfoot" on November 29, 1999, for example, representatives from the Blackfoot Confederacy called for the establishment of separate border crossings to assist them in maintaining internal ties across the Canada-U.S. border. For the Blackfoot, as for the Yaquis fictionalized in Silko's *Almanac,* border crossing rights are thus intimately connected to notions of sovereignty and nationhood.

One of the short stories in King's collection *One Good Story, That One* (1993), entitled "Borders," highlights, more explicitly than Silko's *Almanac,* connections between notions of tribal nationhood and struggles for border crossing rights. The unnamed twelve- or thirteen-year-old narrator in King's story "Borders," his twenty-two-year-old sister, Laetitia, and his mother live on the Blood Blackfoot reserve near Standoff. The boy's absent (and presumably white) father is from "Rocky Boy on the American side" (133). It is the father's citizenship rather than the children's membership in the Blackfoot nation, a sovereign national body, that allows them to "go and come as [they] please" across the border (133). The novel describes the border crossing between the two actually existing towns thus: "Coutts was on the Canadian side and consisted of the convenience store and gas station, the museum that was closed and boarded up, and a motel. Sweetgrass was on the American side, but all you could see was an overpass that arched across the highway and disappeared into the prairies. Just hearing the names of these towns, you would expect Sweetgrass . . . would be on the Canadian side, and that Coutts, which sounds abrupt and rude, would be on the American side. But this was not the case" (135–36). The narrator remembers how, when he was seven or eight years old, Laetitia simply walked across the land border into Sweetgrass, Montana, to catch a bus to Salt Lake City, Utah.

The story opens five years later when the narrator and his mother are about to leave their home on the Blackfoot reserve in Alberta to visit Laetitia. Unlike her daughter, the mother encounters great difficulties at the official border crossing between Alberta and Montana, a relatively remote stretch of the border where fewer problems with indigenous border crossings have been reported than along other parts of the boundary. Because the narrator's mother refuses to respond to the U.S. American border guards' questions about her citizenship and place of residence with anything other than "Blackfoot," she is not allowed to enter the United States. When they turn back, the Canadian border guard also does not readmit her since she insists on identifying herself as Blackfoot. The mother and her son are stuck, for three nights, in the no-man's-land of a duty-free store located between Coutts and Sweetgrass. Only when the media start covering what they perceive to be the story of "Indian[s] without a country" (145) is the family finally allowed to cross into the United States without having to frame their citizenship in terms of belonging to a particular nation-state.

There is no indication that their admission constitutes anything other than an exception to the rule. This is in line with actual policy. While a recently established Blackfoot cultural sensitivity training program for border agents has, for example, led to fewer arrests and detentions, individual border agents decide on their own how to handle each border crossing incident (Taliman 16). Even though the mother's courageous act only challenges rather than changes official border crossing rules, the story's ending confirms the Blackfoot view of international borders. "Borders" leaves us with the final image of a disappearing international boundary, marked by flags as the obligatory symbols of nations, when the mother and son cross back into Coutts. The narrator watches the border through the rear window of the car "until all you could see were the tops of the flagpoles and the blue water tower, and then they rolled over a hill and disappeared" (147).

King's more recent novel *Truth* transforms the location of "Borders," the Canada-U.S. border near the Blackfoot reserve, into a water boundary. Besides a brief allusion to a café owner from the Blackfoot Blood reserve who knew the narrator's father (87) and a German who is said to speak good Blackfoot (202), however, the novel never identifies the characters' tribal affiliation as clearly as "Borders." Instead, *Truth* sets out to develop an explicitly hemispheric form of pan-Indianism at the site of the international boundary. The water separates the fictional Bright Water, a Canadian Indian reservation, and Truth, an adjacent U.S. American railroad town. The communities of Truth and Bright Water are separated by a half-completed bridge across the Shield River, the failed construction of which is claimed to be responsible for the area's economic depression. Residents of Truth tell Bright Water to "keep your kids on their side of the river" (41), expressing their perception of the border as a natural division between two nationally and ethnically different, hierarchically organized, and antagonistic communities. Yet the division is clearly not that simple, as members of the native community reside on both sides of the border. Off-reservation Indians like the narrator, fifteen-year-old Tecumseh, his mother, Helen, and his father, Elvin, live in the U.S. town of Truth, whereas Tecumseh's grandmother and his cousin Lum reside on the reservation in Bright Water.

In the opening pages, the novel's setting is described thus: "Truth and Bright Water sit on opposite sides of the river, the railroad town on the American side, the reserve on the Canadian side" (1). The shift in King's fiction from a land to a water boundary underscores the arbitrary nature of national borders. The novel notes that the water boundary has "been here since the beginning of time" (*Truth* 52) and thus predates any national division. As Marian Botsford Fraser writes, water boundaries are intrinsically different from land borders: "there can be no cut line on water" as water lines "make a mockery of the notion of mathematically precise boundary" (Fraser 69; 71). King's focus on the water portion of a national border also suggests contemporary Blackfoot struggles to defend their position on water rights against proposals, codified in the FTAA, to export water from the Great Lakes basins for sale to the West and to Europe.

As opposed to the difficulties that the characters in King's story "Borders" face when moving across the national boundary, in *Truth,* native people cross the border frequently and without much trouble even though they are still subjected to border racism. One character in the novel describes the fluid nature of the portion of the border around the reserve by saying that there are "[l]ots of places to cross" (141). Despite the danger it represents, the unfinished bridge appears to be the most convenient (and fastest) way to cross for people who cannot afford or do not desire to engage in the other two ways of border crossings. These include taking "Charlie Ron's ferry" or "the toilet," a bucket suspended over the river on a cable, or making a forty-minute car trip to an official border crossing at Prairie View.

Just as the Mexico-U.S. line in Silko's novel creates smuggling opportunities for members of transborder tribes like the Yaqui, the Canada-U.S. boundary enables its own plethora of illegal activity for some Blackfoot. Indigenous people, especially members of transnational border tribes, often justify this type of cross-border movement by claiming that their sovereign status renders them immune from such nation-state policies as taxation. Other native people, however, characterize these views as perversions of sovereignty since they exacerbate threats to tribal autonomy, exposing border tribes to additional pressures from nation-states to enforce their portion of the border against threats like terrorism and undocumented immigration (Hill 64).

Elvin transports cigarettes, stereo equipment, motorcycles, garbage, and biohazardous waste across the border and even considers bringing in guns for an "Indian Days" celebration. He describes the garbage ironically as "[t]he new buffalo" (153). Bright Water's chief, Elvin's brother Franklin, keeps accepting waste for extra money even though the community's landfill has officially been closed. After Tecumseh helps Elvin unload the barrels of medical waste, they prepare to cross back but have to leave Tecumseh's dog Soldier behind. The narrator reports, "'They won't let dogs across,' says my father. 'Used to be the same for Indians.' He holds up his hands. The gloves are covered with a reddish-black stain. 'Better wash up. No telling where those barrels have been'" (83). Juxtaposing commentary about dogs and Indians crossing the border with the unloading of hazardous barrels, the novel points to the differences in the crossings of people and objects across national borders.

Like Silko, who draws from various tribal traditions to articulate her vision of alliances located in the Mexico-U.S. border landscape of Tucson, King's novel projects onto the Canada-U.S. border space of the Blackfoot a range of other tribal cultures, such as Apache, Shawnee, and Cherokee.[23] Tecumseh's cousin Lum is associated with the Apache Geronimo, who also figures centrally in Silko's depiction of intersections between Yaqui and other U.S. southwestern tribes and who has become an icon of resistance for indigenous people more generally. Like Geronimo, Lum has a bad eye, is a great runner, and meets a tragic end (Ridington 90).

In naming its main protagonist Tecumseh, the novel also points to a Shawnee chief who unsuccessfully attempted to unite the tribes of the Mississippi valley, including Cherokees, Muscogees, Choctaws, Chickasaws, and Seminoles, against invading Europeans. The eventual defeat of Tecumseh and his brother Tenskwatawa, the Shawnee Prophet, paved the way for the U.S. doctrine of Indian removal and led to the Cherokee "trail of tears." This doctrine displaced to Oklahoma the same tribes Tecumseh tried to organize. *Truth* fictionalizes other important Cherokee personages who come to visit Bright Water's celebration of "Indian Days."[24] For example, *Truth*'s central figure, Monroe Swimmer, is one of the novel's tricksters and a "famous Indian artist."[25] The artist's name evokes two characters central to Cherokee history: Swimmer, a Cherokee healer who in 1887 showed the anthropologist James Mooney a book of sacred formulas written in the syllabary devised by George Guess; and President James Monroe, a key figure in the history of Cherokee removals (Ridington 92–93).

While Monroe and Tecumseh's father Elvin were friends once, they now embody different reactions to the colonization of indigenous people and the commodification of their cultures. Elvin "authenticates," with his tribal number, badly fashioned wooden coyote figures designed for sale to tourists; Monroe takes native children's skulls from a Toronto museum where he works and then liberates them in the Shield River of his native reserve. Monroe's acts challenge the widespread practice of collecting Indian artifacts for government institutions or museums in Canada and the United States. Monroe's efforts also foreground indigenous efforts at repatriation that have led to the passage of the 1990 Native American Grave Protection and Repatriation Act (NAGPRA) in the United States and to similar policies in individual Canadian provinces and institutions.[26]

A restaurateur in a Toronto art museum, Monroe also works on nineteenth-century landscape art. This form of art celebrated notions of the land while depicting the demise of indigenous peoples, but Monroe restores "the village and the Indians back into the painting" (133). Once he returns to Bright Water, Monroe continues his anticolonial efforts in the realm of art by setting out to obliterate the community's symbols of colonization. He purchases the "Sacred Word Gospel Church" overlooking Truth, which was built by Indian missionaries, and then paints its exterior the exact color of the prairie landscape so it appears as if the church never existed. Monroe also populates the prairies with papier-mâché and iron buffalo nailed into the ground. He thus reaffirms the central role and sacredness of the buffalo for Blackfoot tribes. Its demise symbolized not only white expectations about the eventual decline of native populations (which characterized landscape painting) but also the loss of subsistence and of deeper meanings behind preserved cultural traditions that revolve around the animal.

Evoking Silko's vision of the return of the buffalo to the Southwestern borderlands, Monroe tells Tecumseh that "[e]ach day the herd will grow larger and larger. . . . Before we're done, the buffalo will return" (135). Monroe's next project involves buying a residential school (near the fictional town of Medicine River, the setting of King's first novel), where Native Canadian children were, until the late 1960s, converted into "white men."

Tecumseh works as Monroe's assistant on the church "restoration project," and in the absence of other adults who make time for Tecumseh, Monroe becomes his not always effectual teacher (B. Hirsch 148). After they complete the church project, Monroe and Tecumseh look out at the prairie. From a certain angle, they cannot see the church, the bridge, or Truth or Bright Water; the Canada-U.S. border is effectively erased. According to Monroe, it is now "[j]ust like the old days . . . [b]esides the river, there is only the land and the sky" (134–35). Similar to the ending of Silko's *Almanac,* Monroe's speech evokes the sentiment of American Indian millenarian movements that white people would eventually disappear, ancestors would return, and the buffalo would repopulate the prairies.

Truth ends with Monroe Swimmer conducting a giveaway of all his possessions in an Indian ceremony. Even though the ceremony briefly brings members of the community together, it appears to have no lasting effect. Shortly after the ceremony, Lum commits suicide. He has a history of severe abuse by his father and is haunted by memories of a mother who abandoned the family. A runner, Lum moves down the length of the unfinished bridge between Truth and Bright Water, marking the geopolitical border between two countries with his body. He is followed by Tecumseh's dog Soldier until both disappear over the edge. While Lum's body is eventually discovered in close proximity to the barrels of biohazardous waste dumped by Elvin, Soldier, another trickster figure in the novel, is never found. This gives Tecumseh hopes that Soldier "survived the fall but was injured and lost his memory, and that one day he'll remember and come home" (262).

Lum's suicide shows, as King has said, that "there is no salvation for these kids within the community . . . because in many cases what's happened to Native peoples is they've wound up in a position where they're hardly able to protect themselves" (Andrews 168). In the end, Monroe Swimmer's several reclamation projects and his ceremonies cannot save Lum, and Tecumseh does not succeed in getting his parents or other adults to help his cousin. Lum's death points to the tragic lives of many native people and makes him one of the lost Indian children in the novel.

The narrative also alludes, like King's "Borders" and Silko's *Almanac,* to the possibility of tribal members' return to strengthened communities. The novel engages in anticolonial reclamations of individual tribal sovereignty at the same time that it paints various tribal histories and cultures onto the Blackfoot landscape of the Canada-U.S. border. King's work thus questions, like Silko's *Almanac,* artificial dichotomies between pan-tribalism and individual tribal struggles for autonomy. In its defense of indigenous nationhood, its defiance of national borders, and its alliance-building across various Indian nations in the United States and Canada, *Truth* opens up possibilities for change.

American Indian Studies and the Hemisphere

The work of Silko and King emphasizes that indigenous people at both U.S. land borders have encountered similar historical and contemporary challenges, which can potentially engender common positions. The national border areas these two writers chose as the setting for their work recall histories of transnational alliances in the borderlands and also individual tribal battles for internal cohesion against nation-state repression throughout the hemisphere. The contemporary settings of the novels highlight how trade agreements and U.S. border militarization further undermine notions of native sovereignty. The commodification of land inscribed in economic hemispheric agreements that promote open borders and the closing of North American boundaries to movements by people reinforce repressive nation-state policies throughout the hemisphere that have historically promoted the loss of native land and the weakening of aboriginal border crossing rights.

Silko and King fictionalize possible responses to these developments in hemispheric notions of indigeneity that highlight native sovereignty, border crossing, and land rights. The two writers thus chronicle and also influence other forms of hemispheric indigenous activism. As Silko and King insist, such alliances need to acknowledge historical and contemporary conflicts among indigenous tribes as potential impediments to visions of hemispheric tribal unity. In her focus on Mexico-U.S. borderlands tribes, Silko addresses historical tensions among U.S. Southwestern tribes like the Yaqui and Apache. Similarly, King's emphasis on the "medicine line" invokes nineteenth-century histories of failed alliances among Canada-U.S. borderlands nations, and his narrator's name, Tecumseh, alludes to the Shawnee leader's failure to unite tribes of the Mississippi valley against the U.S. doctrine of Indian removal.

Any comparative approach to border tribes along U.S. boundaries similarly needs to take into account each tribal nation's differential historical relationship to the nation-state in which it now resides, relationships that are often codified in treaties. While Mexico-U.S. border tribes like the Tohono O'odham, for example, have demanded that U.S. citizenship be granted to enrolled tribal members living in Mexico, Canada-U.S. tribes like the Iroquois insist on recognizing that their membership in an independent nation is uniquely defined by international treaties between the United States, Britain, and Canada. The Iroquois in particular fear that proposals to grant U.S. citizenship to indigenous people will mean having to give up native citizenship in order to travel within aboriginal territories.[27]

The fiction of Silko and King highlights borders as sites where differential nation-state policies have intersected to create the promise of escape to a neighboring nation. As in the case with undocumented Chinese border crossers, international boundaries with Canada and Mexico did not usually turn out to be long-lasting sanctuaries for indigenous peoples. When several native tribes, including the Sioux and the Nez Perce, fled the U.S. Army into Canada, the Canadian government offered no concrete help, instead urging them to return to U.S. territory. Similarly, Geronimo's flight to Mexico, fictionalized in Silko's *Almanac,* did not provide him with lasting sanctuary from U.S. policies as Mexican troops helped the U.S. Army recapture its most dreaded enemy. Just as Mexico and Canada collaborated to an extent in the enforcement of U.S. Chinese exclusion legislation (discussed in the previous chapter), the colonial regime in both countries contributed to the oppression of native people in the United States and in their own nations. The limited support offered to indigenous peoples from the United States in U.S. neighboring nations points to similarities in the treatment of aboriginal populations across the hemisphere, while also highlighting the limitations of Canada and Mexico's sovereignty vis-à-vis the United States when it came to disputes involving U.S. land boundaries.

In addition to reinforcing existing pan-tribal ties, Silko and King ingeniously place into contact tribal nations across the hemisphere that have not yet been thought of together. In her attempt to creatively forge a network of tribal coalitions, Silko alludes to potential political connections among northern border tribes like the Mohawk and southwestern border tribes like the Yaqui and the Apache. Much of King's border trilogy is similarly marked by an effort to imagine ties among tribes like the Cherokee and the Blackfoot, who have historically not been in contact. The two writers' affirmation of historical affiliations and their attempts to establish new intersections among tribal nations articulate comparative, hemispheric, and at times, internationalist visions of indigeneity.[28]

These visions move beyond entrenched U.S.-centered divisions between specific approaches to particular tribal cultures and more generalized understandings of indigeneity across the hemisphere (and globally). That a more comparative version of academic indigenous studies may be on the rise is exemplified in recent institutional change. Some U.S. American Indian studies programs have moved toward more broadly hemispheric orientations. The Native American Studies department at the University of California at Davis, for example, has changed its focus to include research and scholarship on the indigenous people of North, Central, and South America as a complement to more traditional inquiries within the framework of Native American studies. Similarly, the University of Buffalo's Department of American Studies, which coordinates one of the strongest American Indian studies programs in the United States, has adopted a hemispheric lens.

Reminiscent of Yamashita's stress on the pan-ethnic character of Asian American civil rights struggles (discussed in the previous chapter), the works of King and Silko foreground the pan-Indian implications of the Red Power movement for possible future coalitions. Silko's work in particular moves beyond the rather limited notions of affiliation that have evolved from U.S. civil rights movements and their emphasis on shared histories of marginalization, or sometimes, as in the case of Chicanismo, on appeals to common bloodlines between Chicana/os and indigenous people.

Silko broadens her definition of indigeneity to include, for example, Euro-Americans and people of Asian and African descent. She points to intersections among the plight of homeless people and landless immigrants from Latin America with indigenous struggles for the return of land. Silko also highlights political intersections, fictionalizing support by radical environmentalists whose interest overlaps with native attempts to protect land and its resources from neoliberal abuse. And, finally, the movement she imagines gains the help of a Korean American computer hacker who entered the country as an undocumented immigrant via the Mexico-U.S. border.[29] The fate of this undocumented immigrant points to the larger historical and contemporary intersections of struggles for indigenous rights with anti-immigration initiatives that have also weakened the abilities of indigenous peoples to cross borders freely. Even though the similarities among Aboriginal peoples and other cultures have historically been insufficient to create alliances, Silko expresses the hope that they will do so in the future.

4   The View from the South

In THE MID-1990s, Mexico's foremost living writer, Carlos Fuentes, dedicated a work of fiction entirely to the contemporary Mexico-U.S. border. While some of Fuentes's earlier work had already addressed historical events in the border region, the publication of *La frontera de cristal* in 1995 (translated in 1997 as *The Crystal Frontier*) signaled the new importance accorded to this location by a writer mostly based in the country's capital, which had long snubbed its northern borderland. In the novel, Fuentes describes *la frontera méxico-estadounidense* as "an enormous bloody wound, a sick body, mute in the face of its ills, on the point of shouting, torn by its loyalties, and beaten, finally, by political callousness, demagoguery, and corruption" (244).[1]

His powerful description is reminiscent of Gloria Anzaldúa's famous characterization of *la frontera* as *"una herida abierta"* (an open wound) in *Borderlands/La Frontera*.[2] At the same time, Fuentes's language also highlights a view of borders not often pursued in Chicana/o literature. This literature is largely known for its focus on U.S. communities and their relation to the U.S. nation, but in his work, Fuentes develops a more comparative North American lens. Pointing to the border's "torn loyalties" and to corruption in both countries as they manifest themselves at the seams of the two nations, *The Crystal Frontier* examines the northern Mexican border area in relation to both the United States and to notions of Mexican nationalism (*mexicanidad*).

The novel's concluding story, "Río Bravo, Río Grande," vividly represents Fuentes's overall attempt in *The Crystal Frontier* to place into dialogue Chicana/o and Mexican notions of the Mexico-U.S. border. In this story, a young Chicano activist transports literature by Chicana/o writers, such as Sandra Cisneros, Denise Chávez, and Alberto Ríos, into Mexico, while bringing into the United States the fiction of northern

Mexican border writers like Federico Campbell. Often called *literatura de la frontera* (literature from the border), the work by Campbell and by such other authors as Rosina Conde focuses on the connection between Mexico's center and its northern areas, thus questioning Mexico City-based views of the border region as a "hinterland." This work shows that, especially since the 1990s, the region has experienced significant change, including enormous population growth, the surge of a new, female workforce for maquila assembly production, and the continuous emigration of men (and increasingly also women) to the United States.

Compared to *literatura de la frontera* by Campbell and Conde, Fuentes develops a more explicitly comparatist view of the Mexico-U.S. border and the transnational relationship it represents. His work emphasizes the historical and contemporary effects of U.S. empire while also drawing attention to the Mexican state's participation in maintaining the United States' role as a hegemonic hemispheric power. Fuentes highlights how the two governments, and particularly the elites dominating them, have collaborated in creating a contemporary infrastructure that has further deepened Mexico's dependency in the realms of trade and labor.

As an alternative to the nationalism tied to Mexico's corrupt government, Fuentes articulates various nationalisms that are divorced from their state-sponsored forms. Fuentes particularly stresses the progressive roots of *mexicanidad* in indigenous thought and in the Mexican Revolution. As a place where political revolutionary figures like Francisco Madero, Francisco "Pancho" Villa, and Venustiano Carranza led movements of national importance, the northern border set the context for the emergence of the Mexican nation and its corollary, a distinctly Mexican notion of national identity. The Mexican Revolution enabled the passage of the 1917 Constitution, which contained some of the most socially advanced pieces of legislation in the world. Article 123 granted workers the right to organize, and Article 27 enabled the distribution of land to peasants (Otero 7).

The northern border was also influential in the construction of new, anticolonial forms of national identity. Associated with the work of Minister of Education José Vasconcelos, the version of *mexicanidad* that rose to prominence highlights the nation's racial origin in the New World encounter between Europeans and indigenous people. *Mexicanidad* places the origin of the Mexican population in the mixture of European and pre-Columbian cultures, symbolized in the union of the Spanish conqueror Hernán Cortés and the indigenous woman Malitzin, or La Malinche. The focus on *mestizaje* sets *mexicanidad* in explicit opposition to dominant versions of U.S. nationhood, which have largely dismissed the influence of indigenous peoples. Even though the emphasis on indigeneity has more affinities with central Mexican thought, Vasconcelos's focus on a strong dualism between the Anglo-Saxon and the Ibero-American world was undoubtedly shaped by his upbringing, schooling, and later exile along the Texas-Chihuahua borderlands.[3]

When *mexicanidad* gained state-sponsored status in the 1920s, the influence of the northern border on this concept was largely forgotten. Instead, the northern border was relegated to a marginalized position, onto which continuing anxieties about the dominance of the United States in the hemisphere could be projected. Increased economic integration since the 1960s and particularly the 1980s and 1990s in the context of NAFTA has resuscitated these anxieties.

To describe his alternative vision of hemispheric relations, Fuentes highlights new forms of *mexicanidad* that are emerging in the Mexican diaspora in the United States and in the northern border area and that he sees as the starting point for conceptions of anticolonial nationalism independently of the nation-state. In its focus on progressive elements of Mexican nationalism and the shortcomings of the Mexican state, *The Crystal Frontier* arrives at a more complex picture of globalization in the hemisphere than do prevailing border studies. In this sense, the novel opens up the possibility for dialogue among approaches to borders and their relationship to nationalism and U.S. empire in U.S. American, Latin American, and Chicana/o-Latina/o studies.

The Northern Mexican Border in Academic Scholarship

Narratives about the northern Mexican border, a seeming periphery within a peripheral third-world country, have so far occupied a marginalized position in popular and scholarly discourses, both in the United States and Mexico. In U.S. American studies, Mexico has long functioned as an object of representational analysis or as a mirror image of U.S. preoccupations rather than as a geography whose theory and fiction (besides magical realism and dependency theory) may be worth studying.

Historical and contemporary representations of Mexico by U.S.-based Anglo writers tend to portray the country as a land of vice, excess, and corruption as well as an imaginary escape for U.S. Americans from problems in their own country.[4] Moreover, the inequities in U.S. and Mexican publication and distribution venues and the fact that much imaginative work from or about the border has not been translated into English have made its inclusion into an English-language curriculum problematic.[5]

In Mexico, the study of the northern border has equally been marginalized. Luis Alberto Urrea has characterized the Mexican view of the Baja Californian portion of the border thus: "Tijuana itself is not welcome in the Motherland. Tijuana is Mexico's cast-off child. She brings in money and *gringos,* but nobody would dare claim her" (20). Few Mexican institutions, including those situated close to the Mexico-U.S. boundary, have traditionally been interested in border work. Instead, attention to the Mexican border has manifested itself in declarations that its proximity to the United States makes it more susceptible to attacks by U.S. American culture and thereby less "Mexican." Centrist or state-sponsored representations also often foreground violence and oppression as a warning directed at "illegal" border crossers from Mexico.

Chicana/o representations have also had little to say about the northern Mexican border. In fact, Chicana/o fiction and scholarship rarely venture on to the Mexican side of the border. In *RetroSpace,* one of the few existing analyses of Chicana/o representations of Mexico, Mexican immigration, and Mexican national identity throughout the 1980s, Juan Bruce-Novoa has shown that this work has produced largely idealized and monolithic notions of *mexicanidad.* He argues that Chicana/o representations revalue shared pre-Columbian or mestizo elements of Mexican culture or depict Mexican immigration and its relationship to Chicana/o communities. This thematic focus informs portrayals of Mexico as a source of nostalgia for a lost paradise or as a place for disillusioning encounters between Chicana/o or Mexican American protagonists and the Mexican "homeland."

Such views are grounded in Chicana/o civil rights activism and its later development into cultural nationalism. The rise of Aztlán signaled a shift from direct civil rights action that often involved notions of transnational solidarity with working-class Mexicans to that of identity formation. The new interest in forging a collective identity shaped more symbolic views of Mexico as the place of ancestral origin of Chicana/os.

The 1980s and 1990s borderlands concept in Chicana/o-Latina/o studies that has replaced Aztlán has transformed the border into a metaphor for theories of cultural difference and diasporic identity. María Socorro Tabuenca Córdoba, for example, has critiqued the largely figurative usage of the border as a synonym for Chicana/o identities as creating "a multicultural space in the United States" (154) that does not recognize the northern Mexican border. Robert McKee Irwin similarly posits that even if Chicana/o border work pays attention to Mexico, it does so to address U.S. questions of identity. In this way, McKee Irwin writes,

Chicana/o border studies has "perpetuate[d] or even reinforce[d] barriers that prevent both dialogue with Mexican scholars based in Mexico and the study of Mexican texts that speak to issues of U.S.-Mexico relations and border culture" ("Toward" 511).

Only recently have Chicana/o scholars called for work that would take seriously the claim that the field explores connections among between Mexican Americans and Mexicans.[6] The emergent framework of Latino studies, which attempts to bridge the fields of Chicana/o-Latina/o and Latin American studies, appears to provide an answer to these calls.

But some practitioners have already warned that the focus of Latina/o studies could minimize internal social, political, and class distinctions. Like the internationalized Asian American studies perspective described in chapter 2, a Latino studies framework threatens to obscure important social divisions and lines of affiliation by insisting that "seemingly transparent lines of panethnicity and panethnic nationalism" can guarantee progressive politics and connections to important social movements and marginalized social groups (Chabram-Dernersesian 106). In the case of border writers, such a descent-driven approach threatens to overlook differences between Mexican intellectuals and U.S. Chicana/o writers, while marginalizing divergent national context of production, reception, and dissemination.

Suggestions for the collaboration between Latin American and American studies within hemispheric frameworks that could potentially also address border literature have been much more tentative than emerging Latina/o perspectives. In 1995, at the inception of transnational lenses in U.S. American studies, Gregory Jay cautioned that extending the field into Latin America could repeat the long history of U.S. imperialism toward the region on an academic level. Even though he briefly considers the possibility of a hemispheric perspective by drawing on Chicana/o border studies, Jay ultimately debunks this alternative in favor of limiting American studies to an examination of texts produced within the borders of the United States. As Jay writes, calling "for an end to the study of a national American literature means calling for an end to the study of a national Mexican or Canadian or Colombian literature. Do 'we' in the United States want to prescribe to such an abandonment of local and regional cultural traditions?" (182). Jay usefully reminds us of U.S. imperialism as an important component of any hemispheric work. But his view also threatens to transpose the theoretical preoccupations of U.S. American studies, especially the field's dismissive attitude toward U.S. nationalism and its uncritical equation with the nation-state, onto other countries in the Americas and the fields that have traditionally been involved in their study.

Other U.S. Americanist scholars have more readily embraced the hemispheric perspective. John Muthyala and Paul Jay, for example, have argued for a theoretical framework that would replace the U.S. American studies focus on the nation-state with an emphasis on cultural zones like the Southwest and the South. Both of these zones are in part defined by their historical and contemporary connections to Latin America and the Caribbean, respectively. The two scholars ground their proposals in the works of Chicana/o border theorists like Gloria Anzaldúa and José David Saldívar and in postcolonial scholarship by Paul Gilroy and Homi Bhabha. But they never address Latin American (or Caribbean) scholarship on these questions or consider the necessity of involvement with these fields.

More recent work by Anna Brickhouse and Debra Rosenthal, which originated in English departments affiliated with American studies, responds to 1990s calls for hemispheric perspectives. Brickhouse and Rosenthal depart from the somewhat programmatic nature of these calls by thoroughly engaging with scholarship from comparative literature, Latin American, Latino, and Caribbean studies. Their work reconfigures U.S. literary history, particularly that of the nineteenth century, by focusing on interlinked questions of race and empire that have been at the heart of attempts to internationalize U.S. American studies.

For Latin Americanists, the production of alternative narratives about a region over which the United States exerts overwhelming dominance seems a more complicated undertaking. Whenever Latin American scholars have articulated regional, inter-regional, or continental approaches to humanistic study, these have tended to take the form of inter-*Latin* American work aligned with anticolonialist agendas rather than inter-American work. Those few Latin Americanists who have employed an inter-American perspective have often done so in order to understand and respond critically to historical or contemporary phenomena of a hemispheric nature, especially those created by neoliberalism and free trade that affect their own countries.

Some U.S.-based Latin Americanists who focus on Mexico and its border region have already reacted to U.S. Americanists' proposals for hemispheric work. Robert McKee Irwin, for example, has promoted a "multilingual cross-cultural dialogue" that would "expand Chicano studies or even American studies (in the sense of studies of the Americas) into the field of Latin American studies" (McKee Irwin, "Toward" 521). McKee Irwin argues that any hemispheric framework will substantially change U.S.-based American studies, but he focuses mostly on questions of language. He believes, for example, that "the next generation of American Studies professors ought to be able to read scholarly publishing in Spanish, to understand and respond to scholarly discourse in Spanish, to feel comfortable teaching Spanish-language texts, and to interact intelligently with the large number of native Spanish speakers or heritage speakers who take their classes," as well as to "carry out their research in Spanish" (McKee Irwin, "Qué hacen" 314–15).

Mexicanidad de la frontera

Since the 1980s, the northern border has been one of the most intellectually active regions in Mexico, as manifested in the large-scale production of cultural criticism, imaginative work, and historical accounts.[7] While the El Paso–Juárez area, the most heavily industrialized and integrated zone, figures as the literary center of the Mexico-U.S. border, Tijuana has also attracted much literary attention.

Of the much larger number of northern border texts, the work of the Tijuana-born Campbell and Conde is available in English translation. In contrast to Fuentes's *literatura fronteriza,* which has become known in Mexico and to a lesser extent in the United States, *literatura de la frontera,* like that by Campbell and Conde, has not yet entered the Mexican (or U.S.) mainstream (Castillo and Tabuenca Córdoba 27). This is due to a range of factors. A literary marketplace that would have allowed the consolidation of an audience was long absent from the northern borderlands, and the national Mexican market showed little interest in border work. Mostly published in regional journals, small presses, or anthologies, *literatura de la frontera* is often associated with theories of regionalism and aesthetic marginality. As Joseph Hodara points out, *literatura de la frontera* tends to employ the less popular genres of criticism, the short story, and poetry instead of the novelistic form.

Compilations of several pieces, either assembled by the authors or their editors, the works of Campbell and Conde focus on the contemporary northern border. Unlike *The Crystal Frontier,* however, these works do not adopt an explicitly transnational framework. Like northern border residents more generally, writers of the border may feel that because of their constant interactions with the United States, questions about the interrelationships of the two nations are so obvious that they do not need to be engaged. Mexican border residents generally claim that constantly reasserting their national identity in relationship to the United States is unnecessary. They may be less susceptible to idealized images of their northern neighbor than residents of the capital, who are exposed to more abstract views of the United States through television and imported consumer commodities (García Canclini, *Consumers* 143). In addition, writing of the border is influenced by the conditions surrounding its production. Northern Mexican authors may see their potential audiences and literary markets located within a regional and national plane rather than in a transnational or international framework.

Federico Campbell, the author of some ten books, has become most famous for *Tijuanenses* (1989), translated by Debra Castillo as *Tijuana: Stories on the Border* in 1995. Together, the four stories and one short novella in the collection focus on Tijuana and its relationship to Mexico City and, partially, to the United States. Well-known in Mexico for his work as a reporter and journalist, Campbell, a Guggenheim recipient, has lived in both of these locations. He sharpened his inter-American expertise as the Washington, D.C., correspondent for a Mexican news agency. For a few decades now, he has been leading the life of a prominent man of letters in the Mexican capital. Yet Campbell periodically returns to Tijuana to visit relatives or friends or take part in literary conferences.

Rather than a systemic examination of the border, *Tijuanenses* represents Campbell's backward glance at the city of his birth and adolescence from the first decades of the twentieth century until the 1980s and into the more recent present. He describes a border *mexicanidad* torn between influences from Mexico City and the southwestern United States. Campbell has said that his work does not participate in the type of academic inquiries into the border region that have recently began to emerge in Mexico, such as studies "by anthropologists, sociologists, journalists and El Colegio de la Frontera Norte" (Johnson).

In his book, Campbell highlights the constant pull exerted on northern Mexican border residents by both Mexico City and the United States. The last story in the collection, "Insurgentes Big Sur," is set in Mexico City (the Distrito Federal). The narrator, who just moved there from Tijuana, describes the capital and Los Angeles as major poles of attraction for the border subject. Cast through popular culture, the influence of these two cities on the border makes residents "turn [their] gaze from one side to another; from Los Angeles to the DF and vice versa, like in Ping-Pong game." But since they can not always properly attribute the cultural influence to one of the two locales, they can't "decide very easily which of the two poles most attracted" them (162).

Other stories in the collection point to Tijuana's migratory, economic, and medial links to Los Angeles as the closest geographic embodiment of U.S. hegemony over the continent. "Everything about Seals" centers on the vague and almost indescribable presence of "Beverly," who is a creation of the narrator's imagination, an object of his sexual fantasies, and a symbol of the cultural domination of the United States. A furtive presence, always escaping to the other side of the street or to another time, Beverly, who is from Beverly Hills (of the other California), arrives in Tijuana as it is experiencing increased invasion by U.S. popular culture and consumerism.

The story "Tijuana Times" looks back to the Tijuana of the narrator's childhood, in the 1950s, right before the city began to step up its current level of expansion. At that time, the city was a livable place "of no more than a hundred thousand inhabitants" (149), but it had already become a well-known party town, attracting U.S. Americans to brothels and night clubs that Tijuanenses would not attend. At the same time, it was a city of "innumerable Tijuanas" which were "superimposed upon each other" (149). Children in the narrator's neighborhood either lived in extreme poverty or barely made it into the lower middle class. Independent of their class status, however, everyone in the neighborhood seemed to have the same opportunities: the children could either emigrate to Los Angeles, stay in Tijuana, or fight in Korea, while the luckier ones entered a university.

Campbell ends his story by describing the contemporary Tijuana, where, as the narrator reports, only the outlines of the living conditions rather than the conditions themselves have changed. Between the 1950s and the 1980s, Tijuana was the fastest growing city on the continent, its growth stimulated by intensified relations with the United States in the form of tourism, migration from Mexico's interior, and labor export to U.S. agriculture.[8] Campbell shows that Los Angeles has continued to figure as a site of possibility and migration, writing, "Every absence [in Tijuana] is related to an adult destiny on Los Angeles's East Side" (150).

The work of Rosina Conde highlights gender as a variable within new versions of *mexicanidad* that are emerging in the Baja California border region. Like Campbell, Conde is a displaced northern border writer from Tijuana who now resides in the capital and has lived in the United States. She was born in Mexicali, but her middle-class family moved to Tijuana when she was four. After finishing high school there (which was interrupted by one year of schooling in Oceanside, California), Conde studied languages and literatures in Mexico City.

San Diego State University Press recently published *Women on the Road* (1994), an English-language compilation of Conde's works, which originally appeared in small, provincial presses as separate short stories or parts of larger works.[9] Unlike Chicana writers who have forged notions of a feminist consciousness from female Mesoamerican myths, Conde employs a realist mode of narration that displays a panorama of living conditions for Tijuana women in the 1990s and highlights the clash of traditional patriarchal ideas with changing gender roles.

The women in Conde's stories continue to take on the roles of housewives or single mothers, work in jobs related to the garment or U.S.-dominated maquila industry, and consider sex work in Tijuana or immigration to the United States. These choices are clearly affected by conditions of globalization created through the collaboration of the U.S. and Mexican nation-state. Yet, the center of Conde's critique is not so much the northern neighbor or the Mexican state as Mexican men. In border towns, these men are considered valuable commodities. They are either absent, working in the United States on a temporary or permanent basis, or marginally employed in Mexico's informal economy. Conde writes that "in Tijuana there aren't many men, and the few that are around are like the public telephones; they're either occupied or out of order" (Conde 35).

The men in Conde's stories determine the deeply patriarchal nature of gender relations, assigning women value as sex objects or mothers rather than as independent individuals. They set up their daughters or female friends as concubines for wealthy or influential men, suggest that women prostitute themselves to make a living, attempt to control women by manipulating feminist ideologies, refuse to pay women for their labor, declare women devoid of value when they become pregnant, and regard their wives or girlfriends as their enemies. But many of the women protagonists fight back. "The Pearls" depicts a wife who uses the law to get a divorce and most of her house from an abusive, unloving husband; in "Morente," a woman narrates her (imagined?) relationship to a much younger man; and in "Tina, Tinita," the protagonist refuses a former lover's invitation to restart their relationship. "Señora Nina" shows a garment worker who leaves her exploitive employer, and the protagonist in "Volver" defies her children's wishes that she get married just so there is another man in the house. Finally, "Barbarella" is about a young woman's rejection of her father's infantilizing domination over her.

Told in a stream of consciousness narrative, the story "Do You Work or Go to School?" in particular traces the emergence of a new type of female consciousness along the Mexican border. It is the story of eighteen-year old María Elena, who comes from a well-to-do background. Her father buys her a car for her fifteenth birthday, and her family is able to support her when she returns to live with them at the end of the story. Educated and financially independent, María Elena has a degree in tourism, speaks English well, and initially works for an import business. And yet, she believes that only men can enable her personal and professional fulfillment. While María Elena expects her boyfriend Antonio to marry her after she loses her virginity to him, her hopes for her professional future are embodied in a male coworker, Miguel Ángel. He promises her modeling classes in San Diego and a job in a new U.S-owned maquiladora as his assistant public relations manager.

Ironically, both María Elena's boyfriend and her employer use feminist rhetoric to manipulate her into choosing between marriage or her job. Miguel Ángel tells her that she is too intelligent and good looking for marriage with someone who will keep her locked up, while her boyfriend Antonio argues that models are sellouts to capitalist ideology since they turn their bodies into consumer products. As assistant to Miguel Ángel on a maquiladora project, María Elena, however, unwittingly ends up as a sex worker. Miguel Ángel prostitutes her to a potential business client, Leonardo; for her part, María Elena thinks that the client wants to have a long-term relationship with her. When plans for the establishment of the maquiladora factory fail and she loses her job, María Elena realizes the destructive role men have played in her life. She also recognizes that men can be placed in feminized roles: Leonardo is now "looking for a father-in-law who will set him up in business" (36). Like María Elena, who becomes dependent on her family (particularly her father), Leonardo is relegated to economic instability and dependency on another man. But María Elena takes ownership of her own dependency, appropriating a "bimbo" femininity for her immediate material gains. She answers the question in the story's title by saying that she neither works nor goes to school because men want "idiotic little women who won't think and aren't economically self sufficient" (36).

Mexicanidad without the State

Written in 1995 and translated into English in 1997, Carlos Fuentes's *The Crystal Frontier* addresses, like the work of Campbell and Conde, the emergence of new forms of border *mexicanidad*.[10] Much of Fuentes's earlier work already emphasized Mexican history and identity, usually in relationship to the United States. *The Crystal Frontier,* however, most clearly ties examinations of *mexicanidad,* including changes in gender relations such as those at the heart of Conde's work, to the location of the northern border.

Fuentes's novel employs a more explicitly comparative hemispheric lens than the texts by Campbell and Conde, one that sets itself clearly in dialogue with U.S. conceptions of the border. The U.S. settings of several stories foreground the diasporic forms of *mexicanidad* that have been central to Chicana/o studies. In addition, *The Crystal Frontier* highlights the emergence of expressions of border *mexicanidad* in a location where the further deepening of Mexican dependency in the realms of trade and labor has become clearly visible. Fuentes attempts to develop antidotes to the dependency by drawing on early forms of *mexicanidad* as they emerged in response to manifestations of U.S. empire. He especially stresses this ideology's relation to the Mexican revolution and to its roots in indigenous myths.

Fuentes's prominent international position and his part-time residence in Mexico City seem to have exempted him from the difficulties many northern border writers have faced in getting work about the border published, distributed, and marketed. But Fuentes's novel has received much less attention than his acclaimed earlier fiction, and it has been reviewed differently on both sides of the border.[11] While no Chicano/a and American studies scholarship on *The Crystal Frontier* exists, Mexican reviews have largely reappropriated it for Mexico's national tradition, and U.S. Latin Americanists have emphasized its relationship to theories of the northern border.

Reviewers in U.S. popular outlets have generally dismissed *The Crystal Frontier* for its uneven literary quality. They have focused on the nine stories' different styles and on the book's use of national stereotypes when referring to the United States and Mexico.[12] Reviews of *The Crystal Frontier* published in Mexican venues, however, primarily discuss its social and political ideas in relationship to Fuentes's other journalistic and essayistic work. They emphasize, for example, that Fuentes places comments from his own journalistic and essayistic work almost verbatim into the mouths of his fictional characters.[13]

U.S.-based Latin Americanists who have written about *The Crystal Frontier* highlight Fuentes's critique of U.S. society, his focus on the Mexican diaspora, or his aesthetic innovation. Linda Egan, for example, has praised Fuentes's use of fragmented points of view and parodic forms of national stereotypes. She argues that when Fuentes includes a reference to himself as one of the two Mexicans who speak English well (*Crystal Frontier* 57), he authorizes "the narrator's voice at a moment when he chooses to trot out a host of racist stereotypes held by Mexicans about gringos and gringos about Mexicans" (Egan 183). And Debra Castillo has emphasized the novel's focus on the northern Mexican border, which is "forcing itself on the Mexican national imaginary as the fastest growing and most prosperous region of the country" ("Fuentes Fronterizo" 161).

Another important source for disagreement about the novel concerns its potential audience. In his reading of *The Crystal Frontier,* Jason Weiss argues that the novel's didactic account of Mexican history indicates that it was written for the U.S. public, which would require such explanations. Weiss assumes that, even though the novel was originally composed in Spanish and then translated into English, it was written with a transnational or global audience in mind. He goes so far as to argue that "Alfred Mac Adam's fluid translation seems to have rendered the novel its true audience" (L1). Linda Egan, however, has characterized *The Crystal Frontier*'s "background narrator who periodically resurfaces as an omniscient 'public,' or extrafictional, voice . . . employing free indirect discourse to reach deeply into his character's consciousness" as a "Mexican writing for a bourgeois Mexican audience" (Egan 182).

These disagreements over the novel's intended audience evoke Fuentes's own complicated border crossing biography. Despite maintaining a physical distance from Mexico throughout all of his life, for Fuentes, the country has always constituted "an obsessive reality," as Francisco Javier Ordiz Vázquez has put it. Born in Panama in a diplomat's family, Fuentes lived in Washington, D.C., until the age of twelve and then traveled in South America before arriving in Mexico City at sixteen. His mother insisted that the family's home always be Mexican no matter where they lived; they spoke only Spanish and played popular Mexican music (Williams 6).[14]

Today Fuentes divides his time between London and Mexico City. He has described his complicated relationship to Mexico thus:

> I had to imagine Mexico before I ever lived in Mexico, so when I went to live in Mexico, the first thing I had to do was to contrast my imagination of the country to the reality of the country, which is the kind of tension from which literature is born. For me, literature was born from that very dramatic contrast between my Mexican utopia, the Mexico I had to defend . . . against the gringos when I grew up in this country. . . . And I had to oppose a vision that was nurtured very much by my father teaching the history, the geography, the values of Mexico. Then I went and saw the real country, and this created a conflict in me. (Castillo, "Travails" 159–60)

Fuentes's perpetual border crossings have also provided him with a choice of languages in which to write. Critics have shown that Fuentes may have started to compose for an English-speaking U.S. audience in the 1980s when he was a professor of Latin American studies at Harvard and when he completed the final portion of *The Old Gringo* in English (Fox, "Hollywood's Backlot" 64, 78).[15] But Fuentes has disputed that he writes in English. He has said that since everything has already been said in that language, he has chosen to compose in Spanish. In an interview with Debra A. Castillo, Fuentes noted, "[S]ince I have yet to have a dream in English, it becomes very difficult . . . or since insults in English don't mean a thing to me and insults in Spanish do. Again, since words of love in English are alien to me and I make love in Spanish: all these things make it difficult to write fiction if you don't have the background of love and insult and dream" (Castillo, "Travails" 161). While Fuentes here points out the differential role languages play for multilingual individuals, his remarks on the distinct status of the two languages may also be intended to disavow the requirements of an increasingly global literary marketplace that shapes, in particular, the work of well-known writers not situated at international centers of cultural production.

Like Fuentes's other work, *The Crystal Frontier* engages in several forms of aesthetic innovation, which first gained him international reputation during the so-called Latin American boom of the 1960s and 1970s. The boom united Latin American writers across the borders of their own home countries and also created an awareness of Latin American (rather than individual national) politics. *The Crystal Frontier* experiments with the presence of multiple narrators, the switching of points of view, and the coexistence of myth and more "linear" fictional time as well as with more explicit forms of magical realism.[16]

Like the twenty-first-century border fictions about Chicana/o communities examined in chapter 1, *The Crystal Frontier* participates in the tradition of the composite novel. All of the characters in what Fuentes has called a novel, but what critics have often characterized as a collection of short stories, are crossers of what Fuentes terms the "illusory crystal divider, the glass membrane between Mexico and the United States" (*Crystal Frontier* 27).[17] As embodiments of allegorical border types—the Mexican student, the undocumented immigrant, the maid, the contract worker, the Chicano intellectual, and the border patrol agent—Fuentes's characters travel relatively freely among the nine stories that make up *The Crystal Frontier*. Individual stories are connected through the figure of Don Leonardo Barroso, a former government minister. Although he is the protagonist of only a few stories, references to his person appear throughout the book to highlight the sometimes hidden role of elite men in the border system and in inter-American relations.

The novel emphasizes the historical roots of the current unequal relationship between the United States and Mexico in different experiences of colonization and in the competition of colonial powers for territory, which set the context for diverging histories of nation-state formation. What is often forgotten is that the disparity between Mexico and the United States was not always that marked. Differences in the colonial experience and, of course, the loss of half of Mexico's land to the United States laid the context for the immense contemporary gap between the two countries. While Mexico's per capita income was about half that of the United States in 1800, by the end of the nineteenth century, it fell to one-tenth (Raat 53). Fuentes's last and culminating short story "Río Grande, Río Bravo," in particular, integrates into its traditional narrative format italicized poetic passages that foreground what Fuentes calls "Mexico's mythic history." The mythic passages highlight the migration of indigenous peoples to the precolonial Americas, the arrival of various Spanish explorers in the New World who "tell not what they saw but what they dreamed" (234–35), the conquest of Mexico, nineteenth-century conflicts with Texas, the loss of Mexico's territory to the United States, 1920s free-trade agreements between Mexican and U.S. border towns as brokered by Presidents Taft and Porfirio Díaz, the increasing economic integration between Mexico and the United States during World War II, and postwar industrialization. This merging of traditional narrative with myth resembles Karen Tei Yamashita's aesthetic strategy in *Tropic of Orange* (discussed in chapter 2), where she places poetic passages about Latin American history into the mouth of the composite undocumented immigrant figure Arcangel.

The mythical text in Fuentes's short story also critiques elements of institutionalized Mexican nationalism and shortcomings of the Mexican state. Individual passages describe the return of "the plagues of Mexico" as "the corruption, the abuse, the misery of many, the opulence of a few, disdain as a rule, compassion the exception" (261). Fuentes here fictionalizes his assertion in *A New Time for Mexico* that Mexican state-sponsored nationalism has, throughout much of Mexican history, served both progressive and conservative goals. On the one hand, *mexicanidad* functioned to defend the country externally against the far more powerful United States. But on the other hand, Mexican nationalism has also bolstered the hegemony of the one-party state (208), an authoritarian regime that largely dismantled civil society. The 1980s introduction of such major neoliberal restructuring policies as the elimination of subsidies, the dismantling or privatizing of state-run firms, the promotion of foreign capital investment, and the deregulation of most economic sectors paved the way for the passage of NAFTA (Otero 9).

The Crystal Frontier highlights how the two governments, and particularly the elites dominating each of them, have collaborated in creating a liberalized infrastructure, formalized in NAFTA, that has further deepened the United States' position as an empire and Mexico's as a dependent, particularly in the realms of trade and labor. The central figure of Don Leonardo Barroso represents the Mexican ruling class, which, alongside the Mexican state and global caretaking institutions, has been the main architect (and beneficiary) of neoliberal globalization in Mexico. Besides cross-border smuggling and land speculation, Barroso is involved in the two related forms of Mexico's labor exportation: he enables direct out-migration, primarily by men, in the form of contract labor, and he owns an assembly plant in Ciudad Juárez that hires predominantly female workers. This form of export-oriented production is not well integrated into Mexico's national economy; it is conducted in the realm of intrafirm commerce, which is placed completely at the service of the United States or other countries.

The story "Malitzin of the Maquiladoras" depicts a day in the lives of four Mexican women who work in Barroso's maquiladora. It is described as a plant that assembles "toys, textiles, motors, furniture, computers, and television sets from parts made in the United States, put together in Mexico at a tenth the labor cost, and sent back across the border to the U.S. market with a value-added tax" (120). The women workers come from different rural regions of Mexico, and most had to leave behind their families and sometimes their children. Many of them become the breadwinners of their families.

On the surface, these changes in the structure of gender and familial relations seem to provide women with more power. As the omniscient narrator of "Malitzin" explains this view, "plants liberated women from farming, prostitution, even from machismo itself . . . because working women soon became the breadwinners in the family. Female heads of households acquired a dignity and strength that set them free, made them independent, made them modern women" (127). However, similar to Rosina Conde's insistence on the continuing marginalization of Mexican border women in the context of changing gender relationships, Fuentes's story shows that rather than empowering women, work in maquilas continues their historical marginalization in Mexican society. Women are exposed to abominable working conditions, including overt sexual harassment, prohibitions against unionizing, and inadequate child care.

Instead of portraying the workers as mere victims in the tradition of La Malinche, the story shows them as agents of resistance. Fuentes establishes a new type of gendered border positionality that addresses Mexico's acquiescence to U.S. empire by revaluing female indigenous myths inscribed in *mexicanidad*. He draws on what he has called the coexisting multiple histories of Mexico, which represent "a horizon of latent, promising or frustrated, never fully achieved potentialities" (*A New Time* 16). *A New Time for Mexico* is titled after Enrique Florescano's work, which posits that the Mexican Revolution established a new time for Mexico, revolutionizing the state, disposing of the old oligarchy, and promoting the rise of new political actors (*A New Time* 66). At the same time, these cultural changes resulted in the growing acknowledgement of Mexico's combined Indian, mestizo, and European heritage in the notion of *mexicanidad* (*A New Time* 66–67).

Fuentes has singled out post-Revolutionary definitions of *mexicanidad* that emphasize Indian history as part of mestizo identity. He has declared Indian beliefs to be the "secret repository of all that we have forgotten and disdained: ritual intensity, mythic imagination, caring for nature, the relationship with death, communal ties, the capacity for self-government" (*A New Time* 201–2). Fuentes has often acknowledged that he begun his writing career under the influence of Octavio Paz's *El laberinto de la soledad*, the best known of a series of state-sponsored works that appeared between the 1940s and 1960s. Paz emphasized that at the basis of the union between the Spanish conqueror Hernán Córtes and La Malinche is the devaluation of the raped Native woman.

Fuentes draws on and inverts Paz's insights about the gendered nature of Mexican nationalism. "Malitzin of the Maquiladoras" is titled after the indigenous woman Malitzin, Dona Marina or La Malinche, who was given to Cortés and became his translator, mistress, and the mother of one of his children. Only after Mexican independence and the consolidation of *mexicanidad* did her story become that of La Malinche, symbolizing the humiliation and oppression of the indigenous people at the hands of Spaniards. By associating female maquila workers with this myth, Fuentes links the colonial history of Spanish conquest and its dependency upon gender stratification to the neocolonial exploitation of Mexican women by U.S. and other foreign-based companies.

Marina, the main figure in "Malitzin of the Maquiladoras," is most clearly related to the legend of La Malinche. Her boyfriend, Rolando, whom she meets for sex once a week in a hotel in El Paso, appears to be an important businessman who uses his cell phone to make deals on both sides of the border. To Marina, Rolando represents a means of realizing her fantasies of escape from Juárez by traveling to an ocean that she has never seen. But, like the conqueror Hernán Cortés, Rolando only uses women to his advantage. His cell phone turns out to have no batteries; rather than being a businessman, he appears to be involved with a shady organization that orders the assassination of Leonardo Barroso. By the end of the story, Fuentes's Marina becomes an empowered Malitzin; she leaves Rolando and realizes that she will have to determine her own fate.

Besides La Malinche, Fuentes associates the story's characters with three other instantiations of myths about indigenous women—La Llorona, María Candelaria, and the Virgin of Guadalupe—that have been central to *mexicanidad*. One of the story's heroines, Candelaria, is linked to the legend of María Candelaria, who, like La Malinche, is often portrayed as either a victim or a traitor to her own people. Wearing traditional peasant clothing assembled from different regions of Mexico, Candelaria points to a tale of an indigenous woman who was stoned to death by her village for allowing herself to be seen naked. Fuentes inverts this myth by portraying his heroine Candelaria as the most politically active of all the women workers. She lives with an outspoken antigovernment union leader, risks repercussions for her own activism, and tries to involve other women in political work.

Another maquila worker, Rosa Lupe, is dressed in a Carmelite habit and sandals all year. Her refusal to change into standard factory work gear is punished by sexual harassment from two different supervisors. Rosa Lupe's character is reminiscent of the Virgin of Guadalupe, who is often seen as the very essence of *mexicanidad*. The Virgin has functioned as a symbol of popular resistance during the Mexican Revolution and in 1950s–1970s Chicano civil rights struggles, especially those led by César Chávez, and she has also appeared on the banners of Mexican peasant uprisings.

The Virgin myth is intricately connected to that of the indigenous woman La Llorona, "the Weeping Woman," who cries at night by the river in search of her lost children. A combination of indigenous Mexican and European traditions, various versions of this original Aztec legend characterize La Llorona either as a woman who died during childbirth or, alternatively, as a jilted lover who drowned her children in the river and, driven mad by her actions, haunts riverbanks calling after her victims. In "Malitzin of the Maquilas," the single mother Dinorah loses her young son whom she had tied to a table leg while she was at work and then went to celebrate with her colleagues. When her child is found dead, her neighbors comment on the nexus between globalization that propels people to leave central Mexico for the border and changes within the Mexican family. They remark that "such a thing couldn't happen in the country—families there always had someone to look after the kids" (140). The maquila workers find power in their unity; in the closing pages of the story, they defy the tristesse of their work in a symbolic act of resistance to maquila rules by dancing on the grass in front of the production facility. By revaluing indigenous myths inscribed in *mexicanidad*, Fuentes diverges from strategies employed by Chicana authors, who have rewritten the negative narratives of indigenous Mexican women to signify their own struggles against oppressive elements of U.S. nationalism and Chicano cultural nationalism. Fuentes's critique, instead, is of U.S. imperialism toward Mexico and the collaboration of Mexico's elite in the production of neoliberal forms of globalization at the border.

As she attempts to organize her colleagues against maquila owners and management, Candelaria remains the most strongly activist character in the novel. Other stories insist on progressive forms of *mexicanidad* without its current attachment to the government in Mexico City, both in their border and diasporic incarnations. "Spoils" shows that popular forms of culture from below, such as a cuisine created by the people who "invent and consecrate the dishes" (59), can oppose the spread of commercialized U.S. American chain restaurants, which are devoid of personality and where the food is prepared without expense, imagination, time, or patience.

In "Río Bravo, Río Grande" Serafín Romero, who grew up in a Mexico City *colonia*, organizes a border crossing gang that robs U.S. trains of consumer items and instead fills them with Mexican undocumented workers "so that war can return to the frontier again, so that it's not only the gringos who attack" (265). The Chicano border patrol agent Mario Islas lets an undocumented immigrant go even though he knows that he is not the godson he passes himself off to be. The most positive note in the novel is struck in the depiction of the Chicano intellectual José Francisco. Neither Mexican nor gringo, José embodies an internal border, something "that couldn't happen on either side of the frontier but can happen on both sides" (250).[18] José transports Mexican literature to the United States and Chicana/o writing to Mexico, thus enabling the kind of transnational meeting of minds that challenges the unequal institutional conditions for the production and consumption of culture on both sides of the border. In the closing pages of *The Crystal Frontier,* José tosses this literature in the air to "let the words fly" (266).

These fictionalized representations of new and often gendered forms of anticolonial being exemplify Fuentes's attempt to highlight progressive elements of nationalism and its ability to attach to structures other than the nation-state. Fuentes wants to retain the nation-state; he imagines a better government that can sponsor a more progressive form of Mexican nationalism. In "Río Grande, Río Bravo," Fuentes chronicles the desire of northern border residents to be as "prosperous, rich, democratic" as the United States, but he points to a different responsibility, the need to be "governed by laws, not tyrants, [to] . . . create a state that will see to it that laws are respected but that won't succumb to despotism" (260). The answer to the erosion of Mexican sovereignty in a globalized context thus is not to wish for complete absorption into the United States. Rather than abandoning nationalist policies or the state, Fuentes imagines an "interdependent world of independent nations" (*A New Time* 209), whose decision-making power is centered in the realm of national sovereignty.

"Río Grande, Río Bravo" ends the novel with a pun on Porfirio Díaz's well-known characterization of the Mexico-U.S relationship: Mexico— "so far from God, yet so close" to the United States. Fuentes transforms this saying from its singular focus on Mexican dependency in relation to the United States to an acknowledgement of the negative consequences that the power imbalances will eventually have on both sides. He ends his novel with the words "poor Mexico, poor United States, so far from God, so near to each other" (266).

Mexicanidad in Inter-American Studies

As *The Crystal Frontier* revalues historical and contemporary elements of *mexicanidad* in relationship to the potentially progressive role of a reconfigured Mexican nation-state, the novel points to the need for more complex inter-American analytical frameworks. Compared to the revolutionary ideas set forth in Leslie Marmon Silko's and Karen Tei Yamashita's work (discussed in previous chapters), Mexican authors are less insistent on the necessity of systemic change when approaching Mexico-U.S. border relations. Campbell shows how the northern border relates to the Mexican capital and to the U.S. side of the border, and while Conde places the power of opposition in the hands of individual women, she does not seem as interested in the structural nature of gender inequities or of Mexican-U.S. relationships.

Similarly, Fuentes never calls for a change in the current political and economic structures of Mexico-U.S. relations or for an uprising of oppressed peoples. In fact, in his political commentaries Fuentes has often attacked visions of radical social and political transformation. He is on record as opposing any break from the established political system in Mexico (Morton 45). In *The Crystal Frontier,* Fuentes instead stresses the possibility of resistance to neoliberal change through personal acts of courage and empathy as well as through anticolonial versions of Mexican national identity that are based on reconfigured and hybrid mythologies of Mexican nationalism and Chicana/o border thinking.

Perhaps as a sign of his having moved to the liberal center, Fuentes has been far less critical of NAFTA than many of the U.S. ethnic writers examined in this book. He has asserted that the agreement can be beneficial as long as it is amended by social measures. In *A New Time for Mexico,* Fuentes has opined that NAFTA needs to be strengthened by adding a social component that is directed at better wages, more jobs, education, and job training (172). In a more recent interview, Fuentes has even praised former president Vicente Fox for his embrace of neoliberalism as part of a North American Common Market. Fuentes suggests that "NAFTA benefits Mexico, not just the US" ("Latin America" 8). Fuentes has also been less than supportive of the Zapatista struggle in Chiapas, declining an invitation to support the EZLN. In the stead of revolutionary violence he has emphasized the need to pursue dialogue through legal channels, through "strict adherence to the spirit and the letter of democracy" (*A New Time* 127). These political views complicate his revaluation of indigenous Mexican myths as elements of new progressive forms of Mexican nationalism.

Read together, Mexican border representations raise important theoretical questions about deepening Mexico-U.S. integration. Fuentes's *The Crystal Frontier,* in particular, depicts *la frontera méxico-estadounidense* as a site of Mexican anticolonial self-definition and a location where the interests of U.S. and Mexican elites dominating individual governments intersect in the creation of neoliberal conditions. Fuentes thus adds to the criticism of U.S. empire and the U.S. nation-state an emphasis on the role of the Mexican nation-state and its elites in the creation of global infrastructures. A contemplation of his work and that of northern border writers may move an emerging inter-American studies beyond well-intentioned warnings of U.S. imperialism that fail to take into account the preoccupations of the geographies and academic fields it tries to encompass.

5 A Border Like No Other

TOUTED AS the "world's longest undefended border" throughout much of its history, the five-thousand-mile Canada-U.S. boundary has recently become defined as yet another potential threat to the United States, porous to the influx of disease, undocumented immigrants, and Middle Eastern terrorists.[1] The September 11, 2001, attacks in the United States have consistently and falsely been linked to the Canada-U.S. border across which some of the terrorists supposedly entered the country. Singled out for blame were Canada's "permissive" refugee laws and its more liberal nonvisa requirement policies with a host of countries, including many that are ideologically opposed to the United States. The idea that Canada functions as a "pathway for terrorists" has also been linked to reports of increased undocumented immigration via the northern border since the late 1980s.[2]

Reports of SARS (Severe Acute Respiratory Syndrome) outbreaks in Toronto in 2003 and the discovery of tainted beef in 2004, which prompted the United States to temporarily close down its northern border, further solidified the view of this boundary as a national security risk for the United States.

These shifts in the image of the Canada-U.S. border and in the way border security has been enforced are especially noteworthy for their similarities to contemporary discourses about and changes at the Mexico-U.S. boundary. Contemporary inter-American scholarship has, however, all but ignored Canada and its boundary with the United States. What Margaret Atwood has called "the one-way mirror of the Canadian-American border" (385) apparently does not allow recognition of Canadian particularities in the United States. Most U.S. cultural productions depict Canada as a "smaller" version of the United States. If they recognize the existence of differences at all, they view Canada as "a kind of fantasy land through which Americans contemplate their own country's shortcomings and envision a simpler and more aesthetically satisfying world" (qtd. in New, *Borderlands* 88).[3]

The view of Canada as an extension of the United States is also grounded in the belief that Canada's majority population is ethnically similar to that of the United States or that the diversity internal to Canada can be thought in terms of U.S. multiculturalism.[4] This perception partially explains the critical neglect of Edith Eaton's depictions of the Canada-U.S. border (discussed in chapter 2) and the limited interest in the work of Thomas King (the subject of chapter 3) in the United States.

As it has emerged in English Canada and in a few U.S. universities in the 1940s, Canadian studies work has formulated more nuanced accounts of the Canada-U.S. relationship as a case study of U.S. empire in the hemisphere, while there remains a lack of scholarship on the actual geography of the Canada-U.S. border.[5] Because integration with the United States has not been primarily achieved through border locations, in Canada "the border" often functions as a symbolic designation for conditions facing all of Canada vis-à-vis its hegemonic neighbor. Sixty percent of the Canadian population, currently 32 million people, live within one hundred miles of the U.S. boundary.[6] The border often figures as a descriptor of their condition and as a symbolic site for Canadian efforts to resist the intrusion of a more powerful culture.

At the same time, the border has also symbolized cultural nationalist attempts to articulate the country's distinctiveness vis-à-vis the United States. Such attempts first emerged in response to increased U.S. domination after World War II, which gathered force throughout the 1960s and 1970s, and have intensified since economic hemispheric integration under the 1989 Canada-U.S. Free Trade Agreement (CUFTA) and the 1994 North American Free Trade Agreement (NAFTA). Cultural imperialism models posit that Canada has been susceptible to increasing U.S. domination primarily because of its weak sense of nationalism and missing cultural identity.[7] Such sentiments helped create public and elite support for the forging of a unified notion of nationhood. They also enabled the creation of a strong social-democratic welfare state.

The work of Russell Brown constitutes one of several exceptions to the general lack of interest in the Canada-U.S. border. He has shown how French and English Canadian border writing since the 1960s functions to symbolize Canada's marginal position in the world and to signify the possibility of sanctuary for indigenous peoples, slaves, and political dissenters. Transformations throughout the 1980s and 1990s in the context of globalization appear not to have inspired much new border writing. In fact, at the turn of the twenty-first century, Canadian authors seem to be generating fewer portrayals of their own country, which includes the border with its southern neighbor (New, *History* 293). Declining interest in the country's distinctiveness and the need to appeal to a now global, U.S.-dominated commercial publishing market may explain why many authors tend to set their fiction in locations other than Canada or to situate their writing in places that appear to be in the United States (Heninghan 77). Decreasing government funding and enthusiasm for arts and culture and increasing reliance on corporate sponsorship have further frayed the national affiliation of artists and writers.

Often supported by the Canada Council and other governmental or provincial institutions devoted to the enhancement of Canadian arts, a few authors have, however, continued to at least obliquely wrestle with changes at the border.[8] These writers include authors of color and immigrant background, some of whom may not even have been considered part of the Canadian canon that was created at the height of cultural nationalism. Their work tends to articulate explicit parallels to the Mexico-U.S. boundary, perhaps also to appeal to the greater interest a transnational audience would have in events at the southern border.

This English-language border fiction from the 1980s and 1990s indicates a shift away from the cultural nationalist focus on the border as a line of (largely cultural) distinction between national identities. Instead, the Canada-U.S. boundary comes to symbolize a more complex set of notions. The border signifies Canadian internal diversity and its difference from ethnic frameworks in the United States. Some representations also separate progressive elements of Canadian nationalism from its association with the nation-state to critique the insufficiencies of the state-sponsored cultural nationalist response to U.S. empire. And, finally, the national boundary is represented as an increasingly porous divide that, while continuing to mark Canada's declining autonomy vis-à-vis the United States, also highlights the country's relationship to other parts of the hemisphere.

Diversity and Diaspora

Several contemporary border representations employ the Canada-U.S. boundary to symbolize issues of cultural or diasporic identity. Thomas King's oeuvre, discussed in chapter 3, could be included in this category since it complicates assumptions about facile parallels between U.S. borders and a particular ethnic culture. Two other (sometime) Canadian residents have addressed similar issues. Clark Blaise, a U.S. American citizen with Canadian ties, and Guillermo Verdecchia, a Canadian citizen of Argentinean origin, use the figure of the Canada-U.S. border to examine their own complex identities and to point to overlooked issues of Canadian diversity and diasporic movements in North America. While they show that diversity is configured differently in Canada than in the United States, both artists (like King) are also somewhat influenced by U.S. conceptions of identity in relationship to the border. Verdecchia's work in particular is shaped by U.S. Chicana/o theories of an ethnic borderlands identity.

Blaise was born and grew up all over the United States; he has lived in Canada and in the United States for long periods of time, and he recently left Québec for California. He has called the Canada-U.S. border "the thinnest membrane . . . undefended because it is maintained psychologically" (64). Through comparison with the Mexico-U.S. boundary, Blaise demonstrates that the Canada-U.S. line used to nominally separate French Canada and French New England. Ninety years ago, as he writes, the "legal and psychological border between French Canada and French New England did not exist . . . Families lapped over the edges of the border as they do today in Mexico and south Texas" (29).

In spite of his "lifetime of crossing borders" (60), however, Blaise is often considered a Canadian author. According to his "post-modern autobiography," *I Had a Father* (1993), he was "one of the designated links between Montréal and Toronto" at the inauguration of contemporary Canadian writing in the 1960s (121). The production of Canadian cultural representations and the construction of a national literary history were corollaries to state-sponsored intervention in the areas of broadcasting, professional sports, and book and periodicals publishing.

These attempts were intended to consolidate an elite culture as a bulwark against the infiltration of U.S. mass media.[9] Blaise writes that these efforts ended up shaping rather narrow ideas of Canadian identity that neglected the country's internal heterogeneity; Québécois and immigrant writers like his wife, Bharati Mukherjee, at the time a Canadian citizen of Indian origin, were excluded. As Blaise concludes, "It was a mainstream, white, Ontario-generated, intensely nationalistic affair with little time for issues other than the American domination of Canadian institutions" (121).

It is somewhat ironic that Blaise would have been involved in attempts to construct a national Canadian identity. Not only was he brought up in the United States, but he also identifies with Québec, a part of Canada that usually considers itself a separate nation. At the time he wrote his autobiography, Blaise considered Québec his home because of his French-Canadian father and the fact that he had lived in the province for fifteen years. Yet, Blaise also complicates his self-identification, acknowledging that it denies "the fact that I was never a French-Canadian, never spoke the language as a child, never took a puck in the face for old Québec" (101). He writes that when he feels nostalgia for Québec, it is for his father's world, "a world I never saw, never knew" (29). As it highlights border crossings between Canada and the United States as well as the author's Québécois heritage, *I Had a Father* adds the French and English divide within Canada to an emphasis on the Canada-U.S. border. Blaise's emphasis on Québec questions any assumptions about the Canada-U.S. border's internal homogeneity.[10]

Guillermo Verdecchia's play *Fronteras Americanas/American Borders,* written and first produced in Toronto in 1993, also employs the notion of the Canada-U.S. border to represent Canadian diversity. But this work's focus falls on the Latina/o Canadian diaspora and the increasingly more intricate interrelationship between the United States, Canada, and Latin American countries. *Fronteras Americanas* represents Latin Americans in Canada, who, unlike the country's longstanding communities of blacks, East Asians, indigenous Canadians, and South Asian and Caribbean immigrants, have not yet received widespread attention. Since the major wave of Latin American immigration consisted of those who were granted political asylum during the 1970s and 1980s, Latina/os in Canada are usually associated with notions of exile (Habell-Pallán 175).

One of the few such cultural productions that involve the Latin American immigrant community, Verdecchia's play chronicles the ongoing transition of Latina/o exilic literature into ethnic writing after the emergence of a second generation that was either born in Canada or immigrated there as children.[11] Verdecchia is a playwright, actor, and performer who moved to Canada from Argentina when he was ten. *Fronteras Americanas* won a 1993 Governor General's Drama Award and a 1994 Chalmers Award for Best Canadian Play. It is a two-character show for a solo performer: the characters include Verdecchia, named after the author, who recounts his assimilation to Canadian culture, and Wideload McKennah, his alter ego, an amalgam of Latino stereotypes, someone who "left home to escape poverty and . . . ended up working in de theatre" (53). Wideload's character is used to explore the various Latina/o stereotypes Canadian culture seems to have uncritically accepted from the United States with its longer history of interaction with Latin America.

Just as the stereotypes originated in the United States, much of the rhetoric Verdecchia uses to undermine them is borrowed from U.S. Chicana/o and Latina/o popular culture. Verdecchia specifically draws on the performance art of Guillermo Gómez-Peña, who has also influenced the fiction of Karen Tei Yamashita, as discussed in chapter 2.[12] While Verdecchia's work highlights the northern line, the play sometimes collapses the Canada-U.S. and the Mexico-U.S. boundaries into one North-South distinction named "the Latin-North American border" (21). Verdecchia's persona asks, "Where and what exactly is the border? Is it this line in the dirt, stretching for 3,000 kilometres? Is the border more accurately described as a zone which includes the towns of El Paso and Ciudad Juárez? Or is the border—is the border the whole country, the continent? Where does the U.S. end and Canada begin?" (21).

Verdecchia's play also focuses on what has been left out of U.S. Latina/o discourse, namely, an attention to Canada and the Canada-U.S. border. While Gómez-Peña, for example, performed his *el Brujo* character at the Canada-U.S. border, he did not theorize this specific space in relation to the southern U.S. boundary. *Fronteras Americanas* highlights the decreased mobility of border crossers across the northern boundary despite the "re-drawing [of] the map of America because economics . . . knows no borders" (76). Verdecchia's character protests when he is hassled by a U.S. Customs Agent, saying, "I'm a Canadian citizen—we're supposed to be friends. You know, Free Trade, the longest undefended border in the world" (57). The play thus both erases and reconstructs the northern boundary in relation to Latina/o populations in Canada.

As happens to Blaise in his work, the concept of the border eventually also comes to name Verdecchia's own border crossing identity, which is, despite some shared characteristics, differently constructed than that of the majority of U.S. Latina/os. Verdecchia contextualizes aspects of his own exilic identity—leaving Argentina, growing up an outsider in the small town of Kitchener, Ontario; delaying his "homecoming" to Argentina for fear that he will be imprisoned for not having registered for military service—within a larger, "idiosyncratic" history of the Americas. During his encounter with *el brujo* (one of Guillermo Gómez-Peña's performance characters), Verdecchia is taken through events in Latin America and in the U.S. Chicano movement, which consequently become part of his personal history.

Even though Canada is the place where he "make[s] the most sense" (74) and where he has lived for almost fifteen years, Verdecchia imagines Argentina as his diasporic homeland. But he can only construct this homeland through the memories of family and other expatriates as well as through popular representations. Verdecchia explains, "I feel nostalgia for things I never knew—I feel connected to things I have no connection with, responsible, involved, implicated in things that happen thousands of miles away" (69). Verdecchia's memories of Argentina and his imagined nostalgia can perhaps be better understood through Marianne Hirsch's notion of "post-memory," which she has theorized in relationship to survivors of the Holocaust. Hirsch posits that because the lives of survivors' children are dominated by their parents' memories, the children develop "post-memories" of events that preceded their birth. This form of post-memory is characterized by deep personal connection to an event or place from which the children are separated by generational distance, pointing to the mediation of memory by narration and imagination (8–9).

Verdecchia describes his identity, located somewhere between exile and ethnicity, thus: "I'm not in Canada; I'm not in Argentina. I'm on the Border. I am Home . . . I am a post-Porteño neo-Latino Canadian!" (75). His acknowledgement of an exilic-ethnic hybridity is accompanied by an emphasis on the presence of Latin America and Latina/os in Canada. Asking Canadians to "throw out the metaphor of Latin America as North America's 'backyard,'" Verdecchia says, "[Y]our backyard is now a border and the metaphor is now made flesh. Mira, I am in your backyard. I live next door, I live upstairs, I live across de street" (77). He ends his play by shifting the emphasis from questions of Latina/o Canadian identity to a focus on all Canadians who live on borders, asking his audience, "Did you change your name somewhere along the way? Does a part of you live hundreds or thousands of kilometers away? Do you have two countries, two memories? Do you have a border zone?" (78).

Autonomy, Sanctuary, and U.S. Empire

Like Verdecchia's play, Janette Turner Hospital's novel *Borderline* (1985) emphasizes the Canada-U.S. border's connection to the larger hemisphere by portraying the presence of Latin Americans in Canada. *Borderline* depicts the undocumented immigration of Salvadorans who entered Canada in the 1980s as a means of escaping the U.S. immigration law that required their deportation, even in the face of certain death in their home country.

While it does not highlight the causes of immigration—El Salvador's civil war and U.S. involvement in it—the novel does ask Canadians to realize their increasing connections with Latin America. Thus, despite its limited focus, *Borderline* contributes to inter-American frameworks by identifying differences in national immigration laws and highlighting their importance for theories of ethnicity, diaspora, and exile. Shortlisted for the Victorian Premier's Literary Award and nominated as runner-up for the Australian National Book Award, the novel is a thriller with postmodernist, surrealist, and magical realist overtones. Hospital has acknowledged that she was reading Latin American authors around the time she was writing *Borderline,* in particular the work of Gabriel García Márquez and Jorge Luis Borges (Brydon 20). About *Borderline,* Hospital has written that the "shadowy interplay of reality and unreality (and its political, social and moral dimensions and implications) is the major theme of the book" ("Letter" 560). The novel has been hailed as a piece of fiction "in which nothing ever *is* until it is imagined; once imagined, it can become something else" (qtd. in Schramm 89).

Hospital self-identifies as a nomadic Australian with "enormous feelings of affection for Canada" (Langer 143), where she lived with her family until her recent move to Washington, D.C. (New, *History* 296). *Borderline* is Hospital's third novel and her first set in Canada. As a writer not born in Canada, Hospital has, unlike Clark Blaise and like his wife Bharati Mukherjee, often been left out of the Canadian literary canon. Instead, she has been relegated to the domain of so-called Commonwealth Literature within Canadian literary studies.[13]

In a 1980s interview, Hospital explained her sometime exclusion from considerations as a Canadian writer through comparison with Mukherjee, who eventually left the country and became a U.S. citizen (Langer 144). Hospital reflects on how the exclusionary nature of Canadian cultural and literary nationalism has subordinated internal differences to articulations of a unified national cultural identity, saying: "Canadian nationalism—understandably, because it has had to exert itself over the U.S.—is in that phase of cultural nationalism where it doesn't want to muddy the issue by having non-'pure' Canadians in the literary pool . . . non-native-born Canadians don't really write 'Canadian literature.' . . . there's certainly a feel that you are pushed out if you are not native-born Canadian" (Langer 144–45). As W. H. New recently suggested, although this did not happen with Blaise, Hospital's move to the United States has led to decreased interest in her work within Canada (New, *History* 296).

Several contesting versions of *Borderline*'s story line are told through the third-person narrator, Jean-Marc. Rather than presuming to give voice to the undocumented refugees whose border crossings are depicted in the opening scene of the novel, Hospital has said that she chose an affluent narrator, someone who "cannot *really* know, . . . can never be sure what happened" ("Letter" 563, emphasis in original). The narrator attempts to reconstruct events one year after the disappearance of the novel's two protagonists Gus and Felicity, who meet at a border crossing between Québec and New York State, a thruway for the Massachusetts Turnpike from Boston and L'Autoroute Quinze to Montréal. Gus is an insurance salesman of English-speaking origin from a small town in Québec, and Felicity is an art historian and curator of a private gallery in Boston.

Jean-Marc's narrative voice describes national borders as places where "control is not in the hands" of travelers, who are assessed according to the potential risk they pose (1).[14] The more "ordinary" one's racial, national, or gender background, the easier it is to move across. A "person, preferably of Anglo-Saxon stock, with the decency to have been born in a country familiar to the presiding official . . . shall be deemed to be largely above suspicion, provided he/she does not exhibit vagabond or philandering territorial habits" (30). While Gus embodies this kind of traveler since he is returning north "unseduced by kinder taxes south of the border" (19), Felicity is afraid that she will evoke more suspicion as a U.S. American citizen who was born in India and grew up in Australia.[15] Her complex identity resembles that of Hospital, who has lived in several locations in India, the United States, and in Ontario, Canada.

At the border crossing, Gus and Felicity find themselves behind a refrigeration van from Massachusetts that carries not only dead animal carcasses but also undocumented immigrants from El Salvador. The two protagonists are surprised that these things happen "so far from the Mexican border" (29) with which immigration from Latin, South, and Central America is usually associated. Hospital has said that the idea for her novel originated in the mid-1980s discovery of dead Salvadoran refugees in a refrigerated truck that had been abandoned in New Mexico after crossing the Mexico-U.S. border. Like Hospital, who began to realize the connection of these events to the Canadian boundary in the form of "growing numbers of refugees in Boston and New York and Montreal . . . [and] the underground railway from the Rio Grande to the Canadian border" ("Letter" 561), *Borderline*'s protagonist Felicity similarly discovers the existence of refugee populations from Central America in the northeastern United States and Canada.

Because El Salvador was a U.S. ally, refugees from the civil strife in the country were usually not even considered for possible asylum and then often deported. One official in the novel describes the general distrust toward these refugees: "Fear of death, they try to tell you, but it's green stuff they want" (29). The general denial of refugee status to Salvadorans prompted the emergence not only of the sanctuary movement across the Mexico-U.S. border but also of lesser-known smuggling networks across the Canada-U.S. boundary. These networks transported Salvadorans to Canada after they had been served deportation papers in the United States. In Canada, these refugees would try to reapply for asylum under that country's more liberal refugee laws.

Borderline's immigrants, however, do not make it across the border. Alerted to the arrival of the van by an anonymous tip from Boston, Canadian customs officials arrest and eventually extradite the refugees. Even though Canada allows the entry of El Salvadorans, in this instance Canadian authorities are forced to comply with U.S. immigration law since the refugees had tried to cross "illegally" into Canada. Had they been able to fly there directly and then file their applications, they may have been among the immigrants from several Latin American dictatorships who were granted asylum throughout the 1970s and 1980s.[16] Jean-Marc's reconstruction of events from the accounts of both Felicity and Gus is juxtaposed with a fictitious Associated Press article about the incident. The article reports that two of the undocumented immigrants died of hypothermia and that everyone else was extradited to the United States to be deported to El Salvador.

After the border guards take the immigrants into custody, Gus and Felicity find one half-dead woman hidden inside one of the carcasses that fell from the truck. Felicity refers to her as Magdalena because she reminds her of a fifteenth-century painting of La Magdalena, a picture Felicity hopes to get on loan for an exhibit in her gallery. The woman's real name is unknown; Felicity finds out later that it may be Dolores Marques, La Salvadora, or La Desconocida. She is the unknown or unknowable one, a woman who knows too much about her husband's death during the civil war. Spontaneously, Felicity and Gus decide to smuggle the woman across the Canada-U.S. border to Felicity's cottage in the village of L'Ascension (near Montréal), from which Magdalena mysteriously disappears.

The two protagonists then begin their separate quests for her. A fallen Catholic, Gus sees Magdalena as a way to redeem his own failures, including his many marital infidelities, his drinking, and his shortcomings as a businessman. Reiterating the official Canadian rhetoric of immigrant success (which looks very different from what he himself has achieved as a native-born Canadian), Gus imagines a future life story for Magdalena in which, despite the things that have happened to her, she is "virginal in spirit" (59–60). In these versions, Magdalena recovers, obtains a

Canadian work permit, learns both official Canadian languages, and studies to become a nurse. She marries a rich doctor and has many children, and her son becomes a Supreme Court judge or even Canada's Prime Minister (60).

For Felicity, in contrast, Magdalena figures as a symbol of suffering. Felicity finds similarities between herself and Magdalena based on her own experiences of losing her father, growing up in the midst of poverty and civil strife in India, and, later, feeling displacement in Australia, where she experiences rape and marginalization. In one of Jean-Marc's versions of events, Gus eventually finds Magdalena in a Spanish restaurant in Montréal, where he ends up as a dishwasher—a position usually filled by undocumented immigrants—after his wife leaves him. When Felicity passes Gus's information to the wrong people in Boston and thereby compromises the Montréal location, Gus takes Magdalena back across the border into New York State. After their successful border crossing, both die in a car crash, which was perhaps caused by others in pursuit of them.

Felicity meanwhile becomes involved in a secret underground network of Salvadorans in Boston, a network extending into Montréal. She eventually appears to have perished in an apartment building fire that may have been set by members of either right- or left-wing Salvadoran groups attempting to find Magdalena. Felicity never arrives at a deeper understanding of the refugee crisis. As the narrator tells us, she believes that both groups are equally dangerous: "Wealthy businessmen and their families, who were legal immigrants or residents, were being kidnapped and/ or killed by the leftists. Subversives, flowing across the borders in illegal droves, were being eliminated by right-wing vigilante groups monitoring the external fomenting of disruption within Central America" (126).

At the end of the novel, the narrator Jean-Marc and his friend, Gus's oldest daughter Kathleen, hold on to the possibility that Felicity and Gus are still alive. Hospital has said that she "wanted to recreate in the reader that unbearable need to know, and the sheer inability of ever being able to know" to evoke the refugees' inability to ascertain what happened to the relatives they left behind in El Salvador (Hamelin 107). Like the Salvadoran refugees who are faced with the possibility of their families' death, Jean-Marc and Kathleen cannot contemplate the possibility that their loved ones are dead. In one way, Felicity and Gus (along with Magdalena) become alternate manifestations of those who have been disappeared, *los desaparecidos*. Even though Jean-Marc and Kathleen console each other with the fact that Canada "isn't Latin America [where] things happen . . . that couldn't happen anywhere else" (281), the fates of Gus and Felicity unveil the interconnectedness of the hemisphere, showing that political events in one portion of the Americas affect (people in) other parts as well.

While Hospital critiques U.S. immigration policies and their reverberations in Canada, she missed a chance to examine how Canada's position toward the Salvadoran refugee crisis differed from that of U.S. foreign politics in El Salvador. The novel is also somewhat weakened by an insufficient knowledge of events in El Salvador, misspellings of geographical place names in Latin America, and a superficial understanding of differences among right- and left-wing positions in El Salvador's civil war.[17]

Yet, in contrast to older, idealized representations of the Canada-U.S. border that highlight Canada's role as sanctuary from U.S. realities, such as are found in fiction by Ishmael Reed and Joyce Carol Oates, *Borderline* critically represents Canada as at best a tenuous hideout for refugees from highly politicized U.S. immigration legislation. Events in the novel point toward the dependency of Canadian domestic and foreign politics on the United States in the arena of immigration and refugee law.

Closer relations with the United States under conditions of globalization have further undermined Canada's sovereignty in the domain of immigration. Under massive U.S. pressure, which has intensified since September 11, 2001, Canada has adopted visa and refugee policies that more closely resemble U.S. laws in an attempt to appease threats that otherwise security at the U.S.-Canada border will dramatically increase. Such militarization could have devastating consequences for cross-border trade, tourism, and Canada's ability to attract foreign investment. Canada's acceptance of U.S. efforts to extend control over its borders beyond its own territory resembles events in the early twentieth century, when Canada supported the U.S. exclusion of the Chinese by cooperating with U.S. officials to enforce U.S. exclusion policies and eventually passing similar legislation of its own (as discussed in chapter 2).

Set on the Canadian side of the Alberta-Montana border, another late-1980s representation of the border, Kelly Rebar's 1987 play *Bordertown Café*, was written and first produced in the context of free-trade negotiations between Canada and the United States. In these negotiations, cultural nationalist discourses reemerged as attempts to restrict notions of Canadian national sovereignty to the cultural sphere.[18] *Bordertown Café* complicates some of the assumptions underlying such discourses, which attribute to culture a greater degree of power in shaping national identity than to any other social sphere. The play draws attention to the interlinked cultural, political, and economic differences between the two countries, and Canadian dependency in those areas. Rebar represents these issues in terms of familial conflict, a trope that rarely appears in depictions of the Mexico-U.S. relationship.

Bordertown Café won the Canadian Authors Association Award for Drama in 1990 and was made into a movie in 1992. Like Thomas King's *Truth and Bright Water* (discussed in chapter 3), the play is set "on the Canadian side of the Alberta/Montana border" (Rebar n. pag.), in an unnamed border town that is situated close to Lethbridge. Exhibiting both Canadian and American flags, the café is identified as "the last thing a Canadian sees when he leaves home and the first thing an American sees when he arrives" (15). The play's central character, seventeen-year-old Jimmy, describes the location of the café as "smack dab in the middle of nowhere—correction, the Canadian side of nowhere" (15).

Functioning metaphorically as a border, the café serves as a meeting place for transient Canadian and U.S. truckers as well as for the town "regulars," and it is used to reflect on the larger relationship between U.S. and Canadian national identities. As Deborah Keahey has pointed out in her reading of the play, *Bordertown Café* reiterates a variety of stereotypes to characterize differences between the United States and Canada (31). At the same time, the play also subtly chronicles historical changes in the relationship between the two countries, as symbolized in the several generations of the family that run the café. Influenced by British imperialism, Jimmy's paternal great-grandmother represents the period of Canada's colonial dependence. Jim, her son, spent most of his life on the Canadian Prairie only to marry Maxine, an American, at a time when relations between the two countries were mostly friendly. Their daughter Marlene illustrates the growing dependency of Canadians on their neighbor throughout the 1960s and 1970s. When she is fifteen, Marlene moves to a Wyoming trailer park with a truck driver, Don, who eventually abandons her. Marlene's son Jimmy grows up at the bordertown café, torn between his love for his Canadian mother and his mostly absent U.S. father in ways that represent the uncertain status of the present-day Canada-U.S. relationship.

Jim's wife, Maxine, does not exemplify the tradition of U.S. American self-exile in Canada as a means of escape from problematic U.S. realities; she moved north of the border only (and, as she insists, reluctantly) to marry Jim. Even though she has lived in the Canadian border town for the last thirty some years, Maxine still considers herself a U.S. American. She holds up the United States as the standard against which to judge elements of Canadian identity she dislikes, especially her mother-in-law's rootedness in British culture. Maxine also keeps highlighting the many advantages of the United States in comparison to Canada; these include bigger shopping centers and more conservative national politics. Maxine tries to socialize her daughter and grandson into the values of U.S. American citizenship by teaching them U.S. geography and history. But as Maxine says, despite her efforts, her daughter still turns out Canadian (39). While Maxine blames her daughter for becoming Canadian, Marlene partially holds her mother responsible for talking her into her marriage since Maxine "figgered the sun rose and set on Don [because] he was an American" (68).

As embodied in the protagonist Jimmy, the play's central conflict highlights the economic underpinnings of differences between the two countries and U.S. attempts at domination. Jimmy is asked to decide between staying with his mother in the Canadian border town or moving in with his father and new wife in Wyoming. His is a metaphorical choice between the U.S. parent who tries to seduce him with promises of greater material wealth (like Hospital's salesman Gus), on the one hand, and expectations of loyalty to his comparatively more impoverished Canadian family/nation, on the other. This personal decision parallels larger developments along the Canadian border where Jimmy lives. The presence of the café indicates that it is no longer possible to exist solely on farming, which still constituted a way of life for Jimmy's grandfather. Characterized as an empty landscape of bleak economic prospects and declining populations, the rural prairie is also increasingly in danger of having its emerging oil business taken over by U.S. companies (Keahey 27).

Given the inequity of his own familial and national situation in relationship to the United States, Jimmy initially seems poised to move in with his father. In her desire to change Jimmy's mind and keep him close, his grandmother Maxine suddenly begins to emphasize the dark underside of the United States, such as its overly liberal gun laws, its role as international policeman, and the low quality of its television programming. Highlighting the ways in which mass-media depictions of the good life are often wrongly conflated with the United States, Maxine says, "America is just the place you think it is. It's not the place it used to be" (55).

Jimmy eventually rejects the United States in favor of his Canadian home. He chooses loyalty to his family, region, and country over a father who represents stereotypical qualities attributed to the United States like irresponsibility, mobility, and rootlessness. Jimmy's choice also reflects Canadian resentment toward domination by its more powerful neighbor, metaphorically figured in his absentee father's efforts to lure him away from his Canadian home. In the end, Jimmy reaffirms his regional and national identity as a Canadian borderlander, an identity that is not simply nationalist but also includes hybrid elements because of Jimmy's proximity to the United States. While he identifies himself as having grown up Canadian and wanting to marry "someone same side o' the *border*" (55, emphasis in original), Jimmy also questions the very notion of national identity, expressing his unwillingness to decide between the two identities: "American, Canadian—back, forth—like it *mattered* what a guy was" (47, emphasis in original).

Set in the late 1990s, Michael V. Smith's novel *Cumberland* (2002) does not employ the border as a metaphor for the examination of national differences, as does *Bordertown Café*, or, like *Borderline*, examine a cross-border issue such as immigration. *Cumberland* is one of the few Canadian representations of the Canada-U.S. border that have appeared since the passage of NAFTA and that reflect on the relationship of the two countries as manifested in the border area. Having grown up in the border town of Cornwall, Ontario, Smith fictionalizes a small Canadian industrial town on the border of Ontario and upstate New York. Situated near Massena, New York, this town is located close to the border space Edith Eaton described in her stories about undocumented Chinese immigration around the beginning of the twentieth century, discussed in chapter 2.

Smith's novel addresses Cumberland's economic and social decline after the closing of its factories and mills in the wake of NAFTA. The main character, Ernest, a man in his fifties, loses his job as a mill worker. As he tells us, with the advent of free trade, Canadian mill exports to the United States lost their competitive edge, which had been based on the unequal exchange rate with the U.S. dollar. As Ernie says, "Why would they pay a guy 20 bucks an hour to do a job some other guy will do for half that in the States, or a tenth in Mexico? . . . They were happy to put us to work up here with the exchange on the dollar, but if they aren't paying tariffs now, why not keep the money in their own country and sell it there?" (88).

Although they live along the border, *Cumberland's* characters never cross into the United States, and the novel does not often address the U.S. side. In fact, *Cumberland* creates the impression that very little contact exists between border residents. The lack of contact extends to the once popular but short-lived pastime of cross-border shopping. This form of shopping became popular after the Canadian federal government first imposed the 7 percent Goods and Services Tax in 1990. Canadian citizens would shop in U.S. border towns like Bellingham, Buffalo, Burlington, Detroit, Massena, and Port Huron, where stores boasted greater product choice and lower prices than in Canada. Since economic integration under NAFTA, which has initially meant a sharp decline in Canadian currency and in Canadian living standards, the phenomenon of Canadians shopping in the United States has become less pronounced and appears not to have left much of a mark on the border. But by 2007 the soaring Canadian dollar caused a resurgence in cross-border shopping.

In the novel, U.S. Americans also no longer frequent Cumberland's faltering Westside Mall, which was originally built "at the base of the bridge to the U.S." for the express purpose of attracting shoppers from the other side (92). Today, there are few incentives left for U.S. Americans to cross the border into Canada, where prices are generally higher (Gibbins 158). Instead, U.S. retail outfits have been created in Canada. As fictionalized in *Cumberland*, U.S.-based transnational corporations like Walmart have put out of business traditional Canadian enterprises like Woolco throughout the country, further reinforcing the high degree of U.S. ownership in Canada (Panitch 82). While the novel does not dwell on these observations, it may foreshadow the emergence of a larger body of fiction on Canadian-U.S. border issues and inquiries into Canadian experiences of globalization in the post-NAFTA context.

As they highlight Canada's internal diversity, transformations in the country's political and economic domains, and/or its changing relationship to Latin America, the Canadian border narratives discussed in this chapter constitute rich comparative material for inter-American studies of the contemporary period. The texts examined appraise the country's increasing interdependence with the rest of the hemisphere and its continuing dependency on the United States.

While none of the border fictions argue for a specifically Canadian alternative to empire, each work emphasizes Canadian historical and contemporary particularities that continue to define the country's difference from the United States. Some texts highlight internal distinctions within Canada that are associated with processes of racialization specific to the country. Other fiction focuses on the changing Canadian–Latin American relationship or on increasing dependency on the United States in areas beyond those of culture.

Together, these texts provide complex representations of Canada's changing role in the Americas. They point to the increasing importation of U.S. models for the functioning of state institutions that assault the cultural and political institutions of the Canadian welfare state under the guise of free market policies or initiatives for closer political integration with the United States. Inclusion into an uneven hemispheric economy and increased political cooperation with this southern neighbor have meant the erosion of such stalwarts of Canadian national policy and identity as the health-care system, progressive social welfare policies, and more liberal immigration legislation. As Stephen Heninghan has argued, the "difference characterizing the Canadian experience lies in the traumatic demolition of our national sense of being by Free Trade- and NAFTA-based 'harmonization,' to the point where our particular individual experiences of society have become intangible and inexpressible" (178). Or, as W. H. New has put it, the function of hemispheric integration is "not to enable freer trade across the border but rather to make . . . [Canada] vulnerable to external control" (*History* 285–86).

The concern with Canadian particularities in the face of the U.S. domination that marks Canada-U.S. border narratives is also being recycled in the domain of mass and popular cultures. The emergence of this domain has been closely linked to the creation of state-sponsored culture industries since the 1930s.[19] Examples of recent forms of popular culture engaging with the Canada-U.S. relationship include the segment "Talking with Americans" that was part of the CBC's popular mock news program *This Hour Has 22 Minutes,* CBC's Rick Mercer's *Monday Report,* and a series of Molson beer commercials articulating the particularity (and superiority) of Canadians and of Canadian culture as opposed to that of the imperialistic United States.

In the most famous Molson beer commercial, "I am Canadian," which ran in 2000 in the tradition of similar ads from 1993 to 1998, Canadians are extolled for believing "in peace keeping, not policing," and for supporting concepts of "diversity, not assimilation." Ironically, the Molson beer commercials were highly popular at a time when a large number of Canadians favored joining the United States to share in that country's greater economic prosperity. Many Canadians appeared resigned to the likelihood of a common currency and increasing levels of integration with the United States (Brooks 37).

This is because the commercials exemplified an ongoing shift toward a more assertive and even patriotic form of Canadian nationalism on the level of expression but not political content (Millard, Riegel, and Wright 11). Above all, the Molson commercials signaled that private companies have taken over the function of state institutions as transmitters of a national culture (Millard, Riegel, and Wright 12). Douglas Coupland has commented on this shift from state- to corporate-sponsored nation building, remarking that "around 1980, Canadian history, or the idea of Canadian history, went from being something taught in schools to becoming something that was processed and sold back to us as a product" (7). While the transformation of cultural nationalism from a government-funded endeavor to a private corporate effort in support of product sales reveals the weakening of the Canadian welfare state, it also points to an increasingly "mercantile vision of Canada" as a business rather than a nation (Coupland 138).

Similarly, free trade negotiations in the 1980s, with their attendant rhetoric of open border crossings, supported the reemergence of a strong cultural nationalist rhetoric that resulted in limiting protectionist legislation to the cultural domain. Leaving culture outside of 1980s trade negotiations allowed the Canadian ruling elite to support free trade while at the same time adopting a rhetoric of cultural nationalism that attributes to culture a greater power to shape national identity than the economy or other spheres (Fox, "Cultural" 26). In the 2006 elections, Canada's elite again recycled populist anti-American rhetoric to gain support for its neoliberal agenda, which will ironically place the country more in line with U.S. policy in the arenas of politics and economics.

Ongoing Canadian efforts for further economic and political integration with the United States can thus coexist quite well with (privatized) cultural nationalist discourses that emphasize the importance of national difference primarily in the cultural domain. While cultural nationalism originally arose out of popular left-leaning positions, its commodification in product placement shows that this sentiment can easily be manipulated in support of neoliberal policies that at least purport to strive toward the eventual annihilation of national sovereignty.

Canada and Inter-American Studies

A study of Canadian border fiction shows that the resurgence of arguments about Canadian particularities does not in itself have progressive implications. Neither does a focus on the Canada-U.S. relationship advocated in this chapter. But an enlarged emphasis on North America may offer one possible way of articulating forms of progressive nationalism independent of the nation-state.

There may be a way to separate "Canadianness" from state-sponsored cultural nationalist models that validate the national only when attempting to establish cultural sovereignty from the United States. One possible way to do this is through an emphasis on Canada's specificities that moves beyond the country's relationship with the United States and toward a larger North American framework. As Stephen Heninghan has argued, "'[i]ntegration into the Americas,' approached through the prism of Latin American literature rather than that of globalized commercial policy, opens the door to the exploration and dramatization of our own [Canadian] differences" (79). Such a focus would, for example, enable the articulation of alternatives to empire that are rooted in Canada's specific experiences as a strong and progressive welfare state with a comparatively weak sense of nationalism, its attempts to officially recognize ethnic and racial diversity, its relatively marginal status on a global scale, and its continued oppositional stance vis-à-vis forms of U.S. empire.

John Gray humorously articulated similar ideas in 1994 when he envisioned a Canadian alternative to North America's takeover. He asked, "Will North America one day find its cultural media infiltrated by a collective northern vision with left-of-centre views? Will traditional Canadian concepts of peace, order and good government begin to taint the American ethic of heroic individualism? . . . There may come a time in free-trading North America when the cultural shoe is on the left foot, and the threat is us. . . . Why else would American politicians and lobbyists have expended so much energy—and lies—denouncing 'the Canadian-style health care system,' if they did not sense the blade of a very large cultural wedge, insinuating itself into American life?" (118–19).

Applying this speculative vein of thought to the realities of globalization, Stephen Clarkson has argued for a "post-globalist" Canadian state rooted in the specificities of the country's historical development, especially its political culture. Similar to Latin American thinkers like Nestór García Canclini, Clarkson emphasizes above all the nation-state's unfulfilled potential to represent public interests vis-à-vis neoliberal processes of globalization. He proposes that the Canadian state recuperate its largely unused powers to "recommit itself to its historic task of strengthening its own democracy" by establishing a more equitable society with better public services (Clarkson 426–27).

The rethinking of cultural nationalism in the context of hemispheric interdependency within Canadian border fiction needs to be acknowledged within U.S.-based inter-American frameworks. In comparison to the study of Latin American cultural representations and to French Canadian work, English Canadian fiction and scholarship do not even demand specific linguistic competence, so there is not a barrier preventing English speakers from participating in the field. Reasons for the disregard of Canada are thus to be found elsewhere: in the perpetuation of U.S. stereotypes about the unremarkability of the country that have contributed to a general disinterest in Canada and in power differentials in publishing and distribution networks that make Canadian work less accessible in the United States.

Acknowledging and engaging with these obstacles would ensure that inquiries into issues of U.S. domination, which have fundamentally shaped Canadian studies and Canadian cultural nationalism, also enter hemispheric approaches and thus contribute to the articulation of more sophisticated theories of the United States' role as an empire, albeit a declining one. When Canada eventually becomes part of hemispheric paradigms, these models will also need to honor long-standing fears of U.S. research on Canada as a possible prelude to takeover or a form of scholarship that supports U.S. state goals (Winks 3). One way to do so is for U.S. Americanists to exhibit critical awareness of their institutional position toward work that has originated outside of U.S. borders and that is fundamentally comparative in orientation. Such an informed inter-American studies framework should alleviate the fear that U.S.-based research paradigms will simply be extended to the hemispheric level through transnational categories that include the Mexico-U.S. border.

Conclusion

Border Fictions and Inter-American Studies

THE LITERATURES about U.S. borders discussed in this book point to the multiple histories and cultures of the borderlands with Mexico and Canada, which have too often been ignored by studies that focus on a particular racialized border subject. Border fictions reveal shared interests and intersections among various border communities that have not yet been fully recognized in academic discourse. These texts point to similar exposure to manifestations of U.S. empire and subjugation by neighboring nations as they manifest themselves in border territories. *Border Fictions* draws on these fictionalized commonalities to open up a spatialized lens on the diversity of U.S. land borders, in the process placing into dialogue various hemispheric perspectives that have largely been obscured within separately institutionalized ethnic and area studies.

It is no coincidence that the texts by many of the writers discussed in this book have been largely ignored. Many are read only within a specific national or U.S. ethnic tradition of literary production, or are just beginning to gain attention from a larger number of critics and readers. U.S. ethnic cultural productions have historically been marginalized in the literary marketplace. It took the creation of Chicana/o publishing houses like Quinto Sol, for example, to enable the widespread production and dissemination of bilingual texts about the Chicana/o experience. Particularly since the 1980s, however, mainstream presses have begun to publish a much larger number of multiethnic works in response to the growing demand for multicultural materials in U.S. public schools and university classrooms. In academia and corporate publishing alike, these texts are approached within preestablished categories of ethnic, gender, or regional identities.

The consolidation of the literary marketplace into fewer publishers and the rise of "big box" bookstores and chains have further encouraged the production of work that presents ethnic communities, nations, or regions within easily identifiable identity categories and can be translated into globalized and depoliticized forms of diversity. Border fictions' emphasis on the material specificity of U.S. border areas complicates such categories. Writers like Silko and Fuentes are famous enough that their work is published and translated no matter what the subject matter, aesthetic style, or overall economic "success" of the particular texts. While Silko is usually treated as a representative of the Native American experience or sometimes of U.S. Southwestern fiction, Fuentes is often incorporated into an emerging "Latino" framework that considers U.S. writers of ethnic descent together with authors in Latin America. But critics and readers alike have had problems with Fuentes's *The Crystal Frontier*, a text that articulates an explicitly comparative view of the Mexico-U.S. border, and with Silko's *Almanac*, a novel that develops a global definition of indigeneity.

Less established U.S. ethnic authors have had more difficulty in getting their work published at a time when book sales depend on the creation and maintenance of easily identifiable niche markets. As she writes about the Mexico-U.S. border and borrows from aesthetic and political traditions that are rarely associated with Asian American frameworks, Yamashita faced considerable difficulty in finding a publisher for *Tropic of Orange* (Murashige, "Karen Tei Yamashita" 323). Her novel was accepted by a small publishing house, Coffee House Press in Minnesota, that had also distributed her earlier work. As the press packaged *Tropic* as a "crossover" book, a work of "Chicanismo," it has not been able to market *Tropic* widely and even had trouble keeping it in print beyond its first edition. The conditions surrounding the publication of Yamashita's book have surely contributed to the relative critical silence surrounding her work, even though the inclusion of excerpts from *Tropic of Orange* in the new *Heath Anthology of American Literature* may help redress this oversight.

Works by lesser-known authors published in Latin America and, to an extent, in Canada, also have had great difficulties reaching a large audience. As Ilan Stavans has argued, until the late nineteenth century, literature was usually not read outside its country of origin, not because translations were not available, but because of limited cultural mobility (Stavans 4). Only during the *modernista* movement, spanning from approximately 1880 to 1915, did writers like José Martí become known beyond their national boundaries (Stavans 5). Before the advance of boom writing, cultural productions by Latin American writers were not seriously read abroad, in particular in the United States. But with the advance of the boom and the emergence of a transnational reading audience, Mexico became a recognized giant in the world of Latin American literature, with several Mexican authors, including Carlos Fuentes, Carlos Monsiváis, and Elena Poniatowska, topping the list of all-time literary greats in Spanish-language literature.

Not coincidentally, the "boom" also marked the zenith of attempts to integrate the Ibero-American publishing industry, heretofore dominated by Argentina, Mexico, and Spain. While Spanish-speaking Latin American reading audiences have historically been the principal buyers of Mexican books, Mexico's economic recession, low buying power, and declining interest in reading have led to a decrease in the number of book purchases.[1] Between 2001 and 2004, roughly 10 percent of all Mexican publishers shut down (Bensinger). While small and medium-scale publishing houses still dominate, they are being replaced by conglomerates that are promoting "novelty" and mass consumption products (Smorkaloff 96).

Some Mexican publishing houses have been taken over by the Spanish publishing industry or have agreed to collaborative arrangements with Spanish publishers to gain access to a larger Spanish-speaking market. Spanish publishing industries are also buying up major bookstores and distribution centers ("Cultural Industries"). There are fewer indications of integration with U.S. publishers, except for small-scale projects like the Voz del Colegio and the Binational Press. But some large mainstream presses like Houghton Mifflin and Harper Collins have launched their own series of Spanish-language texts. These series include some Chicana/o authors alongside Latin Americans and Spaniards (Martín-Rodríguez, *Life* 110–11).

Like Edith Eaton at the turn of the twentieth century, who moved from Canada to the United States to be closer to publishing opportunities, Latin American writers often move to countries such as Spain, or to the United States, where they have access to publishers and can get their work published in (sometimes simultaneous) translations. Writers who stay in Mexico tend to set their fiction in locations other than their native country, perhaps to appeal to a global market. They also break with literary traditions, like magical realism, that have been associated with Latin America (Blume). As the example of northern Mexican border authors shows, writing that insists on regional specificity within a national context has largely remained marginalized in the absence of local publishing industries and lack of interest by national publishers in these topics. The work of Rosina Conde (discussed in chapter 4), for example, appears to be more popular in the United States, where she is marketed within Latina/o studies paradigms, than in Mexico, where it exemplifies border writing. The translation of Federico Campbell's work (examined in chapter 4) into English has also further bolstered his position as an acclaimed writer in Mexico.

English-language literature produced in Canada faces slightly different issues. Today, 75 percent of all books read by English-speaking Canadians are imported from the United States (Smorkaloff 92), which leaves little room for a domestic publishing market. As Robert Thacker and Carole Gerson have shown, since at least the late nineteenth century, Canadian writing has been shaped by its proximity to the larger U.S. market. Because of a lack of profitable publishing venues in Canada, writers residing in Canada have tended to either publish their work in the United States or physically move there, which results in their literature becoming increasingly influenced by the expectations of the U.S. publishing industry and reading audience. At the end of the nineteenth century, for example, Canadian expatriate writers produced work that satisfied the U.S. taste for romantic tales and provincial stereotypes, manifested in the fascination with a romanticized, nonurban Canada (Gerson 111; Thacker 132). During that same time period, Edith Eaton modified her work to conform to U.S. expectations of Chinese assimilation. Her Canadian settings fared badly when her work was translated to a U.S. publishing context and they have fared poorly in U.S. academia as well. Once Eaton was integrated into U.S. canons as either an ethnic Asian American writer or a local color author, the Canadian border settings of her early work and her examination of the emergent Chinese undocumented border crosser (a precursor of the Mexican *indocumentado*) became muted.

These developments continue into the present (Thacker 134). Even though the writing of Alice Munro, for example, clearly shows the influence of her home—Huron Country, Ontario—with protagonists and towns reflecting that part of Canada, the specificity of this location is marginalized every time she is included in collections of the best U.S. American short stories. Authors who remain in Canada, however, continue to seek foreign markets for their work, which during most of Canada's recent history has meant publication in the United States. As Stephen Heninghan has argued, contemporary Canadian authors appear to be writing for a global audience rather than a national one. Their work is often set in locations other than Canada or in places that appear to be U.S. American (77).

The continuing production of writing that foregrounds Canadian issues and settings, such as the border texts examined in chapter 5 of this book, is in large part owing to the support of Canadian state institutions interested in the promotion of specifically "Canadian" content. However, as a holdover from the period of cultural nationalism that dominated Canada throughout the 1960s and 1970s, the power of these institutions and their subsequent effect on the shaping of Canadian literature and culture seems to be declining. That even these texts need to appeal to an audience beyond the national context is clear from the references in many of the Canadian border texts to the Mexican-U.S. boundary, a location more familiar to U.S. and transnational audiences.

Thomas King's reception further exemplifies the differential power of national publishing industries and the negative impact of an insistence on national and regional particularity. First editions of his novels appeared in Canadian outfits of U.S. publishing companies, like Penguin and Harper Collins (and also in smaller Canadian publishing houses). While all his work was later picked up by other, major U.S. publishers, like Bantam, Grove, Houghton Mifflin, and the Atlantic Monthly Press, it has received much less recognition in U.S. academic circles than the fiction of other native writers. Even though his name appears to be familiar to U.S. American Indian scholars, critical analyses of King's work have predominantly appeared in Canadian publications, and much of this scholarship tends to neglect the explicit Canadian dimensions of his work or to claim him simply as a U.S. writer.

The ways in which publishing industries shape the hemispheric production of literature need to be examined further to avoid reinforcing the mechanisms of the literary marketplace in the academic realm, as happened in Eaton's case.[2] Clearly, the work of critics has implications for book sales and, partially, for the production of literary works.

In this book, I have argued that border fictions require new interdisciplinary models of academic inquiry that bring together approaches from the humanities and the social sciences to address questions of globalization, U.S. empire, and nationalism of the hemisphere. I am aware that even a model of analysis that moves from identity-based categories toward spatialized inquiries cannot, in itself, avoid the possible emergence of a new niche marketing category, such as "border literature." Yet it is possible that such a model will at least get us to think about different forms of academic inquiry. In its unabashedly transnational focus on two nation-states and their often divergent forms of nationalism, border fiction identifies important distinctions among ideologies of nationalism and institutions associated with the nation-state. Many texts critique the repressive structures and ideologies linked to the nation-state, which are directed at internal populations or, in the case of empires like the United States, also at external nations. As the state sponsors ideologies of nationalism, these structures also become linked to the promotion of restrictive or often falsely homogeneous "imagined communities." Such ideologies usually start out with a progressive, anticolonial message before they become institutionalized by the state and its institutions, or, in the case of U.S. ethnic cultural nationalisms, in an academic environment increasingly dominated by neoliberal ideologies.

At the same time that they critique ideologies of nationalism, many border texts also attempt to recuperate from near oblivion the original anticolonial impetus of nationalist sentiments. These texts search for ways to divorce the articulation of progressive cultural national identities from the nation-state. One could ask, for example: since Canadian nationalism is increasingly becoming privatized and marketed for consumption, why can't this and other anticolonial sentiments also reestablish links with popular movements outside the nation-state?

Many border texts accomplish just that: Fuentes in particular attempts to articulate nationalisms independently of repressive state-sponsored forms. The fiction of U.S. ethnic writers examined in this book similarly works at divorcing various ethnic nationalisms from their institutionalized separatist incarnations to help build pan-ethnic and transnational bridges to similar movements. Some border texts also stress the immense potential of nation-state structures to protect the citizenry from the onslaught of neoliberalism. Perhaps these views embody not so much the wish for a return to the unchallenged reign of nation-states as the recognition that mechanisms for the protection of citizens currently exist only in the (often unused) powers of the nation-state and its institutions. Other such structures will have to be created and will probably be grounded in a mixture of national, international, transnational, and certainly pan-ethnic formations rather than in the wholesale abolition of the nation-state.

Notes

Introduction

1. For accounts of U.S. border militarization, see Peter Andreas, Timothy J. Dunn, and Joseph Nevins.

2. See the September 2004 *Time* special feature, entitled "Who Left the Door Open?," as a sample of the public discourse that conflates discussions of immigration and terrorism. Changes in the function of the Border Patrol constitute the corollary of such discourses. While its primary task had been to police undocumented immigration and drug smuggling at U.S. borders, in March 2003 the Border Patrol became a division of U.S. Customs and Border Protection (CBP) within the Department of Homeland Security. The Department's priority is to prevent terrorists and terrorist weapons from entering the country.

3. Bolton emphasized hemispheric similarities in the struggles for independence of native-born property holders, commonalities among inherited economies based on slave labor, and similarities in the imposition of internal colonial structures on indigenous peoples (Gruesz, *Ambassadors* 8).

4. On the importance of scholarship about the U.S.-Mexico border for transnational perspectives in American studies, see Paul Jay, Amy Kaplan and Donald Pease, John Muthyala ("Reworlding"), Carolyn Porter, John Carlos Rowe, and Priscilla Wald.

5. The field of contemporary border writing is expansive. Examples of contemporary border fiction that exceed the thematic limits of this study include novels by Tanya Maria Barrientos, T. Coraghessan Boyle, DBC Pierre, George Rabasa, and Susan Straight. Also, in "Left Sensationalism," Claire F. Fox points to detective fiction by Lucha Corpi, Rolando Hinojosa, Gabriel Trujillo Muñoz, Janice Steinberg, Paco Ignacio Taibo II, and Judith Van Gieson.

6. For theories of U.S. imperialism, see Michael Denning ("Globalization"), Michael Hardt and Antonio Negri, Amy Kaplan, Amy Kaplan and Donald Pease, Emmanuel Todd, and Immanuel Wallerstein. For all of its problems, Hardt and Negri's claim about the decentered nature of contemporary forms of empire may

simply be anticipating a future where the United States has lost its role as global hegemon.

7. While the War of 1812 ended in a territorial statement, 1840s conflicts between the United States and Canada over land straddling Maine and New Brunswick and over Oregon territory resulted in treaties stipulating that England cease territory to the United States.

8. Mexico's industry may indeed be moving away from cheap labor maquilas toward higher-end production of auto parts and electronics, which requires advanced technology, better-trained labor, and higher salaries.

9. For a comparison of approaches to the Berlin Wall and the Mexico-U.S. border, see Sadowski-Smith.

10. These measures include new permanent-resident cards, tighter security screenings for asylum seekers, accelerated deportations, and an increase in border guards.

11. Currently, about 1,000 U.S. Border Patrol agents work along the Canada-U.S. border, which constitutes roughly triple the 2001 force but a fraction of the 9,600 agents who patrol the Mexican boundary (Gillies n. pag.).

12. Mary Louise Pratt notes that "on the regional periphery . . . the short story cycle has been most likely to make its appearance" and adds that such work establishes a "basic literary identity for a region or group, laying out its descriptive parameters, character types, social and economic settings, principal points of conflict for an audience unfamiliar either with the region itself or with seeing that region in print" (187–88).

13. See Henry Louis Gates Jr. and Gerald Vizenor on the trickster-coyote in African American and U.S. American Indian writing. Jeanne Rosier Smith discusses the use of tricksters in various U.S. ethnic literary traditions.

14. For examples of recent work on magical realism as a global genre, see Wendy B. Faris and Frederick Luis Aldama.

15. The Borderlands Project and the scholarship by Matthew Sparke, Victor Konrad, Beth LaDow (*Medicine*), and Thomas F. McIlwraith (and, in literary studies, the work of Jennifer Andrews and Russell Brown) constitute exceptions to the dearth of scholarship on the Canada-U.S. border. To my knowledge, Canada-U.S. border studies have not become an institutionalized object of study in Canada. In Mexico, few institutions have been interested in border work. With the exception of the Department of the Humanities in Hermosillo, Sonora, and the Autonomous University of Baja California, which has a professorship in regional literature, no other border institutions have permanent courses dealing with contemporary regional literature (Castillo and Tabuenca Córdoba 25).

16. Richard Gwyn has described Canada as a "state-nation" where state, business, and elite interventions were needed to create a sense of national identity.

17. For the distinction between *literatura de la frontera* and *literatura fronteriza*, see Debra Castillo and María Socorro Tabuenca Córdoba (27).

18. While some U.S.-based Americanists like Cyrus Patell have understood

internationalization to mean more comparative work on U.S. ethnic and racial groups, others, like Jane C. Desmond and Virginia R. Domínguez, have employed it in reference to the global study of the United States as an area, emphasizing foreign-based scholarly perspectives on U.S. culture and thereby resituating the field's traditional institutional sites of power.

19. For a more comprehensive historical account of inter-American scholarship since the 1940s, see Sophia McClennen.

20. Gustavo Pérez-Firmat, Earl E. Fitz, José David Saldívar (*Dialectics*), and Hortense Spillers produced influential examples of mid-1980s and early 1990s inter-American research. Fitz included texts from the United States, Spanish America, Brazil, and English and French Canada. Pérez-Firmat's collection initiated the ongoing dialogue between Latin American studies and comparative literature. Saldívar advocated a pan-Latino focus on cultural production that has affinities with African and Native American literatures, while Spiller's collection forged intersection between U.S. communities and other parts of the hemisphere, including Spanish America, the Caribbean, and Québécois Canada.

21. The trans-Pacific foregrounds links between Asian America and various Asian countries. Paul Gilroy's notion of the Black Atlantic has initiated a trans-Atlantic focus on the legacies of the slave trade. Joseph Roach's scholarship on the Circum-Atlantic stresses links between New Orleans, the Antilles, West Africa, and London, and is one of the founding works of New World studies. For examples of this perspective, see Deborah H. Cohn, J. Michael Dash, Vera M. Kutzinski, George B. Handley, Timothy J. Cox, and Jon Smith and Deborah Cohn (eds). It is important to note, however, that the term *New World Studies* is often simply used as a synonym for inter-American studies.

22. For emerging work on connections among New World studies and literature of the Americas, see José Eduardo Limón, and Kirsten Silva Gruesz ("The Gulf").

23. For work on the decline of Canadian studies in Canada, see T. D. Maclulich, and T. H. B. Symons.

24. This language is adapted from Giles Gunn's discussion of interdisciplinarity, which he imagines through the metaphor of heterosexual marriage.

25. However, in discussions of potential collaboration with American studies, it is often forgotten that if it exists at all, in most universities, the field has only been given program status with few faculty positions. A much larger number of U.S. Americanists interested in literary studies works in English departments, which are also embattled but are perhaps in a slightly better institutional position than language or area studies departments.

1. Chicana/o Writing and the Mexico-U.S. Border

1. The novel also draws attention to the ecological current in Chicana/o thought, which can be traced back to connections between the Chicana/o civil rights movement and environmental concerns. Andrea Parra reminds us, for example,

that the threat of pesticide poisoning gave rise to the grassroots organization of César Chávez's United Farm Workers (1099).

2. Rolando Hinojosa's work on Belken county includes, for example, *Klail City* (1987) and *Becky and Her Friends* (1990). Brito, Casares, Gilb, Hinojosa, Islas, Paredes, Rechy, and Troncoso have ties to the Texas-Chihuahua border area. Viramontes was born and grew up in the extended California–Baja California border zone of Los Angeles, but she sets much of her work in Mexico-U.S. border areas.

3. María Amparo Ruiz de Burton's *Who Would Have Thought It?* (1872) and *The Squatter and the Don* (1885) as well as Américo Paredes's *George Washington Gómez* (published in 1990 but written mostly in the late 1930s and early 1940s) exemplify work on the border that was authored before the inception of Chicanismo.

4. Mainly active in California, César Chávez's United Farm Workers' Union (UFW) introduced most of the symbols of Chicanismo and the idea of collective land ownership, which it borrowed from the Mexican Revolution. Reies López Tijerina's *Alianza Federal de Mercedes* in New Mexico highlighted violations of the 1848 Treaty of Guadalupe Hidalgo, which secured community land grants provided in the seventeenth century to Mexican farmers and villagers. José Angel Gutiérrez's Mexican American Youth Organization (MAYO) emphasized community control of institutions and resistance to educational segregation, organizing school boycotts, or "blowouts," in California, Colorado, New Mexico, and Texas.

5. In "El Plan Espiritual de Aztlán" (1989), Alurista wrote, "*we,* the Chicano inhabitants and civilizers of the northern land of Aztlán from whence came our forefathers, reclaiming the land of their birth and consecrating the determination of our people of the sun, *declare* that the call of our blood is our power, our responsibility, and our inevitable destiny" ("El Plan" 1, emphasis in original).

6. Méndez claims in the introduction to *Pilgrims,* however, that the novel had been finished by 1968, before the height of cultural nationalism (2).

7. In his article "Chicano Border Narratives as Cultural Critique," José David Saldívar identifies *Tierra* alongside work by Américo Paredes and Rolando Hinojosa as a border narrative that replaces old racist border history and culture and that signifies the emergence of Chicano oppositional thinking in south Texas (177).

8. José Aranda Jr., for example, discusses the autobiographies of Richard Rodriguez (*Hunger of Memory*) and Cherríe Moraga (*Loving in the War Years*) as precursors to Anzaldúa's critical examination of Chicanismo (24–33). Manuel M. Martín-Rodríguez has identified Anzaldúa's work as having initiated one of two major tendencies in contemporary Chicana/o studies toward "transatlantic reformulations" ("Recovering" 796).

9. For work on Anzaldúa's connection to environmental concerns, see Adamson ("Literature-and-Environment") and Dixon.

10. Ríos has said that "when he was first introduced to Latin American writing, he found it foreign to his schooling but 'familiar and friendly' to his upbringing" (Dunaway and Spurgeon 169).

11. While a bill acknowledging the repatriation in California was signed in 2005, a second bill allowing victims of the program to seek civil damages was vetoed in 2006.

12. Michaelson and Johnson were among the first scholars to criticize the Chicana/o narrative of the Southwest as one of property, possession, and genealogy of occupation, where the borderlands are claimed by Chicano culture.

13. This demographic information comes from the 2000 U.S. Census http://www.laredo.areaconnect.com/statistics.htm. Information about Nuevo Laredo is available at http://www.mexicostartupservices.com/info.php?ID=8.

14. The Border Patrol or other military has, to my knowledge, mistakenly killed at least three U.S. civilians or immigrants. Juan Patricio Peraza Quijada, a nineteen-year-old immigrant from Mexicali, Baja California, was shot to death by Border Patrol agents in San Diego in 2003. In 1997 a U.S. Marine in Redford, Texas, member of the Joint Task Force 6 drug patrol, shot eighteen-year-old Esequiel Hernandez, who thus became the first U.S. civilian killed by a U.S. marine on U.S. soil. In 1992, the Border Patrol in Nogales mistakenly shot and killed Dario Miranda Valenzuela, a twenty-six-year-old resident of Nogales, Sonora.

15. This possibility is prefigured by the actions of the other women protagonists, all of whom give or take something important to the river in an act that changes their lives. For example, Estella, a housewife from Nuevo Laredo, drops into the river a dish of poisoned mole that was supposed to kill her cheating husband, and Lourdes discards a ring she took from a body she found by the international river. One may surmise that the dead man is Sofia's husband, who did not return to Laredo from his work in the Mexican city. He may have been a victim of thugs and growing border crime or he may have drowned in his attempt to swim across the river.

16. These demographic data are available at http://www.elpasotexas.gov/demographics.asp and http://www.dallasfed.org/research/busfront/bus0102.html.

17. These figures are available at http://www.nogales.areaconnect.com/statistics.htm and http://www.en.wikipedia.org/wiki/Nogales,_Sonora.

18. The theme of female self-empowerment runs through Guerrero's collection. For example, the protagonist in "Gloves of Her Own," a play on Virginia Woolf's famous essay "A Room of Her Own," finds independence from her much-venerated grandfather. The last story in the collection, which brings many of the book's characters together in a wedding ceremony, represents hope for a change in gender relations. The happily married newlyweds, who seem to enjoy more equality in their relationship, move into an apartment on Frontera Street that was once occupied by a family in which the man abused his wife.

19. Some Chicana/o literature has already paved the way for such connections. For example, Ríos's "The Curtain of Trees" references intersections among

Mexican contract laborers called *enganchados* who worked on railroad lines in the U.S. West alongside Chinese, German, and Irish workers (*Curtain*). And Pope Duarte's *Let Their Sprits Dance,* though not a border novel, focuses on a barrio in south Phoenix that is also inhabited by African American and Asian American protagonists.

2. Asian Border Crossings

1. Born Edith Maude Eaton in England, the author published some of her work under the name Sui Sin Far (and Seen Far or Sin Fah), which also seemed to have been a term of familial address. In this chapter, I follow the more common scholarly practice of referring to her as Edith Eaton when discussing her texts, even though my citations of her published work use her chosen pen name.

2. The sixty-one-year critical silence after Eaton's death in 1914 was broken by brief discussions of her work in dissertations and dictionaries. After her mention in the 1975 anthology *Aiieeee!* critics like S. E. Solberg and Amy Ling in the 1970s and 1980s helped establish Eaton's position as a pioneering Chinese North American writer. For recent influential work on Eaton, see Elizabeth Ammons, Annette White-Parks, and Dominika Ferens. Some of Eaton's stories have also been included in the *Heath Anthology of American Literature.* For examples of recent work on Chinese exclusion, see Andrew Gyory, Erika Lee, and Lucy E. Salyer.

3. Eaton's biographer, Annette White-Parks, writes that she was able to locate separate printings for only eleven of the collection's thirty-eight selections, which suggests that Eaton wrote some original stories for the volume (White-Parks, *Sui* 196). Most of Eaton's previously published stories were not included (White-Parks, *Sui* 204). I quote throughout from the reprinted version of *Mrs. Spring Fragrance, Mrs. Spring Fragrance and Other Writings* (1995), which contains approximately three-fourths of the stories from the original 1912 text and a sampling of Eaton's uncollected essays, journalistic articles, and short stories.

4. We can only know about those authors who retained their Canadian identity or returned to Canada; many more probably became absorbed into the United States (Gerson 108). The success of Canada's first best-selling author, May Agnes Fleming, relied on serials contracted with U.S. popular magazines that contained few references to Canada. At the height of her career, Fleming also moved to New York to be closer to her publishers (Gerson 111). Sara Jeannette Duncan (a *Post* editorial writer), who became a major figure in the Canadian canon, is another of the many Canadian women who left for the United States to work in publishing or journalism (Gerson 108–9). In addition, important figures like Charles G. D. Roberts, Bliss Carman, and Gilbert Parker published their work in the United States during the latter part of the nineteenth century (Thacker 132).

5. Early Chinese authors, mostly students or diplomats who had been sent by the Manchu court, brought by missionaries, or arrived on their own for advanced education in the United States, produced autobiographical writing (Yin

52–53). Unlike their countrymen who lived in segregated urban ghettos, most of these writers assimilated into mainstream U.S. intellectual and cultural life. They perceived ignorance and common misconceptions about Chinese civilization rather than economic and social conditions as the root of racism and thought that by providing correct information on Chinese culture, they would win sympathy and acceptance for Chinese immigrants (Yin 54).

6. Edith Eaton's parents, Edward Eaton and Lotus Blossum, migrated to North America when she was about two but soon returned to England. The second migration took place in 1871 or 1872. The family first went to Hudson City, New York, and then traveled on to Montréal (White-Parks, *Sui* 18).

7. Besides claiming Japanese descent, Winnifred also wrote under a variety of other pen names and literary personas, such as Winnifred Mooney, Winnifred Babcock Reeve, and Winnifred Eaton Reeve. These names made her appear to be a working-class Irish American, a British author, or an Englishwoman in the Canadian west (Roh-Spaulding 27–28). While Winnifred was more successful than her sister during her lifetime, today Edith's work is more widely taught, analyzed, and anthologized.

8. For example, Elizabeth Ammons and Valerie Rohy label Eaton a local color writer and group her work with that of other U.S. "West Coast" authors, and Eric Sunquist identifies her as a regionalist writer who first recorded the urban experiences of the Asian community on the West Coast.

9. Dominika Ferens believes Eaton's stories use a "parable" form that resembles ethnographic fiction about Asians (108). Sean McCann also comments on Eaton's idiosyncratic style, both in orientation and method (McCann 79). Neither critic links such statements to assumptions about regionalism, however.

10. See Ammons and Ferens. Ferens argues that Eaton's focus on Chinese family life within melodramatic conventions that emphasize love and marriage marginalized the problems of the predominantly uprooted male culture in Chinatown society (*Conflicting* 57). Other scholars have, however, also emphasized Eaton's sympathetic depictions of interracial characters and relationships before they began to be outlawed in sixteen U.S. states after the 1880s (Yin 114).

11. The most important legacy of pan-Asian American movements like the college-based Asian American Political Alliance (AAPA) was the institutionalization of Asian American studies. The first programs were established at San Francisco State College and, later, at the University of California at Berkeley (Espiritu 35–36).

12. Gordon H. Chang notes that the about fifty million people who can be considered products of Chinese migration to over one hundred countries since the fifteenth century include, for example, Taiwanese and Vietnamese Chinese who speak various different dialects, such as Mandarin or Cantonese (135–36). Postcolonial Asian populations, such as Filipinos, Indians, Koreans, and Vietnamese, now form the majority of Asian America, but their histories of European colonial and imperial warfare or, alternatively, of their domination by neighboring Japan

are not usually presented as the normative face of Asian America (Nguyen and Chen).

13. For work on Asian immigration to Latin America, see Aihwa Ong and Evelyn Hu-DeHart (*Across*).

14. In her essay "We Wear the Mask," Annette White-Parks reads Eaton's use of the trickster as a precursor for much of the tricksterism commonly found in contemporary multiethnic fiction. Eaton's later stories, such as "A Chinese Boy-Girl," take up similar themes of interracial relationships and gender bending in formally and stylistically more complex ways.

15. White-Parks writes that six short stories and one essay of Eaton's, her first creative writing about Chinese, were written in Montréal but published in little magazines in the United States, such as *Fly Leaf, Lotus,* and *The Land of Sunshine* (*Far* 84–85). Ferens mentions that four of the ten stories Eaton published in *The Land of Sunshine* were postmarked in Montréal; one of those was "The Smuggling of Tie Co" (83, 95).

16. But one of Eaton's U.S.-based stories, "The Land of the Free," depicts the detention of a merchant's newborn child by U.S. authorities upon arrival in San Francisco. And in "Mrs Spring Fragrance," a Chinese American merchant who has lived in Seattle for many years mentions to his neighbor that his brother is being detained in accordance with exclusion law. Recently, Ferens also discovered "The Persecution and Oppression of Me," a piece she attributes to Easton. It was published anonymously in the *Independent* in 1911, a New York political weekly, and was considerably more explicit on everyday experiences of racism (4–5).

17. Thanks to Karen J. Leong for pointing out these events.

18. *Tropic* has finally begun to receive some attention from Asian American scholars. In publications in 2004 and 2006, Caroline Rody, Florence Hsiao-ching Li, and Ruth Y. Hsu have framed *Tropic* within Asian American critical frameworks that do, however, not examine potential conflicts between the global direction of the field and the hemispheric orientation of the novel.

19. The characters in *Tropic* embody different traditions of the cultural representation of Los Angeles, such as detective noir, LA disaster fiction, and Hollywood and other mass media representations, to which Yamashita adds Latin American–style magical realism (Gier and Tejeda). *Tropic*'s protagonist Gabriel Balboa, the Chicano news reporter and detective noir aficionado, represents the new interest in hard-boiled fiction in the border areas of the United States and Mexico. See the essays by Claire F. Fox ("Left Sensationalism") and Jennifer Insley on Mexican and U.S. crime fiction about the Mexico-U.S. border and its relationship to Los Angeles and Mexican border cities.

20. Yamashita cites Guillermo Gómez-Peña's book *The New World Border,* from which she also borrows the concept of a performance wrestler in the opening epigraph to *Tropic*. In a piece entitled "Borderama," one of Gómez-Peña's characters states, "[T]hey call me 'Supermojado" (138), and a later slide shows

a "CLOSE-UP OF THE BLEEDING FACE OF A MEXICAN WRESTLER" who is diagnosed as "[o]ne of the first casualties of NAFTA" (145).

21. Other estimates range from 7,000 to 17,300 Chinese undocumented Mexico-U.S. border crossings between 1910 and 1920 alone (Ryo 110). For example, Mexicali, the capital of Baja California, was numerically and culturally more Chinese than Mexican in the early twentieth century, and the city still boasts the highest per capita concentration of Chinese residents in Mexico. The first Chinese to arrive in the area worked for the Colorado River Land Company, a U.S. enterprise that designed and built an extensive irrigation system in the fertile Valle de Mexicali. Some immigrants came from the United States, often fleeing officially sanctioned anti-Chinese policies, while others sailed directly from China. As happened in California, thousands of Chinese coolies were lured to the area by the promise of high wages that never materialized. Many of the Chinese who survived the building of the irrigation system stayed on after its completion, opening bars, restaurants, and hotels (Cummings).

3. Native Border Theory

1. I use the terms *indigenous, native, American Indian, aboriginal,* and *Indian* interchangeably to acknowledge different naming practices throughout the Americas and to draw attention to the political-cultural contexts involved in self-naming and naming by others. I use specific tribal names when referring to particular nations.

2. Discussing Blackfoot nationalism as a case study, Kiera L. Ladner argues that this spatialized understanding of nationhood is rooted in precolonial forms of indigenous nationalism that draw on spiritual stories about the sacredness of a place and that define the history of a nation in terms of its relationship with the Creation.

3. In his assessment of U.S. Native American studies, Russell Thornton laments that the field has not emerged as a separate intellectual entity in higher education and that much important scholarship has been produced by scholars inside and outside academia without formal affiliations with Native American studies departments, programs or centers (Thornton 97).

4. While American Indian studies has been institutionalized as a distinct and interdisciplinary field in Canada and the United States, in Latin America the academic study of indigenous peoples has been largely confined to linguistics and anthropology (Varese 138).

5. The declaration states that indigenous peoples in the Americas are "bound by common origin and history, aspiration and experience" and that "arbitrary lines [between Canada and the United States] have not severed, and never will, the ties of kinship among our peoples."

6. Momaday's Pulitzer Prize helped in particular to convince publishers that Native American literature could be profitably marketed to a U.S. reading public and thus recognized as art rather than as ethnography or anthropology (Peterson 2).

7. Later criticism by Janet St. Clair ("Cannibal"), Jeff Karem, and Alex Hunt emphasizes the novel's problematic linkage of white men's aberrations with homosexuality, which thus functions as a marker of larger evil, including pedophilia, cannibalism, rape, and capitalist exploitation of people and land.

8. Silko's publisher, Simon and Schuster, initially marketed the book as a work of southwestern literature, using blurbs from Tony Hillerman and Larry McMurtry, rather than as Native American literature (Karem 196–97). But in subsequent printings, Simon and Schuster began marketing Silko as an ethnic author, placing comments from Toni Morrison and Maxine Hong Kingston on the book covers of new editions (Karem 196–97). This shift highlights the United States' comparatively greater interest in ethnicity (rather than region) as a marker of authenticity in the present day.

9. Vine Deloria first used the term "Red Power" during a 1966 convention of the NCAI. The symbolic occupation of Alcatraz Island in November 20, 1969, by the "Indians of All Tribes" mobilized shifts toward supratribal civil rights. The weeklong occupation of the Bureau of Indian Affairs building in Washington D.C. in November 1972, named "Trail of Broken Treaties," however, marked a renewed desire to address more specific tribal issues, such as treaty rights and land claims, to involve reservation groups who had not much supported Red Power (Nagel 205).

10. See Louis Owens for a critique of tribal realism.

11. *Almanac* employs a variety of predictive cosmologies shared by indigenous communities throughout the greater Southwest, including Toltec stories of Quetzalcoatl's return; the Aztec myth of Aztlán, which Silko points to as predicting the resurgence of indigenous peoples; the Quiche Maya creation story, and fragments from Chilam Balam, so named for the Mayan priest of the immediate pre-Conquest period who became famous for having predicted the Spanish invasion.

12. For work on Yaqui history, see for example Evelyn Hu-DeHart (*Yaqui*) and Edward Spicer.

13. Silko's vision has parallels in Chicanismo's emphasis on the native component of Chicana/o identity, which is grounded in notions of *indigenismo* that elevated *mestizaje* to a state-sponsored form of *mexicanidad*.

14. Silko has often endorsed prophetic readings of her novel. She has characterized her book as a form of premonition resulting from her research on Mexican and U.S. politics and economics, particularly as it has affected the border area where she lives (Karem 197–98).

15. King's depiction of crazy Coyote as the originator of Christian biblical narratives, for example, is reminiscent of Silko's insistence in *Ceremony* that white people were created by Indian witchery. And the return of the novel's protagonist, the photographer Will Horse Capture, to Medicine River also resembles Silko's emphasis on the reintegration of her protagonists into their Laguna Pueblo communities in *Ceremony* and *Almanac*.

16. On the ways in which native tribes of the Great Lakes regions manipulated competing colonial interests, see Richard White.

17. The first full-time, degree-granting Native studies program was created at Trent University in Peterborough, Ontario, in 1969 (Price, *Native* 9), and others soon followed. Even though indigenous Canadians are sometimes imagined in terms of postcolonial theory (a framework that is also used to theorize South Asians in Canada or Canada's relationship to the United States), this perspective has remained controversial. In his essay "Godzilla vs. Post-colonial," King has rejected the postcolonial label because, as he argues, the term assumes that struggles between white and indigenous cultures have figured as the main catalyst for contemporary Native art. In this sense, the label "postcolonialism" cuts Native peoples off from their precolonial traditions (King, "Godzilla" 11–12).

18. In 1870, Louis Riel, leader of the Métis, sought refuge in the United States from death threats in Canada. In the United States, he worked toward the creation of a pan-native alliance to invade Canada and declare an independent native republic. His failed rebellion in 1885 represented the last great attempt at native unity along the Canada-U.S. border besides the 1890s Ghost Dance religion (Ladow, "Sanctuary" 33–35, 37).

19. Some reviewers seem to find *Truth* less aesthetically accomplished than King's earlier work. Warren Cariou, for example, writes that King "just got so caught up in the machinery of his symbols that there was no room left for complex characters and narrative drive . . . unlike . . . some other allegorical works—including *Green Grass*, where the symbols enhance narrative instead of mastering it" (38–39).

20. About *Green Grass* and its basis in two national traditions, King has said that "there are a number of Canadian allusions, and there are a number of U.S. allusions, and not everybody's going to get them all, but if you get 'em, the book's a lot more fun, and if you don't I don't think it hurts it at all" (Gzowski 68).

21. Other indigenous nations like the Ojibwa and many Salishan tribes have also been defined by their border crossing experiences, their residence on traditional territory that straddles the border, or their having been forced from territory in the United States (Miller 374).

22. Activism for the free cross-border passage of Iroquois people calls for the enforcement of the 1794 Jay Treaty and the 1814 Treaty of Ghent, which allow Indians to cross the border freely without paying duties on their personal goods (Grinde 168–69). The Iroquois' internal separation is today most clearly visible on the Mohawk reservation of Akwesasne (discussed in chapter 2 of this book).

23. King's second novel, *Green Grass*, also integrates Cherokee traditions into its tale about Canada-U.S. Blackfoot. King employs Cherokee syllabary to separate individual chapters and sections, points to the ceremonial opening of storytelling in a Cherokee divining ceremony, and references Star Maiden or Star Woman, a central figure in Cherokee creation and Blackfoot stories (Flick 144, 161).

24. These icons of Cherokee history include John Ross, the principal chief of the Cherokee nation, 1826–1866; George Guess, the Cherokee who devised the Cherokee syllabary; and a young girl named Rebecca Neugin who was three at the time of the removals. Her experiences were published in 1932 by the Oklahoma historian Grant Foreman (Ridington 100).

25. Other trickster figures in the novel are the "cousin dogs" that came with the church (38–39), and Lum's dog, who is called "dog soldier," a term accorded to the bravest men in a tribe, the ones who stay behind and protect people from attack.

26. The 1990 Native American Grave Protection and Repatriation Act provides a process for U.S. museums and federal agencies to return Native American cultural items, such as human remains, sacred objects, and objects of cultural patrimony, to lineal descendants, culturally affiliated Indian tribes, and Native Hawaiian organizations. While no such federal policy exists in Canada, in 2000 the Government of Alberta instituted the First Nations Sacred Ceremonial Objects Repatriation Act. In addition, the 1992 recommendations by the Task Force on First Peoples and Museums have been selectively implemented by individual museums. The Canadian Museum of Civilization, for example, passed a Repatriation Policy in 2001.

27. The Texas band of Kickapoo set the precedent for citizenship demands of Mexico-U.S. border tribes. When the Kickapoo acquired a reservation in Oklahoma, half the band stayed in Mexico, where they survived by hunting, farming, and working as migrant farm laborers in the United States. In 1983 they were recognized as a distinct subgroup of the band in Oklahoma, and they now hold dual citizenship. When on the U.S. side, they live in a village of traditional houses under the international bridge at Eagle Pass, Texas. A smaller sister tribe also exists in Arizona.

28. The analysis of border tribes in the hemisphere could become a sub-area of inquiry, encompassing such tribes as the Yanomami at the Brazil-Guatemala border, the Maya of the Mexico-Guatemala border, the Miskito people of the Nicaragua-Honduras border, the Andean Mapuche of the Argentine-Chile border, the Aymaras between Chile and Bolivia, the Quechuas and Ashaninka in Peru and Ecuador, the Wayyu in Venezuela and Columbia, and the Emerá in Colombia and Panama (Berreiro 2).

29. Silko's notion of affinities among indigenous people and undocumented immigrants from Asia like Awa Gee, is, however, not fleshed out to the same extent as Karen Tei Yamashita's vision of coalitions among Chinese and Mexican immigrants, discussed in the previous chapter.

4. The View from the South

1. The Spanish original reads: "Soñó con la frontera y la vio como una enorme herida sangrante, un cuerpo enfermo, incierto de salud, mudo ante sus propios males, al filo del grito, desconcertado por sus fidelidades, y golpeado,

finalmente, por la insensibilidad, la demagogia y la corrupción políticas" (*La frontera de cristal* 286). The translation of the Spanish title *La frontera de cristal* as *The Crystal Frontier* unfortunately evokes the historical meaning of the U.S. West as the frontier of Anglo expansion; the novel itself does not endorse this view.

2. I do not mean to suggest that Fuentes borrowed the image of the border wound from Anzaldúa. He had already employed similar terms in earlier work. In the conclusion to his nonfictional history of Mexico, *The Buried Mirror* (1992), for example, Fuentes associates the growing numbers of Mexican immigrants and the visibility of Mexicans in the United States with the notion of a scar (342). In *Gringo viejo,* Inocencio Mansalvo says, toward the end of the novel, "[c]on razón, ésta no es frontera, sino que es cicatriz" (175) ["They're right when they say this isn't a border. It's a scar," *The Old Gringo* 185].

3. Vasconcelos's insistence on the anti-imperialist potential of *mexicanidad* as a representative of a larger Latin American union in opposition to the United States was also shaped by his later experiences in Latin American expatriate communities in France, Argentina, and Brazil.

4. For studies of representations of Mexico in U.S. literature, see Cecil Robinson, José Eduardo Limón, José David Saldívar (*Border Matters*), and Daniel Cooper Alarcón.

5. But see, for example, Cinco Punto Press in El Paso and Binational Press, a joint venture between the California State University at San Diego and universities in Baja California. Similarly, much understudied border literature has existed in translation or in bilingual format. See, for example, the work collected by Harry Polkinhorn et al.: *The Flight of the Eagle, La Línea,* and *Borderlands Literature.* See also Manuel José Di-Bella et al. *Literatura de la frontera méxico-norteamericana.*

6. See, for example, Alberto Ledesma and Anna M. Sandoval.

7. Besides Federico Campbell and Rosina Conde, who will be the focus of this chapter, *literatura de la frontera* comprises work by such artists and thinkers as María Socorro Tabuenca Córdoba in Ciudad Juárez; Víctor Zúñiga in Monterrey; and Sergio Gómez Montero and Humberto Félix Berumen in Baja California; as well as Tijuana writers like Luis Humberto Crosthwaite. In addition, the essayists Sergio Gómez Montero, Gabriel Trujillo Muñoz, and Francisco Luna have consistently commented on the literature of Mexico's northern border region (Castillo and Tabuenca Córdoba 145).

8. The Bracero Program, in effect between 1942 and 1964, produced entire neighborhoods of temporary, mostly male, residents in Tijuana and Ciudad Juárez waiting to cross the border. As a result of Operation Wetback, which forced Mexican male laborers to return to Mexico, the population in border cities increased at record levels.

9. Except for *Border Women* by Debra Castillo and María Socorro Tabuenca Córdoba, Conde's work has received little critical attention.

10. Raúl Rodríguez-Hernández remarks on similarities between Fuentes's and Campbell's work on the border, but he focuses on formal similarities in the two writers' use of narrative fragments (142).

11. In the United States, only the Latin Americanists Debra A. Castillo, Linda Egan, Hugo Méndez-Ramírez, and Alfonso González have written on *The Crystal Frontier*.

12. Amanda Hopkinson of the *Independent* argues, for example, that *The Crystal Frontier* is disappointing when contrasted with the work of U.S. Chicano/a writers, whom she characterizes as "more authentic literary voices speaking of Latino borders" (Hopkinson 32).

13. Sergio González Rodríguez, for example, writes that "Fuentes's novel is an exercise in fiction and at the same time a manifesto of ideas. In his role as Mexican essayist he has for years spread these ideas concerning our history and our myths as they are reflected to the outside, in particular, to the United States" (7, my translation from the original Spanish). Support for this assertion can be found in the ending of *The Crystal Frontier*, which reiterates, word for word, Fuentes's argument in *A New Time for Mexico*.

14. Fuentes claims that he first gained consciousness of his Mexican nationality when he lived in Washington D.C. As he watched the movie *Man of Conquest* in 1939 and heard the protagonist proclaim the secession of the Republic of Texas from Mexico, the eleven-year-old Fuentes stood up and shouted "Viva Mexico! Death to the Gringos!" (Williams 7).

15. In "Hollywood's Backlot," Claire Fox argues that having begun composing *The Old Gringo* in 1964 mostly in Spanish, Fuentes resumed writing it almost twenty years later—and then in English—probably spurred on by the prospect of a motion picture contract brokered by actress Jane Fonda (64). Both the English and Spanish versions of the novel were published in 1985, with Fuentes being credited as one of the cotranslators of the English version, which differs in some significant aspects from its Mexican instantiation. Fuentes's increasing bilingualism was also manifested in his subsequent novel, *Cristóbal nonato*, which he composed in both English and Spanish (79).

16. While Fuentes's writing has often been praised for its innovation, the politics of his work have, especially in recent years, been criticized for their left-of-center nature or, alternatively, for moving away from their original leftist ideals. The largely ideological reception of Fuentes's work and persona is reflected in the well-known feud between him and the more conservative Mexican writer and Nobel laureate Octavio Paz.

17. Rafael H. Mohica and Celia Correas Zapata, for example, have registered their skepticism that *The Crystal Frontier* is indeed a novel rather than a collection of short stories.

18. The depiction of the border in psychological terms also borrows from Fuentes's earlier work *The Old Gringo*. In this novel it is a white U.S. American who is said to bear an internal frontier. Fuentes writes that "each of us carries his

Mexico and his United States within him, a dark and bloody frontier we dare to cross only at night" (*Gringo* 187).

5. A Border Like No Other

1. The events of September 11 put an end to efforts for the creation of the proposed common "open and seamless border" between Canada and the United States articulated during the summer of 2001. Proposals to ease U.S.-Canada border restrictions under a "NAFTA-plus" plan were couched in appeals to the long and peaceful history of "the world's largest undefended border" separating two largely similar neighbors (Walker A1).

2. The link between illegal activities at the U.S.-Canada border and terrorism directed at the United States has a long history. It dates back to at least 1997, when the Palestinian Gazi Ibrahim Abu Mezer was prevented from crossing the border with bomb-making material designed to blow up the New York subway system. In December 1999, the Algerian Ahmed Ressam was captured at Port Angeles, Washington, and prevented from blowing up the Los Angeles airport during the millennium celebrations. He later admitted that he had been trained in camps connected to Osama Bin Laden's network.

3. W. H. New points out that, since the nineteenth century, Canada has been construed by U.S. Americans "either as an extension of Europe (and therefore a culture in decline) or as an extension of themselves (with annexation as an inevitable consequence)" (*Borderlands* 73).

4. John Carlos Rowe, for example, theorizes a "North American Studies" that includes "investigations of how the many different Americas and Canada have historically influenced and interpreted each other" (13–14). In referring to Canada in the singular but to the United States in the plural, Rowe reiterates the common view of Canada as an internally homogenous nation.

5. Canadian studies has mainly become institutionalized in English-speaking institutions of higher learning in Canada, whereas Québécois studies is common in French-language universities. U.S.-based scholarship on Canada originally emerged in the 1940s and 1950s in history departments but has recently also extended into other fields, such as economics, business, political science, economic geography, law, anthropology, and sociology (Winks 7–8).

6. As Michael Hart put it in a July 8, 2005, address to the Wilson Center, 80 percent of Canadians live within a two-hour drive of a U.S. shopping center.

7. Richard Gwyn has described Canada as a "state-nation" where state, business, and elite interventions were needed to create a sense of national identity.

8. *Fronteras Americanas, Bordertown Café,* and *Cumberland,* the texts that will be the focus of this chapter, were produced with the support of the Canada Council for the Arts. In addition, *Bordertown Café* was supported by the Manitoba Arts Council and *Cumberland* by the Ontario Arts Council and the Book Publishing Industry Development Program.

9. For a concise characterization of the Canadian literary tradition and its

relationship to cultural nationalism, see Davey. Examples of government intervention include the Canadian Radio and Television Commission's content regulations, which require 30 percent of Canadian popular music selections on the radio, 60 percent of Canadian programming on private TV on a full-day basis, and 60 percent of Canadian programming on public television in primetime (Mulcahy 194–95). Suggestions for similar policies in Latin America can be found, for example, in Néstor García Canclini's *La globalización imaginada*.

10. The Québécois struggle for independence has been considered Canada's only identity-based movement, and Canada's official policy of multiculturalism has been widely interpreted as a means of undercutting Québécois demands for special recognition by bestowing it on other cultural groups. See, for example, Goellnicht's and Mackey's work.

11. For parallels to Verdecchia's depiction of a Latino Canadian diaspora, see also Michelle Habell-Pallán's discussion of Latina/o theater in Vancouver.

12. *Fronteras Americanas* pays homage to Guillermo Gómez-Peña by including a section about a (fictional?) encounter with *el brujo* (one of Guillermo Gómez-Peña's performance characters) in Toronto, where he diagnoses Verdecchia's identity problem as that of a "very bad border wound" (Verdecchia 71). Verdecchia also includes a quotation from Gómez-Peña in the play and in a footnote explains his influential role in U.S. debates on multiculturalism.

13. However, an interview with Hospital was included in the important collection of interviews with Canadian authors, *The Power to Bend Spoons,* edited by Daurio Beverley. As Hospital herself said in an interview, in the mid-1980s she and Mukherjee were listed among the best ten younger Canadian writers (Langer 144).

14. In an earlier short story, "The Bloody Past, the Wandering Future," Hospital has termed the Canada-U.S. border "the desiccating edge of things, . . . the dividing line between two countries, nowhere" (*Dislocations* 184).

15. Gus's description is an ironic commentary on the many Canadians who immigrate to the United States because they are seduced by better economic opportunities and greater individual material wealth and long to be unhampered by the kind of taxation that has allowed the creation and (attenuated) maintenance of the Canadian welfare state.

16. While criteria for political asylum have become severely restricted in the United States, Canada's requirements remain relatively open. In contrast to the United States, which now largely implements the mandatory detention of refugees, Canada applies so-called balance-of-credibility tests that not only accord refugee claimants the benefit of doubt when trying to determine their eligibility but also guarantee Canadian constitutional rights to refugees and entering immigrants. Immigrants can apply for asylum upon arrival in Canada, and their work permits are approved while they wait for the resolution of their cases. Instead of restricting refugee policies throughout the 1980s in the context of rising numbers of refugee claimants, Canada implemented visa requirements for those

countries that produced large numbers of asylum seekers. A visa requirement with El Salvador was introduced in 1978 (Buchignani and Indra 432).

17. Words misspelled include "El Centro Salvatore" (which should be Salvadoreño), "Morazán," a province of El Salvador that witnessed a lot of violence, and "Guadalupe." As a result of Hospital's equation of left and right, Latin America emerges as a chaotic place where both sides terrorize innocent peasants and indigenous peoples in a pointless struggle for power. Although the left were also guilty of atrocities in the civil war, the majority of the sixty thousand dead were killed at the hands of Salvadoran military troops backed, advised, and trained by the United States. Thanks to Claire F. Fox for these observations.

18. Cultural industries in the NAFTA agreement are defined as the publication, distribution, and sale of books, magazines, periodicals, and newspapers; and the production, distribution, sale, or exhibition of film or video, audio or video music recordings, radio communications, and cable TV and satellite programming (Mulcahy 188).

19. Until the 1930s, the Canadian market had largely been dominated by British cultural products, especially journals and books. In response to increasing U.S. domination, Canada began to establish a variety of cultural institutions to provide the state with tools to realize some of the goals of cultural nationalism: Canadian public radio, the Canadian Broadcasting Corporation, and the National Film Board. Another wave of cultural nationalism emerged in the 1960s when the Canadian Film Development Corporation (now Telefilm Canada) was created to promote a feature film industry independent of Hollywood (Rutherford).

Conclusion

1. The Mexican government has made great strides, reducing illiteracy to less than eight percent, compared with around twenty percent two decades ago, which places it leagues ahead of Central American countries (except Costa Rica) and even beyond Latin America's other economic powerhouse, Brazil. Yet this success has not also resulted in an increase in active reading (Bensinger)

2. See Pamela Smorkaloff for an initial examination of these issues.

Bibliography

Adamson, Joni. "Literature-and-Environment Studies and the Influence of the Environmental Justice Movement." *Blackwell Companion to American Literature and Culture.* Ed. Paul Lauter. Oxford: Blackwell, forthcoming.

———. *The Middle Place: American Indian Literature, Environmental Justice, and Ecocriticism.* Tucson: University of Arizona Press, 2001.

Alarcón, Justo S. "The Border: To Cross at the Crossroads in Three Chicano Literary Texts." *Chicano Border Culture and Folklore.* Eds. Arturo Ramírez and José Villarino. San Diego: Marin Publications, 1992. 65–75.

Aldama, Frederick Luis. *Postethnic Narrative Criticism: Magicorealism in Oscar "Zeta" Acosta, Ana Castillo, Julie Dash, Hanif Kureishi, and Salman Rushdie.* Austin: University of Texas Press, 2003.

Alper, Donald K., and Robert L. Monahan. "The Attraction of a New Academic Frontier: The Case of Canadian Studies in the U.S." *Alternative Frontiers: Voices from the Mountain West Canadian Studies Conference.* Eds. Allen Seager et al. Montréal: Association for Canadian Studies, 1997. 173–83.

Ammons, Elizabeth. *Conflicting Stories: American Women Writers at the Turn into the Twentieth Century.* New York: Oxford University Press, 1991.

Ammons, Elizabeth, and Valerie Rohy, eds. *American Local Color Writing, 1880–1920.* New York: Penguin, 1998.

Anaya, Rudolfo A. *Bless Me Ultima.* Berkeley: Quinto Sol Publications, 1972.

Andreas, Peter. *Border Games: Policing the U.S.-Mexico Divide.* Ithaca: Cornell University Press, 2000.

Andrews, Jennifer. "Border Trickery and Dog Bones: A Conversation with Thomas King." *Studies in Canadian Literature* 242 (1999): 161–85.

Andrews, Jennifer, and Priscilla L. Walton. "Rethinking Canadian and American Nationality: Indigeneity and the 49th Parallel in Thomas King." *American Literary History* 18.3 (October 2006): 600–617.

Anzaldúa, Gloria. *Borderlands/La Frontera: The New Mestiza.* San Francisco: Aunt Lute Books, 1987.

Aranda, José F., Jr. *When We Arrive: A New Literary History of Mexican America.* Tucson: University of Arizona Press, 2003.

Arnold, Ellen L., ed. *Conversations with Leslie Marmon Silko.* Jackson: University Press of Mississippi, 2000.

Assembly of First Nations and the National Congress of American Indians. "Declaration of Kinship and Cooperation among the Indigenous Peoples and Nations of North America through the Assembly of First Nations and the National Congress of American Indians." July 23, 1999 http://www.afn.ca. Accessed March 20, 2001.

Atwood, Margaret. "Canadian-American Relations: Surviving the Eighties." *Second Words: Selected Critical Prose.* Toronto: Anansi, 1982. 371–91.

Barrientos, Tanya Maria. *Frontera Street.* New York: Penguin, 2002.

Beauregard, Guy. "The Emergence of 'Asian Canadian Literature': Can Lit's Obscene Supplement?" *Essays on Canadian Writing* 67 (Spring 1999): 53–75.

Becerra, Angela. "Bridging the Two Laredos: The Day the River Turned Red." *San Antonio Living* June 21, 2005 http://www.woai.com/living/books/story.aspx?content_id=15AD48F7-7962-4360-B6F7-FB5CBD483796. Accessed August 1, 2005.

Benito, Jesús, and Ana María Manzanas. "Border(lands) and Border Writing: Introductory Essay." *Literature and Ethnicity in the Cultural Borderlands.* Eds. Jesús Benito and Ana María Manzanas. Amsterdam: Rodopi, 2002. 1–21.

Bensinger, Ken. "Chilling Mystery: Why Don't Mexicans Read Books?" *Christian Science Monitor* February 16, 2005 http://www.csmonitor.com/2005/0216/p01s04-woam.html Accessed July 15, 2005.

Berreiro, Jose. "Direct Divisions." *Native Americas* 28.1 (March 31, 2001): 2.

Beverley, Daurio, ed. *The Power to Bend Spoons: Interviews with Canadian Novelists.* Toronto: Mercury, 1998.

Bevis, William. "Native American Novels: Homing In." *Recovering the Word: Essays on Native American Literature.* Eds. Brian Swann and Arnold Krupat. Berkeley: University of California Press, 1987. 580–620.

Blaise, Clark. *I Had a Father: A Post-Modern Autobiography.* Reading: Addison-Wesley, 1993.

Blume, Klaus. "Young Mexican Writers Bid Farewell to Magical Realism." *The Age* July 15, 2002 http://www.theage.com.au/articles/2002/07/15/1026185155152.html. Accessed August 26, 2004.

Bolton, Herbert Eugene. "The Epic of Greater America." *Do the Americas Have a Common History? A Critique of the Bolton Theory.* Ed. Lewis Hanke. New York: Knopf, 1964. 67–100.

Boyle, T. Coraghessan. *The Tortilla Curtain.* New York: Penguin, 1995.

Brady, Mary Pat. *Extinct Lands, Temporal Geographies: Chicana Literature and the Urgency of Space.* Durham: Duke University Press, 2002.

Brickhouse, Anna. *Transamerican Literary Relations and the Nineteenth-Century Public Sphere.* Cambridge: Cambridge University Press, 2004.

Brito, Aristeo. *The Devil in Texas = El diablo en Texas*. Trans. David William Foster. Tempe: Bilingual Press/Editorial Bilingue, 1990.

Brooks, Stephen. "Comments on 'Here's Where We Get Canadian: English-Canadian Nationalism and Popular Culture.'" *American Review of Canadian Studies* 32.1 (Spring 2002): 35–40.

Brown, Russell M. "Borderlines and Borderlands in English Canada: The Written Line." *The Border as Fiction*. Orono: Borderlands Project, 1990. 13–70.

———. "Crossing Borders." *Essays on Canadian Writing* 22 (Summer 1981): 154–68.

———. "The Written Line." *Borderlands: Essays in Canadian-American Relations*. Ed. Robert Lecker. Toronto: ECW Press, 1991. 1–27.

Bruce-Novoa, Juan. *RetroSpace: Collected Essays on Chicano Literature, Theory, and History*. Houston: Arte Público Press, 1990.

———. "Righting the Oral Tradition." *Denver Quarterly* 16.3 (Fall 1981): 78–86.

Bruchac, Joseph. *Survival This Way: Interviews with American Indian Poets*. Tucson: University of Arizona Press, 1987.

Brydon, Diana. "The Stone's Memory: An Interview with Janette Turner Hospital." *Commonwealth Novel in English* 4.1 (Spring 1991): 14–23.

Buchignani, Norman, and Doreen Indra. "Vanishing Acts: Illegal Immigration in Canada as a Sometime Social Issue." *Illegal Immigration in America*. Eds. David W. Haines and Karen E. Rosenblum. Westport: Greenwood Press, 1999. 415–50.

Calderón, Héctor. "The Novel and the Community of Readers: Rereading Tomás Rivera's *Y no se lo tragó la tierra*." Calderón and Saldívar, *Criticism* 97–113.

Calderón, Héctor, and José David Saldívar, eds. *Criticism in the Borderlands: Studies in Chicano Literature, Culture, and Ideology*. Durham: Duke University Press, 1991.

———. "Editors' Introduction: Criticism in the Borderlands." Calderón and Saldívar, *Criticism* 1–7.

Caldwell, Wendy. "Narrating the Border: An Interview with Lucrecia Guerrero." *South Carolina Modern Language Review* 3.1 (Spring 2004) http://alpha1 .fmarion.edu/~scmlr/V3/newvoice.htm. Accessed October 5, 2005.

Campbell, Federico. *Tijuana: Stories on the Border*. Trans. Debra A. Castillo. Berkeley: University of California Press, 1995. Originally published as *Tijuanenses*. México, D. F.: Editorial Joaquín Mortiz, 1989.

Cantú, Norma Elia. *Canícula: Snapshots of a Girlhood En La Frontera*. Albuquerque: University of New Mexico Press, 1995.

Cariou, Warren. "Native Novels Range from Passionate to Polished." *Canadian Forum* 38.3 (December 1999): 38–39.

Casares, Oscar. *Brownsville: Stories*. Boston: Back Bay Books, 2003.

Castillo, Debra. "Fuentes Fronterizo." *Arizona Journal of Hispanic Cultural Studies* 4 (2000): 159–74.

————. "'Pesadillas de noche, amanecer de silencio': Miguel Méndez and Margarita Oropeza." *Studies in Twentieth Century Literature* 25.1 (Winter 2001): 46–62.

————. "Travails with Time: An Interview with Carlos Fuentes." *Review of Contemporary Fiction* 8.2 (Summer 1988): 153–65.

Castillo, Debra, and María Socorro Tabuenca Córdoba. *Border Women: Writing from La Frontera*. Minneapolis: University of Minnesota Press, 2002.

Cervantes, Lorna Dee. *Emplumada*. Pittsburgh: University of Pittsburgh Press, 1981.

Chabram-Dernersesian, Angie. "Latina/o: Another Site of Struggle, Another Site of Accountability." *Critical Latin American and Latino Studies*. Ed. Juan Poblete. University of Minnesota Press, 2003. 105–20.

Chan, Sucheng. "The Exclusion of Chinese Women, 1870–1943." *Entry Denied: Exclusions and the Chinese Community in America, 1882–1943*. Ed. Chan. Philadelphia: Temple University Press, 1991. 94–146.

Chang, Gordon H. "Writing the History of Chinese Immigrants to America." *South Atlantic Quarterly* 98.1–2 (Winter–Spring 1999): 135–42.

Chávez, Denise. *Face of an Angel*. New York: Farrar, Straus, and Giroux, 1994.

————. *The Last of the Menu Girls*. Houston: Arte Público Press, 1986.

Cheung, King-Kok, ed. *An Interethnic Companion to Asian American Literature*. New York: Cambridge University Press, 1997.

Chin, Frank, Jeffery Paul, Paul Chan, Lawson Fusao Inada, and Shawn Hsu Wong, eds. *Aiiieeeee! An Anthology of Asian-American Writers*. Washington, DC: Howard University Press, 1974.

Chin, Ko-Lin. *Smuggled Chinese: Clandestine Immigration to the United States*. Philadelphia: Temple University Press, 1999.

Chuh, Kandice. "Of Hemispheres and Other Spheres: Navigating Karen Tei Yamashita's Literary World." *American Literary History* 18.3 (October 2006): 618–37.

Chun, Gloria H. "'Go West . . . to China': Chinese American Identity in the 1930s." *Claiming America: Constructing Chinese American Identities during the Exclusion Era*. Eds. K. Scott Wong and Sucheng Chan. Philadelphia: Temple University Press, 1998. 165–90.

Cisneros, Sandra. *Caramelo or Puro Cuento*. New York: Knopf, 2002.

————. *The House on Mango Street*. Houston: Arte Público Press, 1983.

————. *Woman Hollering Creek and Other Stories*. New York: Random House, 1991.

Clarkson, Stephen. *Uncle Sam and Us: Globalization: Neoconservatism, and the Canadian State*. Toronto: University of Toronto Press, 2002.

Cohn, Deborah H. *History and Memory in the Two Souths: Recent Southern and Spanish American Fiction*. Nashville: Vanderbilt University Press, 1999.

Coltelli, Laura. "*Almanac of the Dead*: An Interview with Leslie Marmon Silko." *Conversations with Leslie Marmon Silko*. Ed. Ellen L. Arnold. Jackson: University of Mississippi Press, 2000. 119–34.

Conde, Rosina. *Women on the Road.* San Diego: San Diego State University Press, 1994.

Cook-Lynn, Elizabeth. *Why I Can't Read Wallace Stegner and Other Essays: A Tribal Voice.* Madison: University of Wisconsin Press, 1996.

Cooper Alarcón, Daniel. *The Aztec Palimpsest: Mexico in the Modern Imagination.* Tucson: University of Arizona Press, 1997.

Correas Zapata, Celia. "Carlos Fuentes, *La frontera de cristal:* una novela en nueve cuentos." *Explicación de textos literarios* 25.1 (1996): 117–18.

Coupland, Douglas. *Souvenir of Canada.* Vancouver: Douglas and McIntyre, 2002.

Cox, Timothy J. *Postmodern Tales of Slavery in the Americas: From Alejo Carpentier to Charles Johnson.* New York: Garland, 2001.

"Cultural Industries in the Latin American Economy: Current Status and Outlook in the Context of Globalization." *Publications and Studies Organization of American States* http://www.oas.org/culture/series6_e.html. Accessed July 15, 2001.

Cummings, Joe. "A Review of Chinese Immigration to Mexico." N.d. http://www.mexconnect.com/mex_/travel/jcummings/jcchina.html. Accessed December 1, 2004.

Dash, J. Michael. *The Other America: Caribbean Literature in a New World Context.* Charlottesville: University Press of Virginia, 1998.

Daurio, Beverley, ed. *The Power to Bend Spoons: Interviews with Canadian Novelists.* Toronto: Mercury Press, 1998.

Davey, Frank. *Post-National Arguments: The Politics of the Anglophone-Canadian Novel since 1967.* Toronto: University of Toronto Press, 1993.

Davis, Mike. *City of Quartz: Excavating the Future in Los Angeles.* London: Verso, 1990.

Deloria, Vine, Jr. *Custer Died for Your Sins: An Indian Manifesto.* New York: Macmillan, 1969.

del Pino, Salvador Rodrig. "Miguel Méndez: The Commitment Continues." *Bilingual Review* 19.3 (September 1, 1994): 89–92.

Denning, Michael. *Culture in the Age of Three Worlds.* London: Verso, 2004.

———. "Globalization in Cultural Studies: Process and Epoch." *European Journal of Cultural Studies* 4.3 (August 2001): 351–64.

Desmond, Jane C., and Virginia R. Domínguez. "Resituating American Studies in a Critical Internationalism." *American Quarterly* 48.3 (1998): 475–90.

Di-Bella, Manuel José, Rogelio Reyes, Gabriel Trujillo Muñoz, and Harry Polkinhorn, eds. *Literatura de la frontera México-Norteamericana: Cuentos/U.S.-Mexican Border Literature: Short Stories.* San Diego: San Diego State University, 1989.

Dixon, Terrell. Letter. Forum on Literatures of the Environment. *PMLA* 114 (October 1999): 1093–94.

Duarte, Stella Pope. *Let Their Spirits Dance.* New York: Rayo, 2002.

Dunaway, David King, and Sara L. Spurgeon, eds. *Writing the Southwest.* Albuquerque: University of New Mexico Press, 2003.

Dunn, Timothy J. *The Militarization of the U.S.-Mexico Border, 1978–1992: Low-Intensity Conflict Doctrine Comes Home.* Austin: CMAS Books, 1996.

"Early Immigrant Inspection along the US/Mexican Border." U.S. Citizenship and Immigration Service. January 20, 2006 http://www.uscis.gov/graphics/aboutus/history/articles/MBTEXT.htm. Accessed September 11, 2006.

Egan, Linda. "The Looking-Glass Frontier: Faces in a Buried Mirror." *Bilingual Review* 21.2 (May–August 1996): 179–87.

Eschbach, Karl, Jacqueline Hagan, and Nestor Rodriguez. "Deaths during Undocumented Migration: Trends and Policy Implications in the New Era of Homeland Security." *Defense of the Alien* 26 (2003): 37–52.

Espiritu, Yen Le. *Asian American Panethnicity: Bridging Institutions and Identities.* Philadelphia: Temple University Press, 1992.

Faris, Wendy B. *Ordinary Enchantments: Magical Realism and the Remystification of Narrative.* Nashville: Vanderbilt University Press, 2004.

Ferens, Dominika. *Edith and Winnifred Eaton: Chinatown Missions and Japanese Romances.* Urbana: University of Illinois Press, 2002.

Fetterley, Judith, and Marjorie Pryse. *Writing out of Place: Regionalism, Women, and American Literary Culture.* Urbana: University of Illinois Press, 2003.

Fitz, Earl E. *Rediscovering the New World: Inter-American Literature in a Comparative Context.* Iowa City: University of Iowa Press, 1991.

Flick, Jane. "Reading Notes for Thomas King's *Green Grass, Running Water.*" *Canadian Literature* 161–62 (Summer/Autumn 1999): 140–72.

Flores, Juan. "Latino Studies: New Contexts, New Concepts." *Critical Latin American and Latino Studies.* Ed Juan Poblete. Minneapolis: University of Minnesota Press, 2003. 191–205.

Fox, Claire F. "Cultural Exemptions, Cultural Solutions." *The Fence and the River.* Minneapolis: University of Minnesota Press, 1999. 15–39.

———. "Hollywood's Backlot: Carlos Fuentes, *The Old Gringo,* and National Cinema." *Iris: A Journal of Theory on Sound and Image* 13 (Summer 1991): 63–86.

———. "Left Sensationalism at the Transnational Crime Scene: Recent Detective Fiction from the U.S.-Mexico Border Region." *World Bank Literature.* Ed. Amitava Kumar. Minneapolis: University of Minnesota Press, 2003. 184–200.

Fraser, Marian Botsford. *Walking the Line.* San Francisco: Sierra Club, 1990.

Fuentes, Carlos. *The Buried Mirror: Reflections on Spain and the New World.* Boston: Houghton Mifflin, 1992.

———. *Cristóbal Nonato.* México, D. F.: Fondo de Cultura Economica, 1987.

———. *The Crystal Frontier: A Novel in Nine Stories.* Trans. Alfred Mac Adam. New York: Farrar, Straus, and Giroux, 1997. Trans. of *La frontera de cristal: Una novella en nueve cuentos.*

————. *La frontera de cristal: Una novela en nueve cuentos.* México, D. F.: Alfaguara, 1995.

————. *Gringo viejo.* México, D. F.: Fondo de Cultura Económica, 1985.

————. *A New Time for Mexico.* Trans. Marina Gutman Castañeda and Carlos Fuentes. New York: Farrar, Straus, and Giroux, 1996.

————. *The Old Gringo.* Trans. Margaret Sayers Peden and Carlos Fuentes. New York: Farrar, Straus and Giroux, 1985. Trans. of *Gringo Viejo.*

García, Mario T. *Desert Immigrants: The Mexicans of El Paso, 1880–1920.* New Haven: Yale University Press, 1981.

García Canclini, Néstor. *Consumers and Citizens: Globalization and Multicultural Conflicts.* Trans. George Yúdice. Minneapolis: University of Minnesota Press, 2001.

————. *La globalización imaginada.* Buenos Aires: Paidos, 1999.

————. *Hybrid Cultures: Strategies for Entering and Leaving Modernity.* Trans. Christopher L. Chiappari and Silvia L. López. Minneapolis: University of Minnesota Press, 1995.

Gates, Henry Louis, Jr. *Figures in Black: Words, Signs, and the Racial Self.* New York: Oxford University Press, 1987.

Gerson, Carole. "Canadian Women Writers and American Markets, 1880–1940." *Context North America: Canadian/U.S. Literary Relations.* Ed. Camille R. La Bossière. Ottawa: University of Ottawa Press, 1994. 107–18.

Gibbins, Roger. "Meaning and Significance of the Canadian-American Border." *Borders and Border Politics in a Globalizing World.* Eds. Paul Ganster and David E. Lorey. Lanham: SR Books, 2005. 151–67.

Gier, Jean Vengua, and Carla Alicia Tejeda. "An Interview with Karen Tei Yamashita." *Jouvert* 2.2. (1998) http://social.chass.ncsu.edu/jouvert/v2i2/yamashi.htm. Accessed December 1, 2004.

Gilb, Dagoberto. *The Magic of Blood.* Albuquerque: University of New Mexico Press, 1993.

Gillies, Rob. "Canada No Plans for Guard on Border." *Seattle Post Intelligencer* May 16, 2006 http://seattlepi.nwsource.com/national/1101AP_Canada_US_Immigration.html. Accessed May 18, 2006.

Gilroy, Paul. *The Black Atlantic: Modernity and Double Consciousness.* London: Verso, 1993.

Goellnicht, Donald C. "A Long Labour: The Protracted Birth of Asian Canadian Literature." *Essays on Canadian Writing* 72 (2000): 1–41.

Gómez-Peña, Guillermo. *The New World Border: Prophecies, Poems, and Loqueras for the End of the Century.* San Francisco: City Lights, 1996.

González, Alfonso. "La intensificación de la problemática de la frontera político-cultural en *La frontera de cristal* de Carlos Fuentes y *Columbus* de Ignacio Solares." *Explicación de Textos Literarios* 28.1–2 (1999–2000): 16–21.

González, Jovita. *Dew on the Thorn.* Houston: Arte Público Press, 1997.

González Rodríguez, Sergio. "La frontera de Fuentes." *Reforma* (December 20, 1995): 7.

Gray, John. *Lost in North America: The Imaginary Canadian in the American Dream.* Vancouver: Talonbooks, 1994.

Grinde, Donald, Jr. "Iroquois Border Crossings: Place, Politics, and the Jay Treaty." *Globalization on the Line: Culture, Capital, and Citizenship at U.S. Borders.* Ed. Claudia Sadowski-Smith. New York: Palgrave, 2002. 167–80.

Gruesz, Kirsten Silva. *Ambassadors of Culture: The Transamerican Origins of Latino Writing.* Princeton: Princeton University Press, 2002.

———. "The Gulf of Mexico System and the 'Latinness' of New Orleans." *American Literary History* 18.3 (October 2006): 468–95.

———. "Translation: A Key(Word) into the Language of America(nists)." *American Literary History* 16.1 (Spring 2004): 85–92.

Guerrero, Lucrecia. *Chasing Shadows: Stories.* San Francisco: Chronicle Books, 2000.

Gunn, Giles. "Interdisciplinary Studies." *Introduction to Scholarship in Modern Languages and Literatures.* Ed. Joseph Gibaldi. New York: Modern Language Association of America, 1992. 239–61.

Gwyn, Richard. *Nationalism without Walls: The Unbearable Lightness of Being Canadian.* Toronto: McClelland and Stewart, 1995.

Gyory, Andrew. *Closing the Gate: Race, Politics, and the Chinese Exclusion Act.* Chapel Hill: University of North Carolina Press, 1998.

Gzowski, Peter. "Peter Gzowski Interviews Thomas King on *Green Grass, Running Water.*" *Canadian Literature* 161–62 (Summer/Autumn 1999): 65–76.

Habell-Pallán, Michelle. "'Don't Call Us Hispanic': Popular Latino Theater in Vancouver." *Latino/a Popular Culture.* Eds. Michelle Habell-Pallán and Mary Romero. New York: New York University Press, 2002. 174–89.

Hamelin, Christine. "'Novelist as Urgent Quester': An Interview with Janette Turner Hospital." *Australian and New Zealand Studies in Canada* 9 (June 1993): 106–11.

Handley, George B. *Postslavery Literatures in the Americas: Family Portraits in Black and White.* Charlottesville: University of Virginia Press, 2000.

Harder, Bernie. "The Power of Borders in Native American Literature: Leslie Marmon Silko's *Almanac of the Dead.*" *American Indian Culture and Research Journal* 24.4 (2000): 95–106.

Hardt, Michael, and Antonio Negri. *Empire.* Cambridge: Harvard University Press, 2000.

Hart, Michael. Address to the Wilson Center, Washington, DC. July 8, 2005.

Harvey, David. *The Condition of Postmodernity: An Enquiry into the Origins of Cultural Change.* Oxford: Blackwell, 1989.

———. *The New Imperialism.* Oxford: Oxford University Press, 2003.

———. *Spaces of Hope.* Berkeley: University of California Press, 2000.

Heninghan, Stephen. *When Words Deny the World: The Reshaping of Canadian Writing.* Erin: Porcupine Press, 2002.

Hill, Richard, Sr. "Border Check." *Native Americas* 18.1 (March 31, 2001): 64.

Hinojosa, Rolando. *Becky and Her Friends.* Houston: Arte Público Press, 1990.

———. *Klail City.* Houston: Arte Público Press, 1987.

Hirsch, Bud. "'Stay Calm, Be Brave, Wait for the Signs': Sign-Offs and Send-Ups in the Fiction of Thomas King." *Western American Literature* 39.3 (Fall 2004): 145–75.

Hirsch, Marianne. "Family Pictures: *Maus,* Mourning, and Post-Memory." *Discourse* 15.2 (Winter 1992): 3–29.

Hodara, Joseph. "Escritura y frontera noroeste Mexicana: Bases para una investigación." *Estudios interdisciplinarios de América Latina y el Caribe* 5.1 (June 1994) http://www.tau.ac.il/eial/V_1/hodara.htm. Accessed June 3, 2005.

Hopkinson, Amanda. "The Crystal Frontier." *Independent* (May 31, 1998): 32.

Hospital, Janette Turner. *Borderline.* New York: E. P. Dutton, 1985.

———. *Dislocations.* Toronto: McClelland and Stewart, 1986.

———. "Letter to a New York Editor." *Meanjin* 47.3 (Spring 1988): 560–64.

Hsiao-ching Li, Florence. "Imagining the Mother/Motherland: Karen Tei Yamashita's *Tropic of Orange* and Theresa Hak Kyung Cha's *Dictee.*" *Concentric* 30.1 (January 2004): 149–67.

Hsu, Ruth Y. "The Cartography of Justice and Truthful Refractions Found in Karen Tei Yamashita's *Tropic of Orange.*" *Transnational Asian American Literature: Sites and Transits.* Eds. Shirley Geok-Lin Lim et al. Philadelphia: Temple University Press, 2006. 75–99.

Hu-DeHart, Evelyn. *Across the Pacific: Asian Americans and Globalization.* Philadelphia: Temple University Press, 1999.

———. *Yaqui Resistance and Survival: The Struggle for Land and Autonomy, 1821–1910.* Madison: University of Wisconsin Press, 1984.

"Huge Alien-Smuggling Ring Used Canada's Refugee System." *Globe and Mail* [Toronto] December 11, 1998: A1.

Hunt, Alex. "The Radical Geography of Silko's *Almanac of the Dead.*" *Western American Literature* 39.3 (Fall 2004): 256–78.

"Indigenous Peoples and the Free Trade Area of the Americas." An Alternative Summit, Call for Papers, Panels, and Involvement. Salle Kondiaronk, Huron Reserve. Part of People's Summit of the Americas. Québec City. April 19–21, 2002 http://www.nadir.org/nadir/iniativ/agp/ftaa/noticias_nl/indigenous.htm Accessed June 1, 2004.

Insley, Jennifer. "Border Criminals, Border Crime: Hard-Boiled Fiction on the Mexican-American Frontier." *Confluencia* 19.2 (Spring 2004): 38–49.

"Island Channel a Magnet to Illegal Immigrants from Asia." *Detroit Free Press* February 9, 2000 http://www.freep.com/news/statewire/sw6128_20000209.htm. Accessed February 9, 2000.

Islas, Arturo. *Migrant Souls: A Novel.* New York: Morrow, 1990.

Jay, Gregory S. *American Literature and the Culture Wars.* Ithaca: Cornell University Press, 1997.

Jay, Paul. "The Myth of 'America' and the Politics of Location: Modernity, Border Studies, and the Literature of the Americas." *Arizona Quarterly* 54.2 (1998): 165–92.

Johnson, Reed. "His Treasured Tijuana." *Los Angeles Times* November 1, 2004 http://www.zocalola.org/press_release.html. Accessed March 2, 2005.

Kaplan, Amy. *The Anarchy of Empire in the Making of U.S. Culture.* Cambridge: Harvard University Press, 2002.

Kaplan, Amy, and Donald Pease. *Cultures of United States Imperialism.* Durham: Duke University Press, 1993.

Karem, Jeff. *The Romance of Authenticity: The Cultural Politics of Regional and Ethnic Literatures.* Charlottesville: University of Virginia Press, 2004.

Kaup, Monika. *Rewriting North American Borders in Chicano and Chicana Narrative.* New York: Peter Lang, 2001.

Keahey, Deborah. *Making It Home: Place in Canadian Prairie Literature.* Winnipeg: University of Manitoba Press, 1998.

Keller, Gary D. "A Crossroad Marks the Spot: Miguel Méndez, Master of Place, and the Bilingual Press/Editorial Bilingüe." *Bilingual Review/La Revista Bilingüe* 19.3 (September 1994): 1–98.

King, Thomas. "Borders." *One Good Story, That One.* Toronto: HarperPerennial, 1993. 131–47.

———. "Coyote Lives." [Interview with Jeffrey Canton.] *The Power to Bend Spoons.* Ed. Beverley Daurio. Toronto: Mercury Press, 1998. 90–97.

———. "Godzilla vs. Post-Colonial." *World Literature Written in English* 30.2 (1990): 10–16.

———. *Green Grass, Running Water.* Toronto: Harper, 1993.

———. Introduction. *All My Relations: An Anthology of Contemporary Canadian Native Fiction.* Ed. Thomas King. Toronto: McClelland, 1990.

———. *Medicine River.* Markham, Ontario: Viking, 1990.

———. *Truth and Bright Water.* Toronto: Harper, 2000.

Konrad, Victor. "The Borderlands of the United States and Canada in the Context of North American Development." *International Journal of Canadian Studies* 4 (Fall 1991): 77–95.

Kumar, Amitava. Introduction. *World Bank Literature.* Ed. Amitava Kumar. Minneapolis: University of Minnesota, 2003. xvii–xxxiii.

Kutzinski, Vera M. *Sugar's Secrets: Race and the Erotics of Cuban Nationalism.* Charlottesville: University Press of Virginia, 1993.

Ladner, Kiera L. "Women and Blackfoot Nationalism." *Journal of Canadian Studies* 35.2 (Summer 2000): 35–60.

LaDow, Beth. *The Medicine Line: Life and Death on a North American Borderland.* New York: Routledge, 2001.

———. "Sanctuary: Native Border Crossings and the North American West." *American Review of Canadian Studies* 31.1–2 (Spring/Summer 2001): 25–42.

Langer, Beryl. "Interview with Janette Turner-Hospital." *Australian-Canadian Studies* 9.1–2 (1991): 143–50.

Larsen, Neil. "The 'Boom' Novel and the Cold War in Latin America." *Modern Fiction Studies* 38.3 (Autumn 1992): 771–84.

"Latin America: Looking North or South? Erasing the Border of Time—An Interview with Carlos Fuentes." *New Perspectives Quarterly* 18.1 (Winter 2001): 8–11.

Ledesma, Alberto. "Narratives of Undocumented Mexican Immigration as Chicana/o Acts of Intellectual and Political Responsibility." *Decolonial Voices: Chicana and Chicano Cultural Studies in the 21st Century.* Eds. Arturo J. Aldama and Naomi H. Quinonez. Bloomington: Indiana University Press, 2002. 330–54.

Lee, Erika. *At America's Gates: Chinese Immigration during the Exclusion Era, 1882–1943.* Chapel Hill: University of North Carolina Press: 2003.

———. "Orientalisms in the Americas: A Hemispheric Approach to Asian American History." *Journal of Asian American Studies* 8.3 (2005): 235–56.

Lee, Rachel C. *The Americas of Asian American Literature: Gendered Fictions of Nation and Transnation.* Princeton: Princeton University Press, 1999.

Levander, Caroline F., and Robert S. Levine. "Introduction: Hemispheric American Literary History." *American Literary History* 18.3 (Summer 2006): 1–9.

Limón, José Eduardo. *American Encounters: Greater Mexico, the United States, and the Erotics of Culture.* Boston: Beacon Press, 1998.

Ling, Amy. "Edith Eaton: Pioneer Chinamerican Writer and Feminist." *American Literary Realism* 16 (Autumn 1983): 287–98.

Lowe, Lisa. *Immigrant Acts: On Asian American Cultural Politics.* Durham: Duke University Press, 1996.

Mackey, Eva. *The House of Difference: Cultural Politics and National Identity in Canada.* London: Routledge, 1999.

Maclulich, T. D. "What Was Canadian Literature? Taking Stock of the Canlit Industry." *Essays on Canadian Writing* 30 (1984): 17–34.

Martí, Jose. *The America of José Martí: Selected Writings.* Trans. Juan de Onís. New York: Noonday Press, 1953.

Martínez, Oscar J. *Border People: Life and Society in the U.S.-Mexico Borderlands.* Tucson: University of Arizona Press, 1994.

Martín-Rodríguez, Manuel M. *Life in Search of Readers: Reading (in) Chicano/a Literature.* Albuquerque: University of New Mexico Press, 2003.

———. "Recovering Chicano/a Literary Histories: Historiography beyond Borders." *PMLA* 120 (May 2005): 796–805.

Massey, Doreen B. *For Space.* London: Thousand Oaks, 2005.

Massey, Douglas. Foreword. *Smuggled Chinese: Clandestine Immigration to the United States.* Ed. Ko-Lin Chin. Philadelphia: Temple University Press, 1999. ix–xiv.

McCann, Sean. "Connecting Links: The Anti-Progressivism of Sui Sin Far." *Yale Journal of Criticism* 12.1 (1999): 73–88.

McClennen, Sophia A. "Inter-American Studies or Imperial American Studies?" *Comparative American Studies* 3.4 (2005): 393–413.

McCracken, Ellen. "Hybridity and the Space of the Border in the Writing of Norma Elia Cantú." *Studies in Twentieth Century Literature* 25.1 (Winter 2001): 261–80.

McIlwraith, Thomas F. "Transport in the Borderlands, 1763–1920." *Borderlands: Essays in Canadian-American Relations.* Ed. Robert Lecker. Toronto: ECW Press, 1991. 54–79.

McKay, Robert R. "Mexican Americans and Repatriation." *Handbook of Texas Online* http://www.tsha.utexas.edu/handbook/online/articles/MM/pqmyk.html. Accessed December 3, 2005.

McKee Irwin, Robert. "¿Qué hacen los nuevos Americanistas? Collaborative Strategies for a Postnationalist American Studies." *Comparative American Studies* 2.3 (September 2004): 303–23.

———. "Toward a Border Gnosis of the Borderlands: Joaquín Murrieta and Nineteenth-Century U.S.-Mexico Border Culture." *Nepantla* 2.3 (2001): 509–37.

McKenna, Teresa. "'Immigrants in Our Own Land': A Chicano Literature Review and Pedagogical Assessment." *ADE Bulletin* 91 (Winter 1988): 30–38.

Méndez, Miguel M. *Peregrinos de Aztlán.* Tucson: Editorial Peregrinos, 1974.

———. *Pilgrims in Aztlán.* Trans. David William Foster. Tempe: Bilingual Press/Editorial Bilingüe, 1992. Trans. of *Peregrinos de Aztlán.*

Méndez-Ramírez, Hugo. "Estrategias para entrar y salir de la globalización en *La frontera de cristal* de Carlos Fuentes." *Hispanic Review* 70.4 (Fall 2002): 581–99.

Meyer, Melissa L., and Kerwin Lee Klein. "Native American Studies and the End of Ethnohistory." *Studying Native America: Problems and Prospects.* Ed. Russell Thornton. Madison: University of Wisconsin Press, 1998. 182–216.

Michaelson, Scott. "Between Japanese American Internment and the USA Patriot Act: The Borderlands and the Permanent State of Racial Exception." *Aztlan* 30.2 (Fall 2005): 87–111.

Michaelson, Scott, and David E. Johnson. "Border Secrets: An Introduction." *Border Theory: The Limits of Cultural Politics.* Eds. Scott Michaelson and David E. Johnson. Minneapolis: University of Minnesota Press, 1997. 1–39.

Miki, Roy. "Asiancy: Making Space for Asian Canadian Writing." *Privileging Positions: The Sites of Asian American Studies.* Eds. Gary Y. Okihiro, Marilyn Alquizola, Dorothy Fujita Rony, and K. Scott Wong. Pullman: Washington State University Press, 1995. 135–51.

Millard, Gregory, Sarah Riegel, and John Wright. "Here's Where We Get Canadian: English-Canadian Nationalism and Popular Culture." *American Review of Canadian Studies* 32.1 (Spring 2002): 11–34.

Miller, Jay. "Canadian Native Studies in the United States." *Northern Exposures:*

Scholarship on Canada in the United States. Eds. Karen Gould, Joseph T. Jockel, and William Metcalfe. Washington, DC: ASCUS, 1993. 373–81.

Mohica, Rafael H. "*La frontera de cristal: Una novela en nueve cuentos.*" *World Literature Today* 71.2 (Spring 1997): 354–61.

Mojica, Barbara. "Mysteries of Woman and of Glass Borders." *Américas* 49.1 (January/February 1997): 62–64.

Momaday, N. Scott. *House Made of Dawn.* New York: Harper and Row, 1968.

Moraga, Cherríe. *The Last Generation.* Boston: South End Press, 1993.

———. *Loving in the War Years: Lo que nunca pasó por sus labios.* Boston: South End Press, 1983.

Morton, Adam David. "The Social Function of Carlos Fuentes: A Critical Intellectual or in the 'Shadow of the State'?" *Bulletin of Latin American Research* 22.1 (2003): 27–51.

Mulcahy, Kevin V. "Cultural Imperialism and Cultural Sovereignty: U.S.-Canadian Cultural Relations." *American Review of Canadian Studies* 30.2 (Summer 2000): 181–206.

Murashige, Michael S. "Karen Tei Yamashita." *Words Matter: Conversations with Asian American Writers.* Ed. King-Kok Cheung. Honolulu: University of Hawaii Press, 2000. 320–42.

———. "Karen Tei Yamashita: An Interview." *Amerasia Journal* 20.3 (1994): 49–59.

Murphy, Gretchen. *Hemispheric Imaginings: The Monroe Doctrine and Narratives of U.S. Empire.* Durham: Duke University Press, 2005.

Muthyala, John. "*Almanac of the Dead:* The Dream of the Fifth World in the Borderlands." *Literature, Interpretation, Theory* 14 (2003): 357–85.

———. "Reworlding America: The Globalization of American Studies." *Cultural Critique* 47 (Spring 2001): 91–119.

Nagel, Joane. *American Indian Ethnic Renewal: Red Power and the Resurgence of Identity and Culture.* New York: Oxford University Press, 1996.

Nevins, Joseph. *Operation Gatekeeper: The Rise of the "Illegal Alien" and the Making of the U.S-Mexico Boundary.* New York: Routledge, 2002.

New, W. H. *Borderlands: How We Talk about Canada.* Vancouver: University of British Columbia, 1988.

———. *A History of Canadian Literature.* 2nd ed. Montreal: McGill-Queen's University Press, 2003.

Ngai, Mae M. *Impossible Subjects: Illegal Aliens and the Making of Modern America.* Princeton: Princeton University Press, 2004.

Nguyen, Viet Than, and Tina Chen. "Editors' Introduction to Postcolonial Asian America." *Jouvert* 4.3 (2000). http://social.chass.ncsu.edu/jouvert/v4i3/ed43.htm. Accessed April 29, 2003.

Norden, Christopher. "Ecological Restoration as Post-Colonial Ritual of Community in Three Native American Novels." *Studies in American Indian Literatures* 6.4 (Winter 1994): 94–106.

Norrell, Brenda. "Indigenous Border Summit Opposes Border Wall and Militarization." October 31, 2006. http://americas.irc-online.org/amcit/3648.

Oates, Joyce Carol. *Crossing the Border: Fifteen Tales*. New York: Vanguard Press, 1976.

Ong, Aihwa. *Flexible Citizenship: The Cultural Logics of Transnationality*. Durham: Duke University Press, 1999.

Ordiz Vázquez, Francisco Javier. "Carlos Fuentes y la identidad de México." *Revista Iberoamericana* 58 (April–June 1992): 527–38.

Otero, Gerardo, "Mexico's Double Movement: Neoliberal Globalism, the State, and Civil Society." *Mexico in Transition: Neoliberal Globalism, the State, and Civil Society*. Ed. Gerardo Otero. Nova Scotia: Fernwood Publishing, 2004. 1–17.

Owens, Louis. *Mixedblood Messages: Literature, Film, Family, Place*. Norman: University of Oklahoma Press, 1998.

Palumbo-Liu, David. *Asian/American: Historical Crossings of a Racial Frontier*. Stanford: Stanford University Press, 1999.

Panitch, Leo. "Globalization, States, and Left Strategies." *Social Justice* 23.1–2 (Spring–Summer 1996): 79–90.

Paredes, Américo. *George Washington Gómez: A Mexicotexan Novel*. Houston: Arte Público Press, 1990.

———. *"With His Pistol in His Hand": A Border Ballad and Its Hero*. Austin: University of Texas Press, 1958.

Parra, Andrea. Letter. Forum on Literatures of the Environment. *PMLA* 114 (1999): 1099–1100.

Patell, Cyrus R. K. "Comparative American Studies: Hybridity and Beyond." *American Literary History* 11.1 (1999): 166–86.

Payant, Katherine. "Borderland Themes in Sandra Cisneros's *Women Hollering Creek*." *The Immigrant Experience in North American Literature: Carving Out a Niche*. Eds. Katherine B. Payant and Toby Rose. Westport: Greenwood Press, 1999. 95–108.

Paz, Octavio. *The Labyrinth of Solitude: Life and Thought in Mexico*. Trans. Lysander Kemp. New York: Grove Press, 1961.

Peña-Delgado, Grace. "At Exclusion's Gate: Changing Categories of Race and Class among Chinese Fronterizos, 1890–1900." *Continental Crossroads: Remapping U.S.-Mexico Borderlands History*. Ed. Samuel J. Truett and Elliott Young. Durham: Duke University Press, 2004. 183–207.

Pérez-Firmat, Gustavo, ed. *Do the Americas Have a Common Literature?* Durham: Duke University Press, 1990.

Perkins, Clifford Alan. *Border Patrol: With the U.S. Immigration Service on the Mexican Boundary, 1910–54*. El Paso: Texas Western Press, 1978.

Peterson, Nancy. "Introduction: Native American Literature—From the Margins to the Mainstream." *Modern Fiction Studies* 45.1 (Spring 1999): 1–9.

Pierre, DBC. *Vernon God Little*. New York: Canongate, 2003.

"Plan espiritual de Aztlán, El." *Aztlán: Essays on the Chicano Homeland.* Eds. Rudolfo A. Anaya and Francisco A. Lomelí. Albuquerque: Academia/El Norte Publications, 1989. 1–5.

Polkinhorn, Harry, José Manuel Di Bella, and Rogelio Reyes, eds. *Borderlands Literature: Toward an Integrated Perspective/Encuentro internacional de la literatura de la frontera.* San Diego: San Diego State University, 1990.

Polkinhorn, Harry, Rogelio Reyes, and Gabriel Trujillo Muñoz, eds. *The Flight of the Eagle: Poetry on the U.S.-Mexico Border/El vuelo de águila: Poesía en la frontera México-Estados Unidos.* Calexico: Binational Press, 1993.

Polkinhorn, Harry, Gabriel Trujillo Muñoz, and Rogelio Reyes, eds. *La Línea: Ensayos sobre literatura frontizera México-Norteamericana/The Line: Essays on Mexican/American Border Literature.* San Diego: San Diego State University, 1987.

Porter, Carolyn. "'What We Know that We Don't Know': Remapping American Literary Studies." *American Literary History* 6.3 (Fall 1994): 467–526.

Pratt, Mary Louise. "The Short Story: The Long and Short of It." *Poetics: International Review for the Theory of Literature* 10.2-3 (June 1981): 175–94.

Price, John A. *Native Studies: American and Canadian Indians.* Toronto: McGraw-Hill Ryerson, 1978.

"Proclamation Restoring the Independence of the Sovereign Nation State of Blackfoot." November 29, 1999 http://membres.lycos.fr/Wild_West/Indiens16.html. Accessed March 20, 2001.

Purcell, Mark, and Joseph Nevins. "Pushing the Boundary: State Restructuring, State Theory, and the Case of the U.S.-Mexico Border Enforcement in the 1990s." *Political Geography* 24.2 (February 2005): 211–35.

Quintana, Alvina. *Homegirls: Chicana Literary Voices.* Philadelphia: Temple University Press, 1996.

Raat, Dirk W. *Mexico and the United States: Ambivalent Vistas.* Athens: University of Georgia Press, 1996.

Rabasa, George. *Floating Kingdom.* Minneapolis: Coffee House Press, 1997.

Rebar, Kelly. *Bordertown Café.* 1989. Winnipeg: Blizzard Publishing, 1992.

Rechy, John. *City of Night.* New York: Grove Press, 1963.

Reed, Ishmael. *Flight to Canada.* New York: Random House, 1976.

Ridington, Robin. "Happy Trails to You: Contexted Discourse and Indian Removals in Thomas King's *Truth and Bright Water.*" *Canadian Literature* 167 (Winter 2000): 89–106.

Ríos, Alberto Alvaro. *Capirotada: A Nogales Memoir.* Albuquerque: University of New Mexico Press, 1999.

———. *The Curtain of Trees: Stories.* Albuquerque: University of New Mexico Press, 1999.

———. *The Iguana Killer: Twelve Stories of the Heart.* Albuquerque: University of New Mexico Press, 1984.

———. *Pig Cookies and Other Stories.* San Francisco: Chronicle Books, 1995.

Rivera, Tomás. *Y no se lo tragó la tierra/And the Earth Did Not Devour Him.* Trans. Evangelina Vigil-Piñon. Houston: Arte Público Press, 1987.

Roach, Joseph. *Cities of the Dead: Circum-Atlantic Performance.* New York: Columbia University Press, 1996.

Robinson, Cecil. *Mexico and the Hispanic Southwest in American Literature.* Tucson: University of Arizona Press, 1977.

Rocco, Raymond A. "Latino Los Angeles: Reframing Boundaries/Borders." *The City: Los Angeles and Urban Theory at the End of the Twentieth Century.* Eds. Allen J. Scott and Edward W. Soja. Berkeley: University of California Press, 1996. 365–89.

Rodriguez, Richard. *Hunger of Memory: The Education of Richard Rodriguez.* Boston: D. R. Godine, 1981.

Rodríguez del Pino, Salvador. "Miguel Mendez: The Commitment Continues." *Bilingual Review/La Revista Bilingüe* 19.3 (September 1994): 89–92.

Rodríguez-Hernández, Raúl. "Viajes con Charley: Desplazamiento cultural e identidad en las fronteras de la modernidad." *Texto Crítico* 4.8 (Winter 2001): 137–47.

Rody, Caroline. "The Transnational Imagination: Karen Tei Yamashita's *Tropic of Orange.*" *Asian North American Identities beyond the Hyphen.* Eds. Eleanor Ty and Donald C. Goellnicht. Bloomington: Indiana University Press, 2004. 130–48.

Roh-Spaulding, Carol. "Beyond Biraciality: 'Race' as Process in the Work of Edith Eaton/Sui Sin Far and Winnifred Eaton/Onoto Watanna." *Asian American Literature in the International Context: Readings on Fiction, Poetry, Performance.* Eds. Rocío G. Davis and Sämi Ludwig. Münster: Lit Verlag, 2002. 21–35.

Romo, Ito. *El Puente = The Bridge.* Albuquerque: University of New Mexico Press, 2000.

Ropp, Steven Masami. "Secondary Migration and the Politics of Identity for Asian Latinos in Los Angeles." *Journal of Asian American Studies* 3.2 (2000): 219–29.

Rosenthal, Debra. *Race Mixture in Nineteenth-Century U.S. and Spanish American Fictions: Gender, Culture, and Nation Building.* Chapel Hill: University of North Carolina Press, 2004.

———. *Twilight on the Line: Underworlds and Politics at the U.S.-Mexico Border.* New York: W. W. Norton, 1998.

Rowe, John Carlos, ed. *Post-Nationalist American Studies.* Berkeley: University of California Press, 2000.

Ruiz de Burton, María Amparo. *The Squatter and the Don.* Eds. Rosaura Sánchez and Beatrice Pita. Houston: Arte Público Press, 1992.

———. *Who Would Have Thought It?* Eds. Rosaura Sánchez and Beatrice Pita. Houston Arte Público Press, 1995.

Rutherford, Paul. "Made in America: The Problem of Mass Culture in Canada." *The Beaver Bites Back: American Popular Culture in Canada.* Eds. David H.

Flaherty and Frank E. Manning. Montréal: McGill-Queen's University Press, 1993. 260–80.

Ryo, Emily. "Through the Back Door: Applying Theories of Legal Compliance to Illegal Immigration during the Chinese Exclusion Era." *Law and Social Inquiry* 31.1 (January 2006): 109–46.

Sadowski-Smith, Claudia. "U.S. Border Theory, Globalization, and Ethnonationalisms in Post-Wall Eastern Europe." *Diaspora* 8.1 (Spring 1999): 3–22.

Saldívar, José David. *Border Matters: Remapping American Cultural Studies.* Berkeley: University of California Press, 1997.

———. "Chicano Border Narratives as Cultural Critique." Calderón and Saldívar, *Criticism* 167–80.

———. *The Dialectics of Our America: Genealogy, Cultural Critique, and Literary History.* Durham: Duke University Press, 1991.

Salyer, Lucy E. *Laws Harsh as Tigers: Chinese Immigrants and the Making of Modern Immigration Law.* Chapel Hill: University of North Carolina Press, 1995.

Sandoval, Anna M. "*Unir Los Lazos:* Braiding Chicana and *Mexicana* Subjectivities." *Decolonial Voices: Chicana and Chicano Cultural Studies in the 21st Century.* Eds. Arturo J. Aldama and Naomi H. Quinonez. Bloomington: Indiana University Press, 2002. 202–28.

Sassen, Saskia. *Globalization and Its Discontents: Essays on the New Mobility of People and Money.* New York: New Press, 1998.

———. "Nation States and Global Cities." Keynote presentation, Globalicities: A Conference on Issues Related to Globalization. Modern Literature Conference. Comparative Literature Program at Michigan State University. Michigan State University. East Lansing, Michigan. October 19, 2001.

Schramm, Margaret K. "Identity and the Family in the Novels of Janette Turner Hospital." *Canadian Women: Writing Fiction.* Ed. Mickey Pearlman. Jackson: University of Mississippi Press, 1993. 84–98.

Silko, Leslie Marmon. *Almanac of the Dead.* New York: Simon and Schuster, 1991.

———. *Ceremony.* New York: Viking Press, 1977.

———. *Gardens in the Dunes.* New York: Simon and Schuster, 1999.

———. *Storyteller.* New York: Seaver Books, 1981

———. *Yellow Woman and a Beauty of the Spirit: Essays on Native American Life Today.* New York: Simon and Schuster, 1996.

Simcox, David. "Growth without Prosperity Plagues the Borderlands." *Forum for Applied Research and Public Policy* 10.3 (1995): 80–83.

Smith, Jeanne Rosier. *Writing Tricksters: Mythic Gambols in American Ethnic Literature.* Berkeley: University of California Press, 1997.

Smith, Jon, and Deborah Cohn, eds. *Look Away! The U.S. South in New World Studies.* Durham: Duke University Press, 2004.

Smith, Michael V. *Cumberland.* Toronto: Cormorant Books, 2002.

Smith, Paul J. Introduction. *Human Smuggling: Chinese Migrant Trafficking and the Challenge to America's Immigration Tradition.* Washington, DC: Center for Strategic and International Studies, 1997. viii–xv.

Smorkaloff, Pamela Maria. "Shifting Borders, Free Trade, and Frontier Narratives: US, Canada, and Mexico." *American Literary History* 6.1 (Spring 1994): 88–102.

Soja, Edward W. "Six Discourses on the Postmetropolis." *Imagining Cities: Scripts, Signs, Memory.* Eds. Sallie Westwood and John Williams. London: Routledge, 1997. 19–30.

Solberg, S. E. "Sui Sin Far/Edith Eaton: First Chinese-American Fictionist." *MELUS* 8.1 (Spring 1981): 27–39.

Spalding, Mark. "Addressing Border Environmental Problems Now and in the Future: Border XXI and Related Efforts." *The U.S.-Mexican Border Environment: A Road Map to a Sustainable 2020.* Ed. Paul Ganster. San Diego: San Diego University Press, 2000. 105–37.

Sparke, Matthew. "Excavating the Future in Cascadia: Geoeconomics and the Imagined Geographies of a Cross-Border Region." *BC Studies* 127 (Autumn 2000): 5–44.

Spicer, Edward H. *The Yaquis: A Cultural History.* Tucson: University of Arizona Press, 1980.

Spillers, Hortense J., ed. *Comparative American Identities: Race, Sex, and Nationality in the Modern Text.* New York: Routledge, 1991.

Stavans, Ilan. *Mutual Impressions: Writers from the Americas Reading One Another.* Durham: Duke University Press, 1999.

St. Clair, Janet. "Cannibal Queers: The Problematics of Metaphor in *Almanac of the Dead.*" *Leslie Marmon Silko: A Collection of Critical Essays.* Eds. Louise K. Barnett and James L. Thorson. Albuquerque: University of New Mexico Press, 1999. 207–21.

———. "Death of Love/Love of Death: Leslie Marmon Silko's *Almanac of the Dead.*" *MELUS* 21.2 (Summer 1996): 141–56.

Straight, Susan. *Highwire Moon.* Boston Houghton Mifflin, 2001.

Sui Sin Far. (Edith Maude Eaton). *Mrs. Spring Fragrance and Other Writings.* Eds. Amy Ling and Annette White-Parks. Urbana: University of Illinois, 1995.

Sunquist, Eric J. "Realism and Regionalism." *Columbia Literary History of the United States.* Ed. Emory Elliott. New York: Columbia University Press, 1988. 501–24.

Symons, T. H. B. "The State of Canadian Studies at the Year 2000: Some Observations." *Journal of Canadian Studies* 35.1 (2000): 27–52.

Sze, Julie. "'Not by Politics Alone': Gender and Environmental Justice in Karen Tei Yamashita's *Tropic of Orange.*" *Bucknell Review* 44.1 (2000): 29–42.

Tabuenca Córdoba, María Socorro. "*Viewing the Border:* Perspectives from 'the Open Wound.'" *Discourse* 18.1–2 (Fall 1995): 146–68.

Taliman, Valerie. "Borders and Native Peoples: Divided, but Not Conquered." *Native Americas* 18.1 (March 31, 2001): 10–16.

Thacker, Robert. "Canadian Literature's 'America.'" *Essays on Canadian Writing* (Fall 2000) 71: 128–39.

Thornton, Russell. "Institutional and Intellectual Histories of Native American Studies." *Studying Native America: Problems and Prospects*. Ed. Russell Thornton. Madison: University of Wisconsin Press, 1998. 79–107.

Todd, Emmanuel. *After the Empire: The Breakdown of the American Order*. Trans. C. Jon Delogu. New York: Columbia University Press, 2003.

Tomlinson, John. *Cultural Imperialism: A Critical Introduction*. Baltimore: Johns Hopkins University Press, 1991.

Troncoso, Sergio. *The Last Tortilla and Other Stories*. Tucson: University of Arizona Press, 1999.

Urrea, Luis Alberto. *Across the Wire: Life and Hard Times on the Mexican Border*. New York: Anchor Books, 1993.

Valdez Moses, Michael. "Magical Realism at World's End." *Literary Imagination*. 3.1 (Winter 2001): 105–33.

Varese, Stefano. "Indigenous Epistemologies in the Age of Globalization." *Critical Latin American and Latino Studies*. Ed. Juan Poblete. Minneapolis: University of Minnesota Press, 2003. 138–53.

Vasconcelos, José. *The Cosmic Race/La raza cósmica*. Los Angeles: Centro de Publicaciones, 1979.

Vela, Richard. "The Idea of Boundaries in the Work of Alberto Ríos." *Pembroke Magazine* 34 (2002): 115–22.

Verdecchia, Guillermo. *Fronteras Americanas/American Borders*. 1993. Vancouver: Talonbooks, 1993, 1997.

Villalobos, José Pablo. "Border Real, Border Metaphor: Altering Boundaries in Miguel Méndez and Alejandro Morales." *Arizona Journal of Hispanic Cultural Studies* 4 (2000): 131–40.

Viramontes, Helena María. *The Moths and Other Stories*. Houston: Arte Público Press, 1985.

———. *Under the Feet of Jesus*. New York: Dutton, 1995.

Vizenor, Gerald. "Trickster Discourse: Comic Holotropes and Language Games." *Narrative Chance: Postmodern Discourse on Native American Indian Literatures*. Ed. Gerald Vizenor. Albuquerque: University of New Mexico Press, 1989. 187–211.

Wald, Priscilla. "Minefields and Meeting Grounds: Transnational Analyses and American Studies." *American Literary History* 10.1 (Spring 1998): 199–218.

Walker, William. "Canada, U.S. Eye Scrapping Border." *The Star* [Toronto] July 28, 2001: A1, A25.

Wallerstein, Immanuel. *The Decline of American Power: The U.S. in a Chaotic World*. New York: New Press, 2003.

Weaver, Jace. *That the People Might Live: Native American Literatures and Native American Community.* New York: Oxford University Press, 1997.

Weiss, Jason. "At the Frontier: Nine Linked Stories by Carlos Fuentes Explore the Fault Line between Mexico and the United States." *Boston Globe Online* November 26, 1997: L1.

White, Richard. *The Middle Ground: Indians, Empires, and Republics in the Great Lakes Region, 1650–1815.* Cambridge: Cambridge University Press, 1991.

White-Parks, Annette. *Sui Sin Far/Edith Maude Eaton: A Literary Biography.* Urbana: University of Illinois Press, 1995.

———. "'We Wear the Mask': Sui Sin Far as One Example of Trickster Authorship." *Tricksterism in Turn-of-the-Century American Literature.* Eds. Elizabeth Ammons and Annette White-Parks. Hanover: University Press of New England, 1994. 1–20.

"Who Left the Door Open?" *Time* September 20, 2004: 51–66.

Williams, Raymond Leslie. *The Writings of Carlos Fuentes.* Austin: University of Texas Press, 1996.

Winks, Robin W. "Imagining Canada." *Northern Exposures: Scholarship on Canada in the United States.* Eds. Karen Gould, Joseph T. Jockel, and William Metcalfe. Washington, DC: Association for Canadian Studies in the United States, 1993. 1–17.

Wong, Sau-ling. "Denationalization Reconsidered: Asian American Cultural Criticism at a Theoretical Crossroads." *Postcolonial Theory and the United States: Race, Ethnicity, and Literature.* Eds. Amritjit Singh and Peter Schmidt. Jackson: University Press of Mississippi, 2000. 122–48.

Wootten, Leslie A. "The Edge in the Middle: An Interview with Alberto Ríos." *World Literature Today* 77.2 (July 1, 2003): 57–60.

Yamashita, Karen Tei. "Purely Japanese." N.d. http://www.cafecreole.net/travelogue/karen-e.html. Accessed November 4, 2002.

———. *Through the Arc of the Rain Forest.* Minneapolis: Coffee House Press, 1990.

———. *Tropic of Orange.* Minneapolis: Coffee House Press, 1997.

Yañez, Richard. *El Paso del Norte: Stories on the Border.* Reno: University of Nevada Press, 2003.

Yin, Xiao-huang. *Chinese American Literature since the 1850s.* Urbana: University of Illinois Press, 2000.

Index

CPSIA information can be obtained
at www.ICGtesting.com
Printed in the USA
FSOW01n1311290615
8369FS